Journeys

A fascinating story about the journey of a writer of fiction. I read the first 115 pages without pause and then was worried that there weren't going to be enough pages still to read because I didn't want the book to end. It's the interplay between the writer's real life and her imagined characters and situations that make this such a completely intriguing book.

— Gay Morris, Drama Professor, Cape Town

A gem of a book, and like no other. Molteno describes how she set out to help her books to find readers, in places familiar, and places unknown to most of us. The journeys are deeply flavoured and spiced, intensely coloured, and full of the variety of scents, personalities and poetry of Africa and the East. Take the journeys with her, without a map!

— Helen Cooper, Environmental Policy Maker, Hampshire

The inspiring journey of a book and its writer's extraordinary life, from her native South Africa to some of the most dangerous places on earth. If you're looking for insight into what makes us human and to the transformative power of literature and story-telling, this is the book and the writer to read.

— Carol A. Caffrey, Actress, Shropshire

Marion Molteno is one of the finest writers working today, and this book is a treasure that offers insight into the making of her fiction. As with all her books, I find myself inside the very real experience of a thoughtful humanitarian whose values and sensibilities are badly needed in the world today.

— Marylee MacDonald, Writing Coach, Arizona

As fascinating and evocative as her fiction — perceptive, intelligent, drawing on a rich, multicultural set of personal experiences and a love of languages, music and poetry, that adds a richness to her work. It's written with her characteristic openness and honesty, and her values are at the core — her growing recognition that she can 'tell stories in a way that helps those who read them empathise with situations other than their own.'

— Jen Marshall Haugen, International
Development Worker, Angola

A brave book, that lays bare levels of feelings, thought and creativity that, though beautifully written, still feel quite raw. Her description of her growth as a writer and how she is gripped by the magic of fiction is both lucid and engaging, and yet it's about so much more. Above all it's a meditation on the creative process. How the personal and the political interact, and why books can spark action and strike fear in autocratic governments. Illuminating, and surprisingly gripping. Give yourself a treat.

— Gregory Lanning, Documentary
Film Director, London

This daring book reveals why Marion Molteno is as successful as she is in her endeavors. She overcomes a natural modesty and treks out into the world carrying her hope in a kit bag … She is a master of tone. She neither over or under-describes, while keeping resonances through words and entire passages. The reader's imagination fills the rest of the space.

— Mary Clark, Community Worker, New York

About the Author

Marion Molteno is the author of four prize-winning novels and a collection of short stories. She grew up in South Africa where she was active in student opposition to the apartheid regime and spent eight years in Zambia at a time of rapid social change. For most of her adult life she has lived in London, where she has organised English classes for adult immigrants, pioneered the teaching of languages of minority communities in schools, and set up a refugee support network. She was a senior advisor in Save the Children, contributing to its work in over 50 countries, mostly in Asia and Africa. Her handbooks for practitioners have been translated into several languages and used around the world.

Her fiction has won or been shortlisted for several literary awards, including the Commonwealth Writers Prize, the International Indie Book Awards, the International Rubery Book Award, the Atta Galatta Bangalore Literary Festival Book Prize, the David St John Thomas Prize for Fiction, and the London Short Story Prize. A short memoir based on her work in Save the Children won the Fish Publishing Memoir Prize. She studied Urdu with the scholar Ralph Russell, and edits his writing on Urdu literature.

Also by Marion Molteno

Uncertain Light
'A moving and necessary book. An adventurous plot, and characters who will remain with me for a very long time.'
Alastair Niven, Judge of the 2014 Man Booker Prize
'A tender love story, set among the ruins of war and hopelessness.'
Financial Express, India

If You Can Walk, You Can Dance
'An ambitious and gripping story.' *The Independent*
'Illuminating. Very unusual and original.' *Sunday Telegraph*

A Shield of Coolest Air
'Moving and inspiring.' *Independent on Sunday*
'Poignant and deeply empathetic. Her writing has a poet's sensitivity and grace.' *The Scotsman*

Somewhere More Simple
'She eloquently sketches a tale of desire, loss and forgiveness against a backdrop of indifferent sea and sky.' *Financial Times*
'Molteno shows great compassion for and understanding of her characters, allowing the reader to care for them as much as she does.' *Sunday Herald*, New Zealand

A Language in Common
'The most extraordinary book of short stories, straddling in fiction the social divide between white Britons and Asians.'
The Independent
'Powerful portraits. Remarkable understanding of her characters.' *Sunday Times of India*

Journeys
Without
a Map

A Writer's Life

Marion Molteno

Matador
9 Priory Business Park,
Wistow Road, Kibworth Beauchamp,
Leicestershire. LE8 0RX
Tel: 0116 279 2299
Email: books@troubador.co.uk
Web: www.troubador.co.uk/matador
Twitter: @matadorbooks

ISBN 978 1800463 394

British Library Cataloguing in Publication Data.
A catalogue record for this book is available from the British Library.

Printed and bound by CPI Group (UK) Ltd, Croydon, CR0 4YY
Typeset in 11pt Minion Pro by Troubador Publishing Ltd, Leicester, UK

Matador is an imprint of Troubador Publishing Ltd

To my grandchildren
Omni, Isla, Zahira, Theo, Zeph & Zander

Stages on the Journey

DIRECTION OF TRAVEL

HEADING OFF ALONE

IN SEARCH OF READERS

INSPIRATIONS ALONG THE WAY

TRAVELLING WITH A BOOK

IN QUIET PLACES

TRANSITIONS

STORIES NOT YET TOLD

CREATIVE PROCESSES

Direction of Travel

~ 1 ~

Setting Out

My latest novel has just been published. I've packed a copy along with my toothbrush, pyjamas and a change of clothes, and I'm setting out to see if I can help it find readers. I have no idea where I will arrive or who I will meet.

In a journey without a map everything is unexpected. I turn corners and land up in places I have not before heard of. I meet surprising strangers, who jolt me into seeing even my own writing process differently. I start a blog to record impressions.

By the time I have travelled several thousand miles I am turning into an accidental travel writer. Incidents along the way keep reminding me how my other novels came to be. I am taking quick flips back while still pushing forwards, exploring my life as a writer.

The journey itself is forming me. I am learning to accept

what it presents without demanding reasons or logic. Everything potentially connects, and living isn't about arriving.

I get off the bus and walk towards the office of Save the Children in London. My job in adult education is being re-structured out of existence. I have been doing it for 16 years, it's a community, my friends, it has kept throwing up new challenges, and now it's coming to an end. For months I have been applying for others and have been offered an impressive-sounding one at a higher salary. I managed to convince the interview panel (and myself) that I could do it, but I know it is the wrong job for me. Perhaps that is because I have had a glimpse of one that I cannot get out of my mind. Save the Children is looking for an Education Advisor. It will involve international travel, which I couldn't have contemplated earlier, but both my daughters have left home, so —

So I put in an application. I hear nothing, which does not surprise me. I don't have the experience they will be looking for.

After a week of dithering I accept the other job.

A letter arrives from Save the Children inviting me for an interview. I instantly phone job number one, apologise for messing them up, and ask if they can give me two weeks more to decide. They are extremely nice about it, which I don't feel I deserve. Then I take that bus to the Save the Children office, to start reading my way through reports in their Resources Centre.

By the end of day one I know that to work on projects like these would be the most amazing thing I might ever get the chance to do.

By day two I am beginning to see how the role might pan out, and thinking, Yes, I can do it.

By day three I have blocked out of my mind any thought that I might not get it.

Three months later I crossed that road again to start work.

I was based in the London office but constantly travelling to countries where Save the Children was supporting education. In my first two years I was briefly in 30 countries in Africa and Asia, in city slums and rural isolation, the poorest parts that tourists never see. It was the early 1990s. In South Africa, where I had grown up, Mandela had been released from prison. Boundaries across Eastern Europe and ex-Soviet Asia were changing too fast for map-makers to keep up. The news was full of wars and environmental disasters. I arrived in Mozambique in the aftermath of a flood, where whole villages had been washed away. I flew into Mogadishu in a plane carrying medical supplies, to land in a devastated city where anarchy ruled. In Mongolia, a place of punishing winters, I visited pre-schools in small towns where the entire heating system had failed — they had run out of coal.

I had a job to do in each place, guided by local colleagues to whom I must have seemed an ignorant outsider, but who handled this visitor from the head-office with patience and tact, and seemed to get something from the exchange. Early on I promised myself that I would not arrive anywhere without having learnt at least to greet and to say a few words in that language. A few years later my brother counted the language-learning books on my shelves. I had given up at 14, by which time I had faced up to the reality of my role. Despite my efforts, I would arrive everywhere ignorant and only able to communicate through interpreters.

I never stopped feeling humble about all there was to learn in each place. Mostly I was working alongside people of that country, many of them inspiring. Other colleagues were internationals, moving from country to country every few years. Each had a different story of how they had got into this life, but all had been moulded by its unusual possibilities, its frustrating limitations. Everywhere I learnt from children, awed at the resilience with which they handled situations that would have traumatised any child I knew in the more protected world I had come from. I met children in rural Pakistan who were teaching younger children because the teacher hadn't bothered to arrive. Children in Kenya whose parents had died of AIDS and who were now looked after by tired grandparents — those children walked miles to school each day, hungry, but never gave up going. In Rajasthan I sat on the floor of a mud house alongside children who were learning to write by candle light. By day they were out in the semi-desert landscape, hours from home, responsible for the family's buffaloes. I asked a girl of eight, 'How do you control such a huge beast?' She said, perkily, 'You just twitch its tail.'

Moving in and out of such environments challenges things we take for granted. When you've just spent two weeks surrounded by skinny children, you can't bear to see how much food we throw away. A tap of running water seems a magic thing, the clutter of possessions we all have, obscene. There were moments I will cherish forever, places I could never have got to, simple experiences that could never have been mine otherwise ... In Mali, moving through the flood lands of the Senegal River in a *pirogue*, a rowing boat with an awning to protect us from the fierce sun, in the company of a tall, quietly competent Malian colleague ... In Laos, watching fishermen cast huge nets out on to a lake ... In South Sudan, sleeping on a canvas bed under the stars, the most peaceful experience possible, yet we were in a pause in a devastating civil war. My diaries for those years are disconnected scraps reflecting the lives of international workers, committed people yet so protected. A bizarre, embarrassing quality in the double-ness of each experience, meeting in places I could never have afforded to go on holiday — a lakeside hotel in Kenya, or a beach resort in Thailand, once overrun by American GIs on leave from Vietnam. Living comfortably while we discussed strategies for responding to situations of extreme deprivation.

Somewhere in the recesses of my mind the germ of a story began to form. But I was so besieged by impressions and issues and encounters — real ones — that the impetus for fiction struggled to get through.

~ 2 ~

The Fictional Impulse

I have been writing fiction since my mid-thirties. At least that's what I thought until I started sorting through old papers. Turns out that at 17 I wrote a play based on the life of Marie Curie (now thrown away unread), and some time before that a play in Afrikaans. I was writing poems (some passable) at 19, and short stories (about nothing – why did I even bother?). There's a draft of a novel I was working on at 20 (probably highly embarrassing, but I'm not even going to look). All into the recycling bag. My memory had blotted them out, despite the fact that I must have chosen to pack them up and get them sent to follow me halfway across the world, and not once but twice.

Then real life took over and my urge to make things up and play around with words went into abeyance until I had had a bit more life experience to draw on.

Ten years later an unusually large dose came my way. We had been living in Zambia for eight years, both of us teaching, and our daughters born there. There was a political crisis and we suddenly had to leave — a place we loved, work, friends, a way of life — to arrive as strangers in a village in Sussex. Our daughters were two and five years old. Robert had just been released from political detention and was in no position to look for a job. He stayed home with the girls while I travelled each day by train to Eastbourne to teach English to foreign students.

We had countless transitions to negotiate, were always tired, yet — extraordinary it seems to me now — I sat up late a couple of nights a week writing after the others were asleep. Wordsworth's definition of poetry as 'emotion recollected in tranquility' hardly applies, because my state was certainly not tranquil; but transmuting experience into fiction is definitely a way of putting difficult things in a box where they are less likely to jump out at you. I thought I was writing a novel but it fell into a myriad pieces and got packed away. Probably destroyed. I no longer remember, and it hasn't emerged in the paper-sorting.

Then a new set of transitions. We knew while we stayed in the village there would be no chance for Robert to find work, so we moved to London. New jobs for both of us, new schools for the girls, finding new people. When eventually things began to settle and small spaces of time opened up, immediately the urge to write reappeared to fill them. By now I understood that novel-writing is not for mothers-with-full-time-jobs, so I was writing short stories. Our younger daughter often took a long time to get to sleep. I would sit next to her bed in the semi-dark, and in that companionable silence the next bit of a story would be writing itself in my head, waiting till I found a moment to get it down. Sometimes I would tuck her up on the sofa in the room where I was writing. Cutting and pasting happened with scissors and sellotape then, and I would be down on the carpet shuffling snippets around. I rationed my writing time, knowing that it was taken at the expense of time that Robert and I needed together. Looking back, I probably didn't ration it enough.

To everyone's surprise, particularly mine, my collection of short stories was accepted by a publisher. Holding *A Language in Common* in my hands felt miraculous — an actual book, as if someone else had done it, or the person I might have been in another life. I was doing radio interviews, getting letters from readers. Now that I had had the heady experience of other people reading my stories, the urge to write was even stronger and I started on a novel. By now our daughters were 11 and 14, Robert was busy with a local education campaign, my job had grown exponentially and I was learning Urdu — it wasn't as if there wasn't enough filling my time. I tried to find a more considerate time and switched to early mornings, waking at five and writing until eight when the day proper began. When friends heard this they used words like 'dedication', but it never felt like that. I never set an alarm. My story woke me, and I would quietly disappear into my own world for those few hours.

They always ended too soon. The rationing of time meant I never sat in front of a computer wondering where to go with my story — it had been growing in some region of my mind in all the hours while my attention was on other things.

It's been like that ever since. I didn't think of it as a job because I've never earned my living doing it. It has been my private eccentricity, something I do when no one is looking. For years I didn't expect anyone to understand what I was doing, and I was glad they didn't ask. All I wanted was to be allowed to do it.

By the time I joined Save the Children my first novel had appeared as *A Shield of Coolest Air* and I was working on a second. I carried my notebooks with me through all the years of arriving in new countries, among people who had to cope with extreme poverty, wars and environmental disasters. In hotel rooms in strange cities I would escape from other people's crises into the details of fictional lives.

Looking back I can see that this too was a kind of therapy. At the time I just knew that to stay sane I had to keep a small space for myself each day, and writing was the way I did it.

~ 3 ~

Into Central Asia

In the late 1990s my work took me to Central Asia — Tajikistan, Uzbekistan, Kyrgyzstan, countries hardly known outside, lands of awesome mountains and sudden fertile valleys, harsh deserts and ancient cultures. Tajikistan had just been through a devastating civil war, and Save the Children was working in the districts most affected, supporting people to rebuild their lives. For 70 years before that all of Central Asia had been part of the Soviet Union. Its institutions had dominated all aspects of life. Now all that had suddenly imploded, and people were struggling to survive the effects of economic collapse. Being there confronted me with aspects of human experience beyond any I had previously been exposed to—

I am in Qurgon Teppe, a small town in the south of Tajikistan, near the Afghan border. The Tajiks I am working with reflect in themselves the complex history of this society. Their grandparents lived through traumatic changes — mass deportations, famine, Stalin's worst excesses, the tragedies of war. Many of their parents came from the mountains, forcibly relocated here to provide labour on the cotton-growing collectives, deserts turned productive by Soviet irrigation schemes, under constant pressure to fulfil production targets set in Moscow. The women my age and younger grew up through an education system that gave them opportunities they would previously never have had. Until things imploded they worked as teachers, youth workers, administrators.

With the collapse of the Soviet Union there was a period of intense upheaval. People who had long been critical hoped for democratic reforms, but when the new state of Tajikistan held its first independent elections, the same ex-Soviet rulers were returned to power through rigged elections. For months mass protests filled the centre of the capital, Dushanbe. There were groups demanding the freedom to openly practise their religion; public adherence to Islam had been heavily constrained but privately had never disappeared. In another city square government supporters gathered, their fear of an Islamic revival ramped up through the ten years the Soviet army had been at war with mujahideen groups across the border in Afghanistan. The panicky government armed its supporters and played on regional loyalties. When state structures crumble and violence is at your door, people retreat into clan and family, and attack out of fear of being attacked. Hundreds of thousands fled, into the mountains, across ice-bound rivers, to exile or death.

The survivors have been coming back, to find their homes taken over by others. Often it is just women and children — their men have been killed in the conflict. Save the Children has channelled international funding to support women with the practical means of starting again: seeds, tools, cows. Now the programme director, Bronwen, has asked me to visit. She and her team of Tajik staff are considering how to support recovery of the part-devastated school system.

She and a driver meet me off a plane from Tashkent, capital of neighbouring Uzbekistan. The journey was so turbulent that we have to stop the car as we crest the first mountains for me to be sick at the roadside. A short pause to take in the extraordinary view over the plains beyond, and we drive on, down into the town. I am to lodge along with a couple of other colleagues in the Save the Children staff house, with carpets on the walls and low bolster-cushions to sit on as we are served delicious Tajik dishes by the woman who manages the house. She bustles around in her highly coloured long dress, a confident, sociable woman in middle age, with a surprising number of gold teeth. She chats vigorously, apparently with no concept that I do not understand. I do a lot of smiling, and soon we are laughing together.

Outside, the wounds of war are still raw. There are bullet holes in the walls of buildings. Government officials tolerate, but only just, an international agency being here because the need is so extreme, but they are tense in their dealings with the programme staff. In a workshop I am facilitating through interpreters things suddenly come to a halt when the (male) education officials stand up furiously and threaten to walk out. The interpreter gives up and it is only afterwards that I learn what sparked the fracas. The (all-female) Tajik Save the Children team were reporting that they have been consulting children in the district to discover what stops them from coming to school, and among the many reasons one is that they have no shoes. It's a long cold walk in winter. A life-time's experience of the Soviet system has made it impossible for the officials to admit that things are not going well, and besides, they are outraged at having their reports challenged by the opinions of children. Bronwen uses all her diplomatic skills to persuade them to stay. They stalk back from the door, take their seats again, their

13

body language eloquent. Their return is a major concession and we had all better behave with due respect now. Stiffly we continue.

I am in some degree of shock. Without understanding a word I had fully expected to see Bronwen marched off and put on the first plane out of the country. After the workshop is over and the officials have departed, the Tajik women gather round, explaining it all to me. Their own body language is pretty expressive too, of disdain. Those stupid men, not willing to listen to children, pretending there are no problems.

But the ice is thin. Just a year ago people here were killing each other.

~

The women who run the programme have all themselves been widowed by war, from both sides of the conflict, yet so soon after its traumas they are here working together to prevent more children from becoming destitute. Bronwen tells me a story about one of them, a woman called Zainab whom I will later get to know. She was challenged by a man from her own clan, angry that she was working with families from the other side of the conflict.

'Why do you help these people?' he demanded. 'It's *they* who killed your husband.'

She said, 'We'll probably never know who killed my husband, but I know it wasn't these children.'

Here are stories, asking to be told.

~ 4 ~

Tentative Connections

I have been here so brief a time, but already I feel close to the Tajik women I am getting to know. They make it so easy. They are outgoing, confident, and those who speak English interpret relaxedly for me with those who don't. Some are in western clothes but most wear the traditional highly coloured dresses and headscarfs. All are proud of being Tajik and its cultural history. Despite everything they have endured, they still have the energy to draw an outsider in to the generous embrace for which Tajik society is famous.

When conversations are going on around me in Tajik, I listen to the sounds, the patterns they make, and how they fit with people's facial expressions and body language. A strange thing is happening. Words I half-recognise fly past me, too fast to catch but familiar. I have the illusion that if I could stay for a few months I might begin to understand what everyone is saying.

The language is Persian. Here it's called Tajik; in northern Afghanistan, Dari; in Iran it is Farsi, but I am told that they are essentially the same language, with no more than regional differences. They share the same historic culture, from the centuries when Persian influence extended from the deserts of what is now Iran to the mountains of Azerbaijan in the north-west, and north-east to the medieval cities of Samarkand, Bukhara, and the mountainous lands where Tajiks lived. Tajiks are proud that many of the great Persian poets were from Central Asia. During the Soviet era the authorities feared the Sufi-mystic influences that pervade Persian poetry, and banned the Persian script, but people's memories kept the words of the poets alive. My friend Zainab tells me that in her family when a child is born the parents hold against its forehead a *divan* — a book of the collected poems — of Hafiz, the great 14th century Persian poet. In the centre of Dushanbe, Tajikistan's capital, is a statue of the man regarded as their national poet, Sadruddin Ayni.

I do not know Persian but I know Urdu, a language that is culturally related. After successive rulers from Central Asia crossed the mountains to the north Indian plains and set up kingdoms in Delhi and beyond, Urdu emerged as a language of communication with their Indian subjects. At a basic spoken level it is very close to Hindi, but it uses the Persian script and its vocabulary draws heavily on Persian, especially its poetic vocabulary. And Urdu speakers share with speakers of Persian everywhere a passion for poetry.

The words that I keep hearing around me in Tajikistan, which give me the illusion that I am on the brink of understanding, are words I have heard in Urdu poetry.

~

I started learning Urdu when I was teaching English to people settled in Britain who had come from India and Pakistan. My teacher, Ralph Russell, was a scholar and translator of Urdu poetry. By now he was 80 years old, a short, comfortably round man with white hair, a huge laugh, and a vivid interest in everyone he met. We met through running a teacher training course together. I had got some way learning Hindi but realised that here was someone I could learn from much more effectively. He took me on as a student, and after an unnervingly short time persuaded me and a few other of his advanced learners to assist in teaching Urdu courses for beginners. I started reading his books introducing Urdu literature to English readers, and edited his articles to produce new ones. He read drafts of everything I wrote, and his steady belief in me fuelled the journey.

Back in Britain after my first stint of work in Central Asia, I asked Ralph to teach me something about the great Persian poets. He did more. From his bookshelves, a never-ending store of surprises, he brought down a small pile of books, among them an autobiography of Sadruddin Ayni himself. He had picked it up when visiting Tashkent once, on his way to India, an Urdu translation from the Tajik original. It's told in a simple, straightforward style but the Urdu vocabulary was beyond me so Ralph read it with me. Ayni, a remarkable man who survived the excesses of two dictatorial regimes, started life as a child of a poor peasant family in the feudal Emirate of Bukhara. Orphaned young, with the support of an older brother he received a traditional Persian and Islamic education and became a leading intellectual and modernist reformer. He challenged feudal authority, was imprisoned by the Emir, and supported the Bolsheviks to win control. In the new society he applied his energies to developing an educational system that for the first time brought literacy within reach of most people. He wrote educational books, was a journalist, a novelist, and above all a poet. He walked a political tightrope but his stature was such that the authorities could not risk eliminating him. He died in 1952, a year before Stalin.

Ayni's story led me to others, writers and dissidents who did not survive. Ralph and I talked about what it would have been like to be a poet steeped in the Persian poetic tradition, yet caught up in the constraints of Soviet Central Asia. Someone whose inner eyes caught, and whose words mirrored, the pressures of a deeply troubled history.

I was imagining the secret life of a fictional, forgotten Tajik poet.

I began making notes, finding people to inhabit the first glimmers of a story.

Two years later I was back in Central Asia, this time with my daughter Star. She was now 24 and I didn't get to see her very often. She was living a travelling life with a group of friends, busking for a living, making up the next stage as they went along — a real journey without maps. Just recently she and her partner had been making a yurt, the tent-home of nomads in Central Asia. I said would she like to come with me, to see the place yurts actually came from?

Star does her own thing while I am busy, and we do things together in moments between my work assignments. In Tashkent we stay in an old Uzbek house, now lived in by an Iranian woman who heads Save the Children's work here. On our first weekend my colleague-friend Layla takes us to see Bukhara. Now part of Uzbekistan, it was for centuries a great centre of Tajik culture, its history still evident in the stunning Islamic architecture, where blue-tiled domed buildings surround open spaces. We watch people working looms to create cloth with traditional patterns. We stand beneath the arches of the old market place, looking at musical instruments for sale – essentially so similar to ones we know, and Star plays, yet hiding different sounds.

Across the border into the Fergana Valley, where three countries weave in and out of each other. Kyrgyz, Uzbeks and Tajiks have lived side by side here for centuries until Stalin's divide-and-rule map-making classified them as separate nationalities. The borders have stuck and cause endless problems. In this very town, Osh, in the year the Soviet Union was coming to an end, there were violent clashes between Kyrgyz and Uzbeks. It started over a dispute about land division on a former collective farm, and spun out of control.

Alfia, my colleague, drives us high into the mountains to meet villagers who are trying to keep the early years of education going through an overwhelming set of transitions. We are outsiders, passing through, privileged to get glimpses of lives lived in response to challenges we can only half imagine. Whatever the faults of the old system, nothing that people are used to can now be relied on. The budget to pay teachers has gone. The few who continue teaching have to be supported by the community that is itself struggling to survive. Layers of older ways are re-emerging. In the pre-school playground an old man demonstrates how they are making felt from the wool of their sheep, something Star has learnt to do in her own travelling life-style. She is down on her haunches, talking to the children. Wordless talk, but the smiles and intention get through.

On our return we pass an isolated homestead, with people outside tending sheep. Star says, 'I wish you could just leave me here.' Alfia stops the car and gets out to talk to them – comes back saying, 'You can stay the night. I'll send the car up for you tomorrow.' Star is excited but embarrassed. They are clearly poor. Should she pay them? Alfia says, firmly, 'People feel privileged to have a guest,' but she and Star gather up whatever food we have in the car to give as a contribution. Star goes with her to the house. I watch as Alfia does some interpreting, then we wave goodbye and set off back down the mountain, leaving her with a peasant family with whom she shares no words.

That night in the town below I sleep lightly from the strangeness of it all, wondering how they are managing.

Our last week together is spent in the far east of Kyrgyzstan, near the China border. I am facilitating a training session for staff from the surrounding countries, in surreal surroundings — a grand hotel set on the edge of a vast lake, Issyk-kul, dark, deep water with soaring mountains all around. I query why we are spending the organisation's money on this kind of accommodation. My colleagues explain. Once this hotel hosted secret meetings of the Soviet governing elite, now it is empty much of the year and offers accommodation at knock-down prices. Midweek the organisers take us walking in the mountains. A stunning environment. We pass a Kyrgyz herding family that lives in yurts, homes that move with them when they have to move for new grazing. Star has her chance to be inside a yurt with them, momentarily part of its everyday life.

We travel back together across the border to the airport in Almaty, in neighbouring Kazakhstan. She will fly back to Britain; I will go on to New Zealand, to receive an award for my latest novel. Anything seems possible. On the long bus journey we talk about the novel I hope I might write.

'I'll dedicate it to you,' I say, 'my travelling daughter.'

But the more I was learning, the less possible it seemed. Where would I find one story to hold together so many disparate strands? Instead of getting clearer it was disappearing off the horizon, far beyond me, the canvas too vast, the issues too complex, the characters not strong enough to bear all that weight.

I wrote a different novel instead.

~

It was published when Ralph was 89. I had retired early to be free to accompany him through what turned out to be his last year. A couple of times he came to listen to talks I was giving about my new book to reading groups in libraries. I see him sitting at the back, saying nothing but smiling broadly whenever there is a positive response from one of those listening.

And then he was gone.

~

A year after his death we were on a family holiday on the Isles of Scilly. Three grandchildren now, being brought to share this place where our own daughters spent their childhood holidays. Star and I had a rare moment alone on the beach while the others had taken the children off. She said, 'Quickly, before they get back, tell me what happened to the Central Asian novel.'

'It never took off,' I said. 'Didn't know where it was going. The bits all fell apart.'

She listened, said, 'Those are just technical problems, Mum. I'm sure it could work.'

When we got home I searched for the piles of notes. The fictional people I had thought couldn't carry the story didn't seem so inadequate after all. Images started coming back to me ...

I started again. But by then I was ten years, three births and one death further on, and it became a different story.

HEADING OFF ALONE

~ 5 ~

A Local Habitation

Writing happens in solitude, scribbling in a notebook or alone at a computer, exploring a private world that is evolving under my typing fingers. When I lift my head I am astonished to find the hours have sped by. I have been in the company of the people who have begun to populate my story.

I am thinking of *A Midsummer Night's Dream*:

> 'And as imagination bodies forth the forms of things unknown,
> the poet's pen turns them to shapes and gives to airy nothing
> a local habitation and a name ...'

I am getting to know the people in my story, one at a time. They connect, but only loosely so far, through the world of international development workers, people trying to do something about dire situations. I have imagined a fictional organisation that has qualities I have seen in all those I have come into contact with, NGOs — Non-Governmental Organisations — humanitarian aid. Those who work for it are beset by funding crises and restructuring and senior managers they think are dysfunctional, but sticking with it, because they care about the work.

I follow them individually. How did each of them come to be who they are? What history do they have with each other? What needs in their own past lives are they having to reconcile with the challenges of the present? But the *story* itself, the central thrust that links all the people I am getting to know — *that* does not hold, perhaps because I never get a run of time to be with them.

And then, deep in an internet search I stumble on a short report in the Washington Post. December 1996. Tajikistan. A road leads up into the mountains. It's winter, early morning. A civil war has been dragging on for four years. A convoy of UN vehicles trundles up the road to find armed men hidden up there, to make sure that they know there is a cease-fire. The convoy disappears round a corner, into the uncertain mountain light.

Then something happens beyond where I can see. Twenty-three people are taken hostage.

I keep searching and find another report from a few weeks later: twenty-one people were released. What happened to the other two? No reference.

I keep searching. There is no further report that mentions them.

That absence of knowing. What do you do when someone close to you just *disappears*?

It's as if I have silently brought a magnet underneath a board of randomly scattered iron filings, lifted it to touch under the centre, and instantly all the filings swivel round – from every side of the board they point in the same direction.

I have it, what connects all of those disparate people whose lives I have been imagining. Each of them knew one of the men who disappeared.

The Midsummer Night's Dream moment has happened. The story has a local habitation: that road into the mountains is where it begins. The man they all knew has a name: Rahul Khan.

~

Now that I have the germs of the story I have entered a peaceful state where I know that all I have to do is make time every day to be with these people, follow the logic of their lives, and it will gradually come together. People occasionally ask me how my novel is going. I say 'fine', but I can't talk about it, it might all disappear if I did.

I'm well into the second year since I restarted and I've only just begun to know where I'm going. But now that I know the story *will* happen, I don't mind how long it takes.

Making time is not easy. Both my daughters, May and Star, have very young children, multiple demands on their time, and I am needed. Robert has had surgery. Several crises, a slow recovery. Keeping ordinary life going seems a full-time job in itself. But there's always the inner journey that proceeds quietly on its own, fitting into odd hours and half hours when they come my way. In hospital waiting rooms, on trains to my daughters.

~

Looking back, I am struck by how sure I was that I understood in such confident detail what was going on for each of the people in the story. I think I've always been someone who watches other people, notices things about what people are feeling. I was the youngest of four growing up – my mother said once that her memory of my earliest years was me watching all the activity generated by three older brothers.

About Rahul particularly? He was one of my original cast of characters but he has taken on new dimensions to fill this role. I am working backwards steadily to fill out his biography, through every stage of his 42 years. He is Indian, from a privileged background, but one which reflects India's divisions, a Hindu mother, a Muslim father. In his own person he represents not just the possibility of creative co-existence, but its necessity.

Further back still, to the lives of his parents, the political upheavals that had formed them. Most of this will only appear in the final story tangentially, if at all, but it is essential for understanding who he is, how he will react, how others will see him. The more I know about these histories, the more he becomes real. From his Muslim intellectual father come the influences of a critical mind, atheist convictions, an internationalist outlook, a love of poetry. How did I know his father so well? Through working with Ralph, hearing his stories of life-long friends, people who came to adulthood at the time of Independence. Through listening to him and his Urdu speaking friends talk, and to recordings he had made of conversations in Urdu with people telling their own life stories.

From Rahul's Gandhian mother's side, his early life followed a path that I have seen in many people, and can imagine in detail, a sensitive person, growing up with privilege but living amidst extremes of poverty and disadvantage. When you can no longer keep looking away, you find something that you can do. He has grown from responding to the needs he sees around him, to wider roles that have brought him by stages to work in difficult international contexts, and now as a UN peace negotiator. He is unusual, impressive, but such people exist. How do I know? That comes from people I met in my Save the Children work, and a decade and more before that, from my own first journeys in India.

I wasn't a 19 year old on a gap year. I was 37, a wife and mother of two young children, yet I set off for two months to travel solo with a backpack.

~ 6 ~

First Sources: India

It's the early 1980s. I am staying in a remote village in Bihar, on land acquired in the *Bhoodan* movement, donated by landlords to the peasants who lived on it. Our friend Larry, an investigative journalist, was years ago a volunteer on a community project here, and he has arranged for me to spend a few days there. A volunteer takes me on a walk through neighbouring villages, whose bare-survival conditions show up how transformatory this project had been ...

We had been in Britain five years. In the English classes I was running my friendships with women from India, Pakistan, Bangladesh had caused an explosion of new interests. I got drawn into their lives, their issues. I had adjustments of my own to living here but they had so many more and I was impressed by the way they handled them. I visited their homes, got to know their families. I was learning Hindi, which seemed an obvious step to putting our relationship on a more equal basis. I listened to Indian music, went on a Saturday workshop to start learning to play the tabla. I read about South Asia's history, its cultures, politics, looking for answers to questions I could hardly frame. I made myself try to look anew at things they found beautiful which I did not, like illustrations of goddesses with six arms. In a family-work life already over busy, how did I find the head-space to explore another culture so persistently? I don't know; only that somehow it became a leitmotif in my own inner journey. A point came where an Indian friend said, 'You'll have to get there yourself', and I knew he was right.

Once the idea took root, I couldn't move around it. Tentatively I explored the possibility of taking two months unpaid leave. To my surprise it was granted. I talked to Robert about going, and him being a temporary single Dad. Our friend Sue, with whom we shared after-school times with our children, agreed to take over my afternoons and be there as a back-up for Robert. He was an excellent father, but still.

I think he assumed he had no choice.

I shut off doubts and went on planning. Women in the English classes enthusiastically gave me addresses of their relatives. 'Please stay with them,' they all said. Robert gave me contacts. He was the editorial director in an independent publisher, Zed Books, and several of his authors were people doing remarkable things in India.

Then I was refused a visa, because I still had a South African passport. Larry got a friend with influence to intervene and vouched for my anti-apartheid credentials. His friend's influence worked and my visa arrived.

Today, a grandmother sharing in the care of my grandchildren, I can scarcely re-enter into the mind of that young mother who chose to go away for two months on a mission of her own. But I have to accept that it's what I did.

In those weeks of travelling I was rarely in a hostel or hotel, for I plotted my route to take in the families of Indian friends back in London. Living for a few days in each household was an unrivalled way to experience India's social diversity, of religions, life situations, attitudes. From a spacious flat in Bombay looking out over the sea I moved to a crumbling multiple-family house in Lucknow, where we drew water from a pump in the courtyard and slept on string beds. In the foothills of the Himalayas I stayed in an ashram with a friend whose grandfather had retired there to meditate. In Qadian in the Punjab I was absorbed into an Ahmadiya community (Muslims considered as non-orthodox), and spent my days with women who never moved out of the house except in a burqa. I learnt what it felt like to go out in one. In Gujarat I was the guest of an Arya Samaj family (a reform movement of Hinduism). I accompanied a head-teacher to her school to watch young girls learn complex *bharata natyam* dance sequences, and realised how little we in the West challenge children to use their extraordinary capacities of memory. Gender roles in homes where I was a guest were never fully predictable. In the household of a polo-playing army officer, stridently 'western' in his attitudes, the women had to engage in subterfuge to do things he accepted in me but would not have countenanced in his own family. In another home I was taken off by the women to sit on the flat roof and learn to winnow the husks off sesame seeds, while it was the man of the house who checked before I retired to bed whether I was 'addicted to bed-tea' in the morning. (I am.) No preconceptions could survive this multiplicity.

On journeys from one to the next, I did what most backpackers do. I had bizarre encounters on trains, and fended off rickshaw drivers when I arrived at a station. I had incidents with locks in cheap hostels. I failed to respond to beggars and felt miserable about it. I discovered the delight of *gane ka ras* (sugarcane juice), watching the cane being crushed by a steel machine that must surely have been 50 years old. I ate delicious *chaat* (cooked snacks) from street stalls, and regretted it when diarrhoea took over. I stood awed before gigantic structures cut into rock, or extraordinary carvings on the walls of temples. As an outsider I was exempt from many of the constraints of class, gender, caste, and could do things like persuade a cycle-rickshaw rider in Jaipur to let me have a go at pedalling while he acted the passenger. I wanted to see how hard it was.

My still-fragile hold on Hindi created some absurd moments. Contemplating the cave paintings in Ajanta (Buddhist and millennia old), I told a young tourist guide that I had written a book about them. He looked deeply impressed, and too late I realised that instead of *parhna* (the verb 'to read') I'd used *likhna* ('to write'). But the blunder got us laughing, and by the end of the day he had invited me home to meet his mother and sisters. They were fascinated by my glasses; they didn't know anyone who wore them, and had assumed they were a fashion item.

India has mega-scale poverty, discrimination, social problems, and also so many remarkable people trying to do something about them. They move before me as I remember. Primila Lewis had helped farm labourers to claim their rights under labour laws; for that she spent 18 months in prison during Indira Gandhi's Emergency, and wrote movingly about her experiences. In Ahmedabad, Ela Bhatt had founded the Self-Employed Women's Association, a kind of trade union for women who supported families with home-based work. She invited me to join a team meeting, and we sat cross-legged in a circle while they talked about their attempts to negotiate better terms from middle-men for rolling *bidi* cigarettes, or collecting recyclable waste. Afterwards a lively young woman who did block-printing on fabric took me home to demonstrate her craft. I hardly know which made the bigger impression, the skill and concentration it required, the repetition, bordering on drudgery, or her energy and confidence, now that she was taking collective action with other women.

A decade and more later, in my work with Save the Children, I saw many similar transformations. My young colleague, Divya, accompanied me on a journey of hundreds of miles to visit initiatives that we were supporting. Mother-and-child health centres in a tribal area of Andhra Pradesh. In Orissa, on land where houses had been flattened by a cyclone, a community-run pre-school and vocational centre. In Delhi, mobile crèches for infants whose mothers carried bricks on building sites. Behind each was a complex history. One organisation was caught up in internal disputes — the original charismatic leader had resisted letting others in on decision-making. In another, there were issues about funding not being properly accounted for. These are predictable human frailties, not unique to this field. None of it diminishes the remarkable phenomenon, that each of these projects had been started by someone who stepped out from the privileged life they had been born into, to try to do something, however modest, for people burdened by extreme poverty, and to confront the socially constructed barriers that prevented them from getting beyond it.

Like Rahul.

The first flickering light in his story goes back all that way. Fragmented, highly coloured moments lodged in memory, to germinate decades later in fiction. Wherever his story would later travel, this is where it began.

~ 7 ~

Following Trails

I have immersed myself in reading. The history of Central Asia. The Persian legacy, 19th century incursions by European powers. I puzzle over the jigsaw map, bizarre boundaries from the Soviet period intersected by complex patterns of ethnic groups. Analyses of political developments since the old order collapsed. Tensions between these unhistorical states.

The civil war in Tajikistan ... How did it happen? Who were the rebel leaders Rahul would be negotiating with? How did he get involved in the first place? I read whatever books I can find. Google searches bring up UN debates long forgotten except by those who were involved in them. UN documents, news stories, international agency reports — I read all I can find in English. I could write a book now about all this, but that's not where I'm headed.

Now I am in the office of Human Rights Watch, London, waiting to meet the director. I pick up a report from the low table in the waiting area. It doesn't tell me much I didn't know but the photos bring home the urgency of the situations these people are working in. When I phoned to make an appointment I used the word 'Research'. That sounds serious enough, but I had to add 'for a novel', which sends a different signal. Not real. Only a novel.

My mind offers a dose of strengthening tonic from Jane Austen: 'It is only a novel … or, in short, only some work in which the greatest powers of the mind are displayed, in which the most thorough knowledge of human nature, the happiest delineation of its varieties, the liveliest effusions of wit and humour, are conveyed to the world in the best-chosen language.'

A door opens. The director himself, a man in his forties I guess, looking harried. Too busy, too much coffee. 'Sorry to keep you waiting. Come in, come in.' His desk tells the same story, piles of reports, memos, interrupted jobs. The telephone rings before we can begin. He takes the call, answering in the same harried tone, then cuts whoever it is short. 'I'll call you back.'

He looks at me. His body language says, I'm here now, can we be quick?

I start with the story. I have never talked about it, so it feels risky. 'At one point I've got my central character working for Human Rights Watch in Central Asia. It would be a huge help if I could check out a few things with you, about how you work.'

He is intrigued. 'Central Asia's not my area, but I can tell you how we work.'

An hour later I emerge, with contacts for two more people.

'And good luck,' he says. 'I look forward to reading it.'

~

Paths I thought were clear become impassable, and others that I couldn't have foreseen open up. An organisation called IWPR, the Institute on War and Peace Reporting, trains local journalists in troubled areas, and they have an office in London. I phone, get through to John McLeod, the political analyst whose articles I found on the internet. He is willing to meet me. I arrive next day and we have a useful chat about conditions in Tajikistan and border troubles with Kyrgyzstan. As I'm leaving he lets drop that he once worked for Human Rights Watch in Tashkent. I stop at the lift entrance. 'When?' At exactly the time Rahul Khan would have been there. Immediately we fix another date so I can hear his stories.

They're hair-raising, but John doesn't seem to think that. Just part of the job.

It turns out he's an avid novel reader. I promise to send him one of my earlier novels. A couple of weeks later I get an email: 'I just finished your book. I was totally absorbed and missed my tube stop twice.' The book I gave him was about music, and it turns out he plays the Irish flute. He sends me recordings. They are wonderful.

He puts me in touch with a woman who was the BBC's correspondent in Tajikistan through all the years of my story. Monica Whitlock is writing a book to a deadline and won't have time to talk, but if I come to her house and don't mind if she ignores me, I can sit and go through her despatches from Tajikistan.

Two days I spend there. She has print-outs of several years worth of despatches, of exactly the period I need. They're on fading paper in a couple of lever arch files. Gold dust. So many details that I could never have imagined accurately, spread out there before me.

~

I need to check something specific with someone in UNHCR, the UN's High Commission for Refugees. Earlier I was often on the edges of things they were doing, heard stories, but now I need to know how they would have handled a particular set of crises. I ask my friends who work on humanitarian issues, does anyone know anyone I could talk to? One friend does. 'One of those extraordinary people,' she says, 'who speak about seven languages. He has worked in UNHCR a long time, in more countries than I could count.' I email, he's willing to chat, and we fix a time for me to phone. There he is in his office in Geneva, dealing with real issues, and here I am living in a world that still exists only in my own imagination, but he puts me at my ease. I have to tell him the actual scenario, which feels really spooky. I have told no one else, and I am superstitious about doing it before the book is finished, but there's no other way I can learn from him what I need to. He laughs, 'I could go to print with the story!', but he gives me the answers I need. We never meet.

~

With so much new information to process, I haven't been properly filing my own notes. I can't now find that crucial news item in the Washington Post, December 1996, that sparked off Rahul's story. Why doesn't it come up again when I search all the possible key words?

Eventually I track it down. The byline is Radio Free Europe in Prague. American funded; they report on countries where the press is censored. I email the journalist who filed the report, Bruce Pannier. He responds immediately, and when he hears that his report has led to a novel, 'Wow! That's amazing!' We have two long calls. I want to know any extra details he can tell me about what was happening at that time. He's keen to help but it's 15 years ago and a lot has happened since so he's struggling to remember. I switch to asking about his own connections with Central Asia. 'I first went on a research project,' he says, 'right after college, when the Soviet Union broke up.' A professor at Manchester was leading a study to check out whether there were people in remote areas who had continued in largely traditional ways, independent of Soviet institutions. He was sent to live with a peasant family way up in the mountains, on the borders of Tajikistan and Kyrgyzstan. That is almost exactly where part of my story takes place, where

Star spent her night wordlessly with a family and their sheep. He starts talking about life in those communities. *That* he remembers vividly, his first experience of such a different life-style.

I ask, 'What about language?' He was fluent in Russian when he went, but the villagers weren't. Soviet officials had hardly ever got up there. He had to learn Tajik, starting with the local mountain dialect for which there are no books. 'You learn by just living it,' he says. 'It's not hard. When you really need to find out things like where to relieve yourself, you learn the words pretty quick.'

~

I am sorting through old notes from Urdu lessons going back 30 years, looking for quotations from Urdu poetry that will connect with the themes of the book. I find among them a condolence card someone sent me after my brother died. 1984. What is this doing here?

John, my oldest brother, was 47 and seemed in perfect health, with far more than the usual share of life-energy. He collapsed playing hockey and died before the ambulance got him to hospital. For my sister-in-law and their three children the loss was incalculable, hugely compounded by the suddenness. My mother, nearly 80, was alone now in our home town, with her grown children scattered across other continents. I flew out immediately to be with her. For two weeks I spent every day in her room in a retirement home, and quietly we let John's continuing existence be with us. Little stories, remembered moments. So huge a presence in so many lives, and now, so suddenly, gone.

This card I am holding — was it waiting for me when I got back? But why is it here among my Urdu notes? I used to go to Ralph's house for an Urdu lesson one day a week on my way to work. Perhaps this card had just come in the post and I had put it in my bag as I left the house, and it got mixed up with my Urdu notes? I take it out to put it elsewhere, and then I see that something is written on the back, in Urdu, a few lines from a poem. It begins:

mujhe mawjazon par yaqin nahin …
I don't believe in miracles …

It's about dying. Perhaps Ralph quoted them to me when I was talking about John and my mother, and I scribbled them down on the nearest thing to hand?

I want to find the whole poem. Frustratingly, I hadn't noted the name of the poet, but one of Ralph's Urdu-scholar friends will surely know. Lovers of Urdu poetry know so much by heart. I email Professor Naim in America. He recognises the lines but can't remember who the poet is. He passes it to a friend, and the answer comes back, it is by Faiz, probably the most famous 20th century Urdu poet. And Faiz based it on one by a Soviet-era poet, Gamzatov.

The name rings the faintest of bells. I track it down to a slim volume from Ralph's bookshelves that came to me after his death, but which I have not yet properly read. English translations of poems by Gamzatov. So the thought behind the lines is Gamzatov's, via Faiz, via Ralph, to me.

The rhythm of the poem is in my feet as I take my morning walk on the common. The three men, speakers of three different languages, were all of a generation. Faiz was a few years older than Ralph, Gamzatov a few years younger. All three were Marxists. Faiz visited the Soviet Union several times, where he got to know Gamzatov. Ralph and Faiz knew each other well. Ralph had stayed in his house on his visits to Lahore. Perhaps he had once heard Faiz himself recite this poem?

I do an English translation:

I do not believe in miracles. But this I wish, that when the time comes
to lead me out from this bustling world, that I just once will be allowed
to leave the grave, so I can come and stand at your door and call for you.

If you should need a partner in grief then I will be there, to
   comfort you.
If not, then I will turn once more, to set out on the road to
   oblivion.

It's obvious why Ralph gave it to me after John's death. But now, reappearing after his own, it's almost as if he is sending me a message. Not just from himself, but from all the people I have lost, who are close to me still. Comforting me, and turning once more.

The words, both in Urdu and in English, recite themselves in my brain as I sleep. They are there when I wake. As I sit at my computer working on my story, the poem infiltrates itself, becomes part of it.

~ 8 ~

Nearly There

Steinbeck's advice to writers of fiction: 'Abandon the illusion that you are ever going to finish.'

Yet I think I am near. The story has its own existence, its own kind of truth, that comes from within and cannot now be tampered with. I have detached from the need to check facts, and let the people in the story follow the paths they have to take, because of who they are.

But it will not be completed until some other mind has absorbed it.

I begin with trusted friends. I listen to their reactions. Each time I learn something new about my own story. Sometimes it's about something incidental, a word, a place, which triggers a certain reaction. Or they are reacting to the relationships which hold up an unnerving mirror, the images bouncing back differently depending on what is going on in that reader's life. People don't always tell me those reactions because they are too personal, but there are clues. I don't change anything in response, but I am constantly considering the order in which things are shared with the reader, the right moment for this nuance, or that revelation.

A few loyal friends read draft after draft. They are on Steinbeck's side – doubting if I will ever let it go.

I have become a wordsmith, working this delicate craft with an almost obsessive attention to detail. I cut words, sentences, paragraphs, whole incidents. I become ruthless, each bit has to justify its continued presence. I print out re-draft after re-draft. At first I worry about all the trees I'm cutting down, then I detach myself from that thought too. Paper is one of my tools, I can't do it any other way.

The discarded drafts provide my grandchildren with one-side-used-paper for drawings, and the entire family with scrap paper for years to come.

My story has a name. *Uncertain Light.*

~ 9 ~

Washed Up by the Tide

I am remembering walking on the sand on the coast of Washington, looking out over the endless Pacific. I have come back after a 30 year absence. The last time I was here was as an exchange student. At my feet now are the crushed shells of a million creatures, battered by the incoming tides. Miraculously intact at the tide-mark is a line of sand dollars, slim flat discs with pricked-out star patterns. Washed up safe by the tide.

Sending a story out into the world feels like trusting something as fragile as these sand dollars to the ocean, hoping the tide will carry it. And if it does? No idea where it will get washed up, or if anyone will ever pick it up. But I know my job won't be finished until someone does.

Uncertain Light floated about, unnoticed, for a couple of years. Over the years I've gathered a lot of loyal readers and a few literary prizes, but I know well that these things do not move agents, and for good reasons. They don't earn anything on a book until it's out there and doing well, so they don't have the luxury of taking on any book they like. They have to double-guess what publishers will think they can sell. Publishers in the UK produce 184,000 new books a year, that is over 500 *each day*. Why would anyone notice this one?

This is my fourth novel. The standard letter I get from agents (if they've looked at the book at all) says, 'You write beautifully but I don't think I'd be able to place it in today's increasingly competitive market.' There's another kind of letter which suggests that if only I would write a novel set among trendy young city-living women, they'd be happy to consider it. Sadly I'm incapable of writing to order, neither sex and the city, nor vampires, nor fast-paced thrillers, nor science fiction, nor any of the other categories that publishers know how to market. The kind of story I tell does have a label in the trade, it's called Literary Fiction. And unless the writer has an already easily recognised name, that spells doom to publishers.

I know I'm in good company. Most writers could paper their walls with reject letters. George Orwell was told that stories about animals don't sell. The publishers who rejected Herman Melville felt the same about whales. The first Harry Potter book was rescued from the reject pile only because an editor thought it might amuse his child. When he did give way to his child's insistence and take it on, he urged J K Rowling to keep on her day job as the book was very unlikely to bring her much income.

Between established writers who get large advances and those who never get published at all spreads a multitude of the rest of us. One-book-wonders who find a publisher first time, and when the second book doesn't do well, don't get taken on again. Slow-burners, excellent writers who are published by independent publishers but never get well known enough to make it into the big league. Various degrees of self-publishing, from which a mere handful of writers will be heard amidst the clamour of on-line voices.

I'm lucky not to have to earn my living through my books. I don't need to worry about whether the book is making money. I don't write to anyone else's deadlines, or even consider parting with my book until I'm absolutely satisfied that this is its final form, however many years that takes. I've never yet persuaded a mainstream publisher that they're likely to make money from any of my books, but I've learnt to follow a maxim Ralph taught me. Expect nothing, hope for everything, and settle for what you can get.

~

When The Women's Press decided to publish my collection of short stories I knew I was lucky but I had no idea how lucky. I was 40 years old. Untested, first-time writers that age do not normally find it easy to attract publishers. If they're going to take a risk, they'd prefer to do it with someone young. Not only that: short stories are even harder to sell than novels. Short stories by a first-time writer are simply likely to sink.

The luck was in the timing. It was 1985, my stories had grown out of my work teaching English to women from India and Pakistan, and at that time there was as yet almost no published fiction reflecting their experiences. I would have been delighted to get even one review, but *A Language in Common* got seven in national and regional papers. Ahmed Rashid, reviewer for The Independent, called it 'The most extraordinary book of short stories ... One of the first attempts to straddle in fiction the social divide between white Britons and Asians.'

Of how you promote a book, get it known, I learnt very little because The Women's Press did it all for me. I was interviewed on BBC's Women's Hour, and on ten regional radio and TV stations. It was translated into Italian and German, and extracts appeared in anthologies. Within a few years it had sold 5,000 copies. I know now that a major publisher wouldn't notice such a figure long enough to sniff at it, but I've heard of plenty of books that have been junked before they reached 1,000. Publishers Weekly tells me that the average sales for books 'traditionally produced' (that is, by larger publishers) is 250 to 300 copies in the first year, and 3,000 over its lifetime. I'm sceptical about how you work out a meaningful average when the scales are tipped in one direction by J K Rowling and James Patterson, but still it's a comforting figure for those of us at the other end.

For my first novel, political timing was against me. *A Shield of Coolest Air* is set among Somali refugees in London, and most novel readers in the UK had then hardly heard of Somalia. I found an agent but she couldn't find a publisher willing to risk such an out-of-the-way topic. I hadn't written it to let it languish in a bottom drawer unread, so after a few more months of getting nowhere, I decided to publish it myself. Attitudes to self-publishing have begun to broaden out in recent years, but there's still an assumption that if you can't find a proper publisher your book is no good. At that time that reaction was universal. I was strengthened against believing it by the support of friends who had loved my stories and read drafts of the novel, and were outraged at the idea of it being rejected. Perhaps also by what you might call a novelist's maternal instinct. Every new mother knows that her own child is beautiful.

I guess I wasn't afraid because Robert was a publisher and could help me learn about the process. He wasn't so sure. Zed Books publishes academic books not fiction, and he knew nothing about marketing fiction, he said. He was anxious that I would build up false hopes and be disappointed, so once he had given me contacts and explained processes I tried not to involve him. From among his colleagues I found people to help me with each step, a designer, copy editor, type setter, printer, advice on ISBN numbers. It all costs, more than I had imagined. Ralph lent me £5,000 which he said I could repay when it became a best-seller, or not at all if it didn't.

Apart from the actual work of producing the book, it seemed all I needed to set myself up as a publisher was a name and a letterhead. I called it Shola Books, easy for English speakers to pronounce but with multi-cultural possibilities. 'Shola' in Urdu means fire, in Tamil a grove of trees, and in Africa it's a girl's name meaning 'one who is blessed'. All of those felt promising. Major publishers have many different imprint names so I assumed no one would bother to check it out. I needed an address (not mine) for the publisher, so Ralph offered his, and (in the unlikely event of anyone ever phoning Shola Books) his phone number. I needed a name for the publisher-person who would be sending out letters with review copies. People take made-up writer names, so why not a made-up publisher name? I kept on the near side of honesty by calling my alter-ego Irène (my middle name) Fair (my mother's maiden name.) If I'd lived in a matriarchy I'd have been 'Fair' from birth, and if I hadn't married before the women's movement got going I wouldn't have changed my name.

Boxes of books arrived from the printer, filling a room of our small flat. I had a launch party with all the friends who had helped me. I produced a flyer and addressed envelopes to everyone I knew (no email in those days) and orders arrived in encouraging numbers. People who had liked *A Language in Common* ordered extra copies to give to friends for Christmas. I turned myself into a mail order centre, parcelling up books, filling a suitcase on wheels every couple of days, and trundling off to the post office.

From Robert I got an introduction to Central Books, a distributor that works with independent publishers. Distributors are critical. They warehouse books, and through travelling reps get them known to bookshop buyers. But bookshops would only take a book if the reps could assure them that people would be coming in asking for it. Which meant reviews. Off went review copies, 50 of them. Friends played the role of promotions people, phoning to try and bring the book to the attention of literary editors. One said, 'I get hundreds of new books on my desk every week. Why should I review this one?' It seemed a good question, so we quickly prepared a sales-talk, and my friends were ready with it for the next phone call.

By now the war in Somalia was often in the news. Perhaps it was this, the very thing that had made publishers think the book would sink, that now helped us get it to float. It got multiple reviews, had to be reprinted after six months, and again six months later. Only books by well known authors stay on the shelves of bookshops more than a couple of months but having it on the bookshop system meant that anyone who heard about it could go in and order it.

Then it won a prize, a minor one called the David St John Thomas Award for Fiction that no one had ever heard of, but still, a literary prize. I got a phone call from a journalist who had reviewed it for The Independent. She hadn't heard about the prize but somehow she had scented a story behind the book and asked if she could interview me for The Women's Page of The Guardian.

Surely now I had arrived as a writer, and the door would open?

It was seven years before my next novel emerged. By now any small name-recognition I might have acquired with my first novel was lost, but after the first crop of rejections it did find an agent. Brian Stone, a wonderful enthusiast, was a partner at a major agency, and he loved *If You Can Walk, You Can Dance*. Briefly I was on a high. He was hugely experienced and handled accounts for big-name writers, so his endorsement really meant something, but the book went through the usual wringer of rejections. He was about to retire and sadly admitted defeat. Where someone of his range of contacts had failed, it didn't seem worth trying another.

So I did it myself again. At least now I knew it could be done; but this time it seemed harder. It got two small reviews. What kept it afloat was the support of friends. In the evenings the front room of our home turned once again into a packing room. I was grateful for each order. Each parcel I sent off represented yet another person who was joining me in this bizarre activity, getting lost in my imaginary world.

Once again I entered the book for prizes, signing the letters with my publisher name, Irène Fair. This was, I decided, possibly the only advantage of being self-published: publishers decide which books to enter for prizes. Had I been taken on by a major publisher there was little chance my book would have been submitted. I knew as I sent copies off that this was fantasy-land stuff, but by now the edges of reality and fantasy had become blurred.

~

I popped in to see Ralph after work one day, to find him on the phone. He was hard of hearing, even with hearing aids, so he often had to get people to repeat things. He was saying, 'Irène Fair? No, there's no one of that name who lives here.' I grabbed the receiver from him and took over the call. It was someone phoning to tell Shola Books that 'one of your authors' had been awarded a Commonwealth Writers Prize. Could I come in and discuss details?

So there I was, going in to their offices to explain that Irène Fair, publisher, and the author of *If You Can Walk, You Can Dance* were the same person. Would they throw me out, or be entertained? The young woman I met thought it was great, lone author defies the odds. It went further up the line, and still no one threw my book out. I had squeaked in before major prize administrators had thought of putting in regulations to prevent books like mine from being entered. It had gone through the process, been judged a winner, so a winner it was.

The roll-call of previous winners was giddy-making. I was following Margaret Atwood, Vikram Seth, Rohinton Mistry, Michael Ondaatje, Alice Munro, Ben Okri. The prize was unique, in being determinedly international. Awards were given in four regions of the Commonwealth (that is, most of the English-writing world except for the United States) for the 'Best Book' and the 'Best First Book' in each region. The organisers did for me all the things a publisher would have done, flying me to New Zealand where the prizes were to be awarded, and where the host team adopted me.

They gave us a whirlwind cultural tour. Art exhibitions. Receptions with a bewildering number of people. Public readings from our books. Visiting the newly opened national museum, Te Papa Tangarewa (Maori for 'container of treasures'). Driving up into the mountains to visit a wine farm in a beautiful valley. Each of us made our own discoveries among our fellow writers, people who became friends for that week, and whose books we would later read with special pleasure.

And the future? Getting a Commonwealth Writers Prize had helped several writers make their names. If I had had a publisher, this might have been my break-through moment. Thousands more copies might have been printed, negotiations made with booksellers to profile the book. But it was just me. I got that wonderful week and £1,000 in prize money, which I spent paying a professional literary publicist to try and get the book placed with a publisher. But because it was already published, none would take it.

Well, that's the way it goes. You win some, you lose some, and I'd had a really good innings.

~

Five years on my new novel, *Somewhere More Simple,* was doing the usual rounds, with the usual rejections. 'You write beautifully, but …'

OK, do it again.

By now we had entered the age of websites. If I wanted this book to come out of something that looked like a publisher, it couldn't be one that did only my book. I thought about all the other people who might need help getting their books out there, and decided to set up a community publishing venture. Each author would have to fund their own book but we could share expertise and resources for promotion. I collected up people who had written books that had been overlooked by mainstream publishers, or been published in short runs and then abandoned, or been published by independent publishers that had gone out of business. There were 16 of us to start with, and a collection of interesting books which definitely shouldn't have been allowed to disappear without anyone reading them. I called it Longstone Books. My daughter's partner, a designer, did us a logo. A friend set up a website. Others agreed to take on the nominal roles of director, editorial advisors, events organisers. Fact began to follow fiction. I did guidelines for new writers who wanted to join us but weren't yet published, and I talked them through all the stages of production. I applied for a grant from a reading agency and organised launches for our books, grouped together by theme. I paid a young student friend to do some of the legwork, and did the rest myself.

So *Somewhere More Simple* came out, published by the respectable-looking independent publisher, Longstone Books. All my loyal readers were still there for me, ordering copies. Its setting on the Isles of Scilly gave me a new angle to get libraries interested. The track record of my previous books got it a surprising number of reviews.

I don't want to be a publisher, I want time to write, but it seemed I couldn't do one without the other. Each time I had taken up the task with the same determination to help this book survive, but each time with less élan. I really, *really* hoped never to have to do it myself again.

And now I was sending *Uncertain Light* out to sea. Waiting for replies. Getting rejections from agents who clearly hadn't even looked at it.

~ 10 ~

Enter: A Publisher

2014, Wiltshire

I'm in a hamlet in rural Wiltshire where for some years we've had a small cottage. I write here whenever I can, at my desk under the window, looking out over fields to a low ridge of hills beyond. We get together with grandchildren here, and for years I have gardened here. It's a small garden but I love it passionately, looking out on it when it's raining, luxuriating in it when it's not. I feel extraordinarily lucky to have this retreat from the world.

In Europe, Crimea dominates the news. In the Arab world it is ISIS. In Nigeria Boko Haram are abducting girls. In West Africa there is an Ebola epidemic. Since I retired from Save the Children I hear these things differently, because people I know are at the front line.

Checking my emails … Another reject from a literary agent. This is probably number 30. I have reached the end, and I'm not waiting any longer. I have to get my book out there. So, regretfully, it's headed for self-publishing.

Then a publisher arrives, coming across the field and up the path.

Hector Macdonald is about the age of my daughters. He is down from London for the weekend, visiting his mother, our neighbour. He's a successful novelist and an innovator who has set up a website for book-lovers. Now he is setting up an unusual independent publisher, Advance Editions. Thousands of people love to post book reviews on-line, he says, so why not offer them the chance to read a pre-final version, and give their reactions when the author can still make use of them? A cute term for it is 'crowd-editing', but it's up to the author what to take on board. To me it sounds like win-win. Getting pre-publication readers is what I do anyway with friends, but this would make it possible to get responses from a much wider group. The real plus is that those who take part are likely to feel a personal connection with the book, so there'll be a ready-made set of fans to help it get known.

Hector is going to test it out initially with three books, different genres. A thriller, his own. A collection of short pieces by a woman journalist about her time in Afghanistan. And for the third, he wants literary fiction. Would I be interested in him looking at my novel?

He gets a copy that day. Within a couple of weeks I get a phone call. He'd like to take it.

He needs me and I need him. How is that for luck?

~

September 2014
Waterloo Station, London. The tannoy is booming, the crowds are pushing, but we find a table in a coffee shop and Hector pulls

out the contract. The signing ceremony — and I feel absurdly delighted. I'm excited not just for my book but also for his project. A major communications company has taken him on. There's been an article in The Bookseller, the book trade's magazine. He's going to debate the idea on BBC with Philip Pullman. Now, like every other publisher, he needs these book to make money, and I hope to goodness they do.

It's a good day to sign a publishing contract. I've just turned 70.

~

October 2014

I am realising quickly how privileged I am to be part of something new, experimental, and therefore spacious. Hector devolves specialist functions — production, e-book, promotion, distribution. He understands enough about each to make good choices, and he sits in the middle, keeping tabs on the whole process. There are no hidebound procedures that must be followed, no Marketing Department deciding what Editorial can do. I've heard stories about writers with mainstream publishers who have had covers they hated thrust on them because the sales people were branding the book for a particular segment of the market. I suffer no such traumas. Hector agrees to use the designer who has done covers for my other novels. Andrew Corbett and I have an ideal writer-designer relationship. We have a long conversation about the book, and he goes away and comes up with something that fits it perfectly.

Hector himself goes through my text with a precise writer's eye. Several of his suggestions push me back to making adjustments which definitely improve it. If we disagree on minor details I'm happy to compromise. Well, usually. A couple of times I won't budge, and he accepts that. We have agreed I would cut the length by 20,000 words. That's a lot of words to throw away, but he's willing to pay an experienced editor to help me do it. A friend in publishing recommends someone who she thinks will do it sensitively, and I couldn't have asked for anyone better.

Now we're onto permissions, specifically, about the quotations of poetry. If you quote lines of popular songs you still have to get copyright permission, and someone's making money out of them for 50 to a 100 years after the death of the song-writer. *Uncertain Light* is full of quotations from poetry but most are from Urdu and Persian poets long dead. The translations are Ralph's, for which I hold copyright — I am his literary executor. The tricky part is the fictional Tajik poet. I needed fragments of his poetry and I borrowed them from a real poet, Rasul Gamzatov, the one whose poem inspired Faiz's. I know this was a weird thing to do but Gamzatov is dead, and unknown to anyone ever likely to read my book. He and my fictional Tajik poet were both Soviet-era poets from Muslim cultures living in remote mountainous areas. Using fragments from his poems seemed a way of making the fictional poet authentic.

'But you have permission?' Hector says.

Actually, no. There is no publisher to give permission. The collection of translations I took them from was published in the early 1970s by a Soviet state publisher that no longer exists. Gamzatov wrote in the Avar language spoken by only a few hundred thousand people in remote mountain villages of Dagestan in the North Caucasus. I can't imagine that anyone there will be reading English novels. I did try to track down the translator and I finally found his son, an academic in the United States. We had a brief email exchange. His father is no longer alive, and the son is not bothered about people quoting the translations.

Hector is still cautious, and takes legal advice.

Well obviously, if you ask lawyers, they're going to say, 'Play it safe.' So I do one final google search to see if there is anyone I can get permission from. Up comes a photo of Putin unveiling a memorial to Gamzatov. Just last year, in Moscow. Apparently Gamzatov is hugely famous in Russia. How did I miss that earlier? He himself translated his poems into Russian. Putin calls him a national hero, the People's Poet. And many Russians read English.

OK, abandon the poems. Hector says, 'Can't you just write some yourself?'

But poems don't just arrive like that, on demand.

I wake at three a.m. with the first line of a poem ready formed. By the end of the week I have produced a small collection of the poems of the fictional poet, Rahman Mirzajanov.

~

November 2014

Hector is often either arriving or departing so train stations are where we meet. This time it is St Pancras, where the trains leave for Europe. Over coffee he says he has unfortunate news. The first two Advance Editions books have been up on the website for a couple of months now, inviting comments, and the response has been very disappointing. The founding premise of his publishing idea was that there would be lots of people out there who would love to put their thoughts about books on-line, but clearly they haven't found the Advance Editions books.

I feel for him, after all the thought and energy, not to mention the funding that he has invested in this project. I understand little about how things do or don't get noticed in among the millions of items of digital information being generated every second, but it doesn't seem to me surprising that some just don't make it. I don't feel his idea was misconceived. Everything is chancy, and there was probably an even chance that it could have worked.

So, he says, he will not be taking on any more books. He will see through his existing commitments, then Advance Editions will close. He will have to rebalance his own activities, and there is a limit to what he can offer post-production. The upshot is, he is offering to release me from our contract if I would like to take *Uncertain Light* elsewhere.

It doesn't occur to me to accept. To go back to looking for agents and publishers? I've been there, and it's a no-man's land.

I tell him I greatly appreciate his support so far, and I want to go ahead as planned. I will do whatever I personally can to try to generate a bigger swell of responses, and even if he can do very little promotion it's still helpful to me to officially have a publisher. I'll do the leg-work, if he will send stuff out as from the publisher, and I hope that the book will earn enough to repay what he has put into it.

We call it the St Pancras Station Agreement.

~ 11 ~

Advance Promotion

So — this bit's up to me.

I have succumbed to the gentle insistence of younger friends that I'm going to need to come to terms with social media. Patient friends help me over the first humps onto Facebook. I am so un-techno-savvy that they hardly understand which bits I don't get. I make notes of all my queries but I can't keep bothering them so I go on a social media training course, whose essential function is to introduce me to the vocabulary that I have apparently been blocking my ears to because I thought I didn't need it. I now know what a hashtag is, understand the 21st century meanings of chat, friend, like, platform, post, sharing, timeline. I privately share the joke with my mother – gone these 25 years, but in her time a lover of precise meanings of words.

I have updated my phone, posted my first photo, and started

reconnecting with friends from Save the Children days, now scattered across the world. It's brilliant. So many people I had lost — they're all out there somewhere.

I still don't get Twitter. How to do it, why you would want to, who will catch my so-short message amidst the flying debris of 350,000 tweets a minute? I feel I ought to get to grips with it and ask the journalist who ran the social media course if I can pay him for a one-to-one session. He comes to my house, does it very patiently, and refuses to accept payment. I have no idea why. He won't budge; so I give him one of my books.

I have barely started tweeting when I get a vivid demonstration of its reach. Someone in Moscow has picked up an Advance Editions tweet, hashtag #centralasia. Ed Lemon is British, doing a PhD on Tajikistan, lived there for two years, speaks Tajik and Russian, and is excited to find that there's a novel coming out that is set there. He interviews me (phone & email) for a journal he edits.

~

The cover design is finalised and now we're sorting out the back cover blurb. Do I know anyone who might give us a comment for it? A famous writer? I don't know any.

Then, reading the latest Man Booker Prize winner, I discover through googling that I know one of the judges, Alastair Niven. He chaired the Commonwealth Writers Prize and was with us in New Zealand the year I was awarded one. Since then he and Robert have served on a board of trustees together. Alastair made the connection, we exchanged a few emails. He suggested we meet for lunch sometime but then was busy and we didn't get round to fixing a date. Now I understand what he was busy with. Reading 154 novels. I can't possibly ask him to read yet another.

It's surprising what obstacles self-interest will overcome. We meet for lunch. Tentatively, I ask him. Psychologically I have an escape clause — it doesn't feel like self-interest, more like a tigress looking after her young.

Alastair is not only eminent, he is also extremely kind. He knows scores, probably hundreds, of the best-known fiction writers yet he has agreed to read my book. We both know he won't give it a serious commendation unless he thinks it merits it; and I'm grateful for that.

There is one person to whom I have to send it before it goes public, Bronwen, who headed Save the Children's work in Tajikistan. She lived there for three years, negotiating highly stressful situations while I just came and went. She is a friend I value yet hardly ever see, for she has been mostly thousands of miles away. Now she is back in Britain looking after her elderly mother, in a small town in Wales where I doubt if any of her neighbours have the least idea what a remarkable life she has led.

I get in touch and tell her what I have been doing. I am nervous she might feel I have been treading on her territory, but she reacts beautifully. Once I have sent it I try not to think about her reading it. She says she doesn't get much time to read, and it will take her a while. Three days later ... I am away from home, awake late at night in my daughter May's home. My phone pings in the dark, an email from Bronwen. She has read it non-stop over a weekend when she should have been doing other things. At two in the morning we have a delightful buzz of emails, while around us others sleep.

After that I feel OK about whatever anyone else might think.

~

December 2014

Life goes into overdrive as Christmas approaches and everyone tries to make plans to see everyone they connect with. All other activities stop until after New Year. This year I'm grateful for the pause. Family and daily life have been going on all the time I've been getting the book ready, but now I can push it firmly into the background. Both daughters and their families are here – one lot journeying down from Yorkshire to join us. Having them all with us is hectic, tiring, and wonderful, and brushes my mind clean.

~

January 2015
It's done. *Uncertain Light* is up on the Advance Editions website. Readers are invited to download the first chapter free, and if that interests them, they can get the e-book of this pre-final version at discount price and post on the website their suggestions for the final edit. A gratifying number of my friends have downloaded the book.

~

February 2015
Comments coming in now, from readers across the world. Hector needs to get it into production soon so I don't have long to decide if I want to incorporate their suggestions.

Over 60 people have commented. Most say they got totally absorbed and loved it. Once I've heard this a few times I can relax. The story works. Knowing that, I can listen to any other points they make without feeling defensive. A couple say, 'I wouldn't dream of making suggestions, it's your book' but there are plenty of small useful points. An Australian reader tells me that a koala isn't a bear, it's just a koala. A Canadian reader says they have prairies not plains. An agricultural consultant who knows Central Asia says he loved the descriptions of landscape, 'But I missed the sheep!' Central Asian sheep are distinctive, with long floppy ears. When you're out of town in nomadic areas they are everywhere. So I put in some sheep. It takes no more than a sentence but lights the picture instantly.

A few say it took them a while to get into the book and then they loved it. That's a warning sign. If they hadn't been friends, they might not have persevered. I have to do something about that.

I get back to them all – can they tell me what didn't work in the early part? They can't, so I have to work it out myself. It's a question of shuffling around the order in which things are revealed to the reader. I've done this so many times, yet it needs doing again.

Only one person makes a comment that impinges on plot. My nephew in Australia says there's one event that relies too much on coincidence. 'I know coincidences happen but it raises the possibility of disbelief, when you probably don't want to.' No, I certainly don't. I look at it again, and immediately see another way that the same thing could have happened. Once I've adapted it, it's obvious that this is how it always was meant to be. Thank you David.

Alastair Niven has sent his comment, generous lines from which we can select what we like to put on the cover. *So* kind. What can I say?

The words we take are 'A moving and necessary novel'.

When I thank him I add, '*Necessary* is an unusual word to use about a novel?'

'Not for me. I have read so many that make you wonder, who needs this? Why did they bother?'

~

March 2015

I'm done. I throw away all the earlier versions and send off the final-final document, happy to see it go. *Hamba kahle*, they say in Xhosa or Zulu, Go gently. Out of my hands now.

~

April 2015

I'm off, taking my 14 year old grand-daughter to meet her cousins in Sydney. Stopover in Singapore, then two weeks of reunion with people I love, in a new place, different winds blowing my head clean. Connecting with nature, noticing shapes and textures with sharpened vision after my long head-down.

Back in Wiltshire, the beauty of an early spring morning. After a lazy breakfast on the patio I somewhat reluctantly go inside, make a cup of coffee, and open my computer. There's an email from a publisher in India.

In the year while *Uncertain Light* was floating about waiting to be picked up by an agent, I had been putting together a new edition of Ralph's writing on the poet Ghalib. It's being published in India. Ralph's knowledge of Urdu literature made him a legend in India and Pakistan and he was never short of a publisher. The proofs arrived for me to check about the time *Uncertain Light* went up on the website. Nice dovetailing, a useful task while I waited. At the same time I emailed some of his friends in India to tell them the book would be out soon, and I happened to mention that I have a novel coming out.

One, a writer herself, replied, 'Why don't you see if you can get it published here?'

A friend of hers had just started as the commissioning editor at a new publisher. Why not try them?

Adrenalin surging, I checked them out. They have the delightful name of Speaking Tiger Books. These are serious players, experienced people. They have announced that they will be doing 35 books this year, aiming to grow rapidly to 80 a year. I am way out of my league here, but I'm getting used to just going for it.

The editor at Speaking Tiger replied promptly, the first time that has ever happened to me from an agent or publisher. She said, 'Yes, send it. We are frantically busy setting up so I wouldn't be able to look at it for a couple of months, but we'll put it out to a reader.'

And now, just two months later, another email from her. 'Have read the novel now, and am glad to say I totally agree with what our reader said. It's a wonderful, accomplished novel, and we would love to publish it in India.'

I've waited a lifetime to get that kind of reply from a publisher.

I still can hardly take it in, that with so much excellent English language fiction being written in India, they are taking on a novel by a non-Indian. I say this to Renuka Chatterjee, the editor. She says, 'We're taking it because we love it. It's not about being Indian or non-Indian, but just having a good story and being able to tell it well. And if anyone is still concerned about nationalities, the pivotal character, Rahul Khan, is Indian anyway.'

They're going to rush it through production to get it out very soon after the UK edition.

This isn't just another publisher, not just another set of potential readers. They will be bringing the story back to one of its sources.

~ 12 ~

Pushing Out the Boat

May 2015

Hector wasn't sure we needed a launch event. It will cost a lot, he said, and won't make any difference to sales. I said, 'Well in that case I'm going to give a party and ask all my friends and the people who have supported me on this book, and as you are one of the main ones, I hope you will come.'

I was pretty sure the other Advance Editions author, Heidi Kingstone, would feel the same. She is a journalist, writes for a living, but this is her first actual book and she is as excited as I am. We can get Daunt's Bookshop in London free in an evening as long as we can get 70 people to come, and since there are three of us launching our books we can easily do that; and maybe people who come for one of us will end up buying the other books too. Hector changes his mind.

So here we are. There was a last minute crisis. The printers were late and the copies of *Uncertain Light* hadn't yet arrived. How can you have a book launch without the book? But they got in late last night, and here they are piled up, with Andrew's beautiful cover. The book itself is a shock — the size of it! So much bigger than I had imagined. I know it's not longer than my other novels, it's all to do with production decisions. The page format is large, the paper is thick, the type-face is large. Large format novels are In, but it looks about the size of *War and Peace* and won't people be put off buying it?

'Don't worry,' a friend says, 'it's really easy on the eye. It'll read quick.'

No worry about numbers, the place is crowded, a rising buzz of conversation. I'm flying on adrenalin, watching friends rediscover friends. In the absence of a podium, Hector pulls up a chair to stand on so he can be seen over all those heads, and we are off. First Hector, then Heidi, and then it will be me. We've agreed ten minutes each to introduce our books. That's as long as anyone can be expected to stand with a glass in their hand listening. Actually it's too long, but it's too late to change that. I am used to speaking in public but this time I have written it out and learnt it, like the script of a play, and rehearsed it walking on the common, talking to the crows.

My turn. A crowd of faces looking up at me, waiting.

I begin with that road into the mountains, the story of how the story came to be.

One journey has ended, another is beginning. What is sure is that this is no longer my story alone. It will take on life in the mind of the reader, and differently for each one.

IN SEARCH OF READERS

~ 13 ~

Fiction A – Z

The book exists. Now how to find readers?

It's in a few bookshops. Who will ever find it there? I have an image of a bookshop I saw in Delhi, so many books there was scarcely room for people to move between them. Even in a well-ordered British bookshop, you never notice how many novels there are until you've got one of your own, hidden under Fiction A-Z. Virginia Woolf used to go into a depression when she walked in and found her book on the bottom shelf. W is the wrong letter to begin with. M is no better.

What you really need is to have the book placed front-facing, the cover tempting the reader, but the only times I spot mine it's like all the rest, just the spine showing. I consider rearranging the shelf while no one's looking.

I restrain myself.

My friends, of course, my loyal reader friends who over decades have read drafts of my books, or bought copies to give as Christmas presents, or got their book groups to read them — Without them I'd be at a loss. Facebook, coming into its own now, a way to tell all those more scattered friends, people I once worked with who now work in countries around the world. But beyond that, to people I don't know?

Reviews are the thing. I did quite well on reviews for my earlier books, but it gets tougher all the time. It's that 500-new-books-a-day situation. Advance Editions has been taken on by an ace promotions firm, looking to get reviews. We meet, talk through possibilities, I give them lists of previous reviews. They try, clearly they try. Nothing comes of it.

My well-wishers offer suggestions. Couldn't my publisher get it on that display table at the front of the bookshop? Ah, that table. Major publishers have entered into contracts with bookshop chains long before books come out to get them there, tens of thousands of pounds worth per title. It's nice to think that someone gets there, but we're not talking about the same league here.

What about the Richard and Judy Book Club? The answer is the same.

Literary festivals?

If you're thinking big, or even middle-sized, forget it. Mainstream publishers are on the case with all of them. Their promotions people scramble to get slots for their new books, and there is an obvious pecking order: well known writers come first. It's logical. To run a festival takes money so the organisers have to charge for tickets to events, and few people will pay to hear a writer they have never heard of.

But why not try?

I trawl the internet to compile an updated list of festivals. There has been an exponential growth of smaller literary festivals. One UK data-base lists 350.

It's a matter of classification what counts as small. They range from the modest home-grown to the rural-but-above-average-income population, and of course publishers will be after those too. Anything that will sell books.

I winnow out those where I clearly have no chance, check out the others to see what kind of writers they took on last year, and for any hint that their organisers might be sympathetic to literary fiction set in other places. Then I draft personalised letters and Hector sends them as from Advance Editions.

Let's see.

~ 14 ~

Early Travels with a Book

My first experience of travelling with a book felt like the wildest fantasy. For a start it was somewhere I would never have got to otherwise, literally on the other side of the world from my daily life. My novel *If You Can Walk, You Can Dance* got me there, through the Commonwealth Writers Prize. One of the hosting team in New Zealand was Carole Beu, a woman of boundless energy and enthusiasm who ten years earlier had set up a Women's Bookshop in Auckland, and it's still going strong. She had been reading her way through the prize-winning books and happened to come to mine last, so she was deep in it through the week we were all together. Each morning over breakfast in the hotel where we were all staying she would tell me where she had got to. Getting the daily bulletin was like reliving my own novel in soap-opera form.

At the end of the week she suggested I enter it for the Listener Women's Book Festival later that year. The organisers (Carole was one) invited publishers to submit new books by women and chose a 'top 20' list, both New Zealanders and international. Local groups across the country then chose from the list the writers that they would like to have visit their town, and an individual tour programme was arranged for each.

But how could I, with no publisher to pay my costs …?

Carole said, 'Just enter, and if it's selected, we'll find a way.'

I did, and they did. The festival's sponsorship covered my costs. A request was put out to independent publishers for one to adopt me for the duration. Jenny Nagle, who had just set up a small press called Addenda, took me on as if I had been one of her authors. She made my travel plans and got me media interviews, including on a prime-time Saturday radio chat show. For ten days I was carried on a wave of generosity across the country, South Island to North Island. In each town local women met me at airports, booked hotels or hosted me in their homes, took me to venues where ready-made audiences waited, delightful people with boundless enthusiasm for books. Bookshops in each town stocked my book. Places that were just names before, have left me with pictures that don't fade … Napier, its town centre in Art Deco architecture, built after most of the city was destroyed in an earthquake … Dunedin, with views over the Otago peninsula, the furthest point south I am likely ever to be … Gisborne, with the sunrise over the endless sea, the first town to see it each day … Christchurch, which 11 years later would suffer a traumatic earthquake. I remember it for a couple of days moving around the city centre from one radio and press interview to the next, an evening reading to a packed hall in a girls' school, then next morning snatching a couple of hours before my flight to walk around the beautiful botanic gardens.

I flew home heady with appreciation, theirs for me, mine for them all. Back to normal life, home to where hardly a bookshop stocked my books.

Salutary, to keep a sense of proportion.

~

When my next novel came out I had just retired, so I had time to give it, if I could find events willing to have me. *Somewhere More Simple* is set on the Isles of Scilly so it had local connections in Cornwall, and an enterprising Reading Development Officer set up talks for me in libraries in six Cornish towns. After that word began to spread and I got invitations to do short library tours in other counties. That gave me the confidence to have a bash at getting into some of the smaller literary festivals.

Festivals in small towns have an atmosphere of their own. I love the lack of pretension, the fact that everything is being done by volunteers, and that they are providing cultural events in a place where everything needs to be homegrown. In that way they are like amateur dramatic societies, which thrive best far from big cities. I remember vividly arriving by train in King's Lynn, on the north Norfolk coast, and thinking, This as far as you can go without landing in the North Sea. If you look at the map you'll see England has a protruding hump on the east, and that's where it is. Centuries ago it was a thriving trading port but it has shrunk and gone into economic decline. Yet in this unlikely small town a group of volunteers organises every year *two* literary festivals, one for poetry and one for fiction, and they've been doing so since 1984. The year I was there all the sessions were packed out. I'm sure none of the 120 people listening had heard of me before. They just all came to everything.

Wells in Somerset was another. Its population is far smaller, 10,000 where Kings Lynn has 42,000, but it has atmosphere in spades, a stunning cathedral and a medieval Bishop's Palace where the literature festival sessions were held. They must have their pick of established authors, so why did they take me? When I asked the organiser later he said that he had been intrigued by this proposal from an independent publisher, about an author he had never heard of, but whose books had won prizes. It all seemed different from the standard publisher's blurb, and he took a risk. He must have backed up his risk with considerable effort, for 70 people came to my session. The bookstall sold out.

Absolutely my most embarrassing book-event moment was at a literature festival in a town where the organiser had, wildly optimistically, booked a small theatre which could have seated 200. There were four people. Everyone else had clearly known it wouldn't be worth the ticket price. If we'd been in a cosy room and could have sat comfortably facing each other it would have been possible to make it feel like a conversation, but here I was on a stage and the organiser, probably to cover his embarrassment, was fiddling with the lighting, so I couldn't even see the faces of those four properly. The challenge to say something that would make them feel they hadn't wasted their time was terrifying. Of course I had prepared, but it deserted me under the stress. I have no memory of what I said. I just remember trying to ignore what I was feeling and summon something that might be meaningful to these unknown people. As soon as I could I got on to asking them questions. Now, writing this, I decided to check back to see what the organiser wrote after the event. I am astonished to see it. 'She generated that feel-good factor where authors interact with readers.'

~

Finally — a positive response! From the Mere Literary Festival. As festivals go this is at the smaller end of small, but it's in Wiltshire, not far from the hamlet where we have a cottage, so I am (almost) a Local Author.

Mere is at the extreme southwest tip of the vast area of chalk downland that includes Salisbury Plain. The town looks up to an almost complete horseshoe of Downs. For anyone not British reading this, 'Downs' are actually 'Ups', hills formed millennia ago from the remains of sea-creatures. It's easy to imagine them having once been under the ocean, for they seem as smooth as if worn by water. Like many small rural towns Mere has a lot going on, with societies of all kinds. A writing group meets regularly and for nearly 20 years they have organised their own literary festival. It's run by volunteers on almost no budget, and raises funds for a local charity which provides transport for elderly people to get to hospital appointments. You'd be surprised how many well-known writers live in the surrounding countryside, so they can usually find enough writers to make an interesting programme.

Last book around, a local newspaper carried an interview with me, and on the strength of that I got invited to judge Mere festival's short story competition. Judging a story competition is a big chunk of work, and as they can't offer to pay, established writers weren't queueing up to do it. It was a salutary exercise. There were hundreds of entries. It reminded me how many people there are out there who are writing, for all the same reasons that I write, and entering competitions in the hope of making a break-through. It also got me thinking more sharply about what makes a good story.

The festival is still going, still being led by the same organiser. So now I have an invitation to talk about *Uncertain Light*.

And now I have to work out what I will say.

~ 15 ~

Appearing Wilfully in Public

The American poet (also playwright and early feminist) Edna St Vincent Millay said, 'Anyone who publishes a book appears wilfully in the public eye with their pants down'.

Speaking in public itself is fine, as long as I have some idea that people might be interested. But questions about your fictional story lead to questions about your own life, and that can be exposing.

I have a vivid memory of a moment when that happened. A friend had got her book group to read *If You Can Walk, You Can Dance,* and they invited me to come and talk to them. It's written through the eyes of Jennie, a young woman who has to flee from the political situation in South Africa and make a new life in other places. People who know that I grew up in South Africa and left for political reasons assume it's autobiographical, and that impression is reinforced by it being told in the first person. Someone in the group checked whether Jennie was me. I said the political context and the places were ones I knew well — I wouldn't have thought of locating a story there otherwise — but the personal story is completely different from my own. A man in the group who had not spoken till then said, 'Well, I'm glad you say it's not autobiographical, because I couldn't stand Jennie.'

It felt, to me, and by the shocked silence clearly also to the others, as personal as a slap in the face. But why should it? I am definitely not Jennie, and in saying so I had given him permission to be outspoken about his attitude to her.

But still.

There is something very personal about having imagined her, and lived with her so long. I'd probably have felt the same if he'd said my (real) child was an obnoxious brat.

Except for the most genre-specific novels (thrillers, vampires, science fiction) it's almost impossible for many readers to keep their reactions to the characters separate from their assumptions about the author. Vivid evocations of childhood lead one to wonder whether the child in the story was in fact the author. Khaled Hosseini's wonderful book *The Kite Runner* ... did he himself experience what happened to the boy? And how about Hisham Matar's novel *In the Country of Men* ? It describes a childhood during politically tense times in Libya in the 1970s, exactly the place and time of his early childhood years. That is of course why he is able to create a picture which feels authentic, but I take his word for it that it's a novel in the sense that the child in the book is not necessarily him, and the incidents described might have happened or might be fictional. It doesn't matter either way. The story is itself, and the skill lies in the telling and the sensitive perception.

Sometimes things we know about the author get in the way. I've never been able to read Lionel Shriver's *We Need to Talk about*

Kevin, though I admire her for tackling so painful a subject, the soul-searching by the mother of a boy who became a mass killer. I felt a wimp for not wanting to read it, and felt (illogically) justified when I learnt that Lionel Shriver does not have children. How could someone who is not a mother know what the mother of such a child would feel? But of course it's not relevant. Any writer of fiction steps way beyond what they personally have experienced. The question is how sensitively she can imagine herself into someone else's life, and I haven't given her the chance to convince me. Maybe one day I will.

Imagination doesn't emerge out of nothing. My stories are not about me, but they have grown out of what life has presented to me. All I can reflect in them is what I have observed and understood about the experience of living. That will move or engage some people and not others. Different people respond to different kinds of story. *If you can walk, you can dance* clearly didn't work for the man in the book group. That may have been because our ways of seeing and experiencing life are too different, or it may also have been something extraneous. A comment like that may tell you more about the person making it than it does about your book.

Now, when I wilfully put myself in the public eye, I try not to bother about whether my pants are in place. I remember the other part of what Edna St Vincent Millay said, less-often quoted: 'If it is a good book, nothing can hurt you. If it is a bad book, nothing can help you.'

The only thing to do it is to shed self-consciousness, and just be myself.

~ 16 ~

Worlds of Words

June 2015, Norwich

I stand in the cloisters of a cathedral that dates from the 12th century, awed by time and the detail of stone craftsmanship. I feel the aura of lives that have passed where I stand. In the 14th century a woman called Juliana, and later 'Julian of Norwich', moved through these echoing corridors in the desolation of repeated plagues of the Black Death. She chose to retreat into a self-isolating, contemplative life, and recorded her mystic experiences in the first book in English that we can be sure was by a woman. For centuries it was lost, but copies have emerged, her words speaking from another time of traumatic upheaval.

History is everywhere. Roman remains are scattered through the town centre. There are signs of the Vikings who sailed up the river. The keep of a medieval castle looks down from a dominating hill. Buildings from different centuries lean against each other. In Juliana's time this was, after London, the country's more important trading city. In our time the city has developed a literary reputation. The University of East Anglia established the country's first MA in Creative Writing here in 1970, and has produced scores of prize-winning writers. It hosts a Centre for Literary Translation. The Writers' Centre, separate from the university, offers short training courses for writers and hosts regular literary events. This one has the impressive title of Worlds Literature Festival. The 'Worlds' reflects who is gathering here, 37 writers from Belgrade and Bangalore, Calcutta and Kyoto, Istanbul and Ithaca, Leipzig and London, Melbourne and Mexico City, Seoul and Sao Paolo, Vilnius and Vancouver, all flying in, as their words have flown before them. A short seasonal migration.

I owe the invitation to be part of this extraordinary gathering to an old but recently re-discovered friend, Jonty Driver. When I was a university student in Cape Town, just getting into political activity, Jonty was the charismatic president of the national students' union, prominent in the anti-apartheid movement. He was held in solitary confinement by the security police and after a traumatic set of experiences came to Britain. We lost touch for years, and now we've reconnected and found that we've both been writing through all those years. I've been catching up on his poetry, he's been reading my novels. As a teacher he inspired in his pupils a love of literature – one of them became a professor at the University in Norwich. Jonty has suggested South Africa connected writers they might invite. Last year it was a Nobel Prize winner, J M Coetzee. This year it's me.

For my early morning walk I go through the cathedral garden to the river, and soon I've left all sense of a city behind. I watch the swans for a few moments, and then get out my book and begin reading aloud. Today it's my turn to take part in an hour of readings open to the public in the Cathedral Hostry, an atmospheric stone building, once part of a medieval monastery. It's a performance, just as acting in a play would be. Maybe harder, because I didn't write this intending it to be read aloud. I've practised, of course, but I need to time it. We each get 15 minutes. Which doesn't feel long when it's your one chance of interesting people in a whole novel.

The swans are obligingly attentive, staring at me with beady audience-eyes.

An elderly woman walks by, supporting her weight on two sticks. With English-politeness she behaves as if there is nothing odd about my reading to the swans. I explain about the event today. 'Ah,' she says, relieved that there is a reason other than that I am mad. In turn, she seems to feel she should explain her sticks. She has a bad back and is waiting for an operation; meanwhile she has to keep moving, to keep the pain at bay.

'Me too,' I say. 'My hip.'

She relaxes further.

'I'll tell you what,' I say, 'take your mind off your back. Come to my reading.'

I tell her where, when. The idea of coming to an event to hear authors read from their books must seem almost as bizarre to her as my reading to the swans.

~

We are here simply to interact with each other, a kind of collective retreat. We have meals together, laugh, listen. We sit in sessions discussing issues to do with the role of writers, with others who work in the field of literature. Translators, lecturers in creative writing, people from cultural and grant-giving institutions. Someone Tweets highlights into the ether. Technicians record the discussions. It's most of a life-time since I had to sit through seminars and I realise I've lost the art. When it gets too theoretical I'm doodling and thinking about how long till the next coffee break. I watch others around the room. The academics have more stamina than me, the younger writers more ambition, hoping to get their own voices heard. Across the room Jonty is looking down in a position that could be either deep concentration or gentle sleep. Probably the latter. I admire the ability to be ambiguous about it.

What I love, and what I'm sure the others like best too, are the times we hear from people about their own writing. There are novelists, poets, literary biographers, critics. There are new writers (one collection of short stories), others whose books sell world-wide. Several span cultural and historic borders. Susan Barker grew up in East London with an English father and Chinese-Malaysian mother, and in her novel, *Incarnations,* she imaginatively tracks millennia of Chinese history through the eyes of a taxi driver. George Szirtes, a child-refugee from Hungary in 1956, is a poet in English — direct, pointed poems that I like immediately — and also a translator from Hungarian. His translation of a László Krasznahorkai book has just been awarded a Man Booker International prize. I try to read it but after a few chapters I give up. George himself describes Krasznahorkai's writing as a 'slow lava flow of narrative'. At the other end of the spectrum in style is Anna Funder from Australia. Her novel *All that I am* recreates the dramatic true story of four German-Jewish intellectuals forced to flee to London in the early 1930s. Why have I never heard of her before? But then I haven't heard of most of the writers here. There are just so many creative people in the world.

Translators are key. Several writers are making their contributions in languages that the rest of us don't know, and it's their translators who do the reading. The one whose thoughts really get to me is a writer from Lithuania, Sigitas Parulskis. Most people in the room have never heard his name, but in Lithuania he has celebrity status, can draw huge crowds, has won every Lithuanian literature prize going. His work has been translated into at least ten languages, but clearly not enough into English. He writes everything — poetry, essays, plays, stories, journalism, and one controversial novel, which is what he's telling us about here. It is based on the hidden stories of Lithuanians who took part in the massacre of Jews during the Nazi occupation. That whole shameful chapter of history had somehow been airbrushed out of consciousness, so that Sigitas, born in 1965, had no idea of what had happened in his own home town until in the 1990s he visited London and saw an exhibition in the Imperial War Museum. It showed all the places where mass killings had happened, and he saw his own town on the map, listing the numbers of Jews murdered there. The English translation, when it comes out, will be called *Darkness and Company*. It won't be an easy story to read; but, to use Alastair Niven's phrase, a necessary one.

Now a Norwegian writer talks about his latest novel. His translator, Deborah Dawkin, talks about the challenges of translating it, and then reads an extract. The reading is unostentatious but riveting. Immediately I am in the house where the story is happening, inside the minds of the people. I thought I could read quite well, but this is in a class of its own. I want to be able to read like her.

Talking to her afterwards I discover that before she became a translator she was a trained actress. It shows. She lives in London. I ask if we can meet when we are both back, for her to give me a couple of sessions of coaching.

~

Back now in London, working with Deborah.

It feels strange reading aloud to one other person. Odd, after decades of reading to my children and grandchildren, but it's different with an adult whom I hardly know. Then I flip the internal monitor switch and imagine she's an audience. Pause. She tells me that I'm not thinking about the words I'm reading, which I instantly realise is true. I'm thinking about how I sound.

84

We go back over it. Now as I see each word ahead of reading it, the sentences seem to plod. Will anyone be interested in this? I realise I am rushing, as if taking it at speed will give it more élan.

Deborah says, 'You're reading the text empty of thought. You have to *think* each thought fresh, *at the moment* you are reading it.'

Trying to do that immediately slows me down. I can feel this is getting somewhere.

After the first session I ask if she'd like a copy of *Uncertain Light*.

Her email three days later says, 'I have just finished reading your exquisite novel. I started yesterday morning and couldn't stop, and now I want to read it all over again.'

I stop worrying about the sentences plodding, and get back to practising reading aloud. Slow this time, slow enough to think each thought fresh.

~ 17 ~

Fiction & Reality

July 2015, Penzance

Dawn over the harbour, and I am alone here to witness it.

Arriving at the western tip of Cornwall has for me a feeling of homecoming, home to where holidays happen. For decades we set off with our daughters on the ferry from Penzance each year for the Isles of Scilly, 30 miles out to sea. We had been three years in Britain when we first discovered them. Our applications to become British citizens were (we hoped) winding through the system (it took ten years in the end), and meanwhile Robert had no travel documents so couldn't leave the country. The long dark winters were getting him down. The map told me that the islands were the furthest south point we could get, and I had heard they grew daffodils in January, so I reckoned they must be warmer and lighter than anywhere else we could go. It was April, and when I look at the photos I see we were all always in anoraks, but our memory was that it was perfect. We went back every year until the girls were beginning to do holidays with their friends. Skip a few years and we started again, with successive boyfriends attached.

By the time I came to write a novel set there, I was looking back over 20 years of holidays and we had taken our first grandchild there. The islands are small enough that with that amount of exposure you can have walked on every headland, explored every cove, and feel, as hundreds of thousands of other holiday-makers feel, that it has got into your soul.

Now I'm back in Cornwall.

~

We started in St Ives. Amazingly, the librarian who hosted my talk on *Somewhere More Simple* eight years ago was still here, and remembered me. She had got her library-based book group to read *Uncertain Light,* and I was invited to talk to them. Robert came with me and we were making a holiday of it. We left our things at the hotel and strolled along the washed-clean beach, looking out over the sea where small boats bobbed. Watched cloud formations move slowly and the sun break through and then disappear. All of it lit by the nuanced light that has always drawn artists to this place.

St Ives library is the kind of place that makes me happy just going into it. It has an art collection, landscapes and seascapes by local artists. It hosts children's activities, a family history group, yoga and pilates classes, a poetry workshop and three reading groups. Plus of course computers, DVDs, and for those who still like to turn the pages, a range of newspapers. It is wheelchair accessible and has baby changing facilities. Libraries like this are the centre of our cultural life, and have made imaginative inner lives possible for generations of children in families that had no books at home. Already they are deeply undermined by government cuts, and if things keep going in this direction we are threatened with losing the fight to keep them free and paid for by our taxes.

There was a bust in the corner of the room we were meeting in, to the benefactor who gave money to set up this library. It had just been installed when I was here last, so I heard a bit about him. John Passmore Edwards was a man I would have liked to meet. Born in 1823, son of a Cornish carpenter, he attended the village school and had almost no access to books in his own childhood. He became a journalist, a freelance writer and lecturer on questions of social reform. He made his wealth by buying several successful newspapers, and with his profits set up a foundation that built 24 libraries, along with numbers of art galleries, schools, drinking fountains, hospitals and convalescence homes. I don't usually go for busts of important men, but I was honoured to have him looking on while we talked about my book.

Robert had decided to come to this event. He was hovering around the back, inconspicuous while I met each of the members of the reading group as they came in. It turned out I hardly needed to have prepared a talk for they all had lots to say. It was a lively couple of hours, made suddenly electric when they realised that the quiet stranger at the back was my husband. Seemed they'd been assuming the novel was autobiography, and they were more than curious to know what he thought about certain things that happened in it. But of course they couldn't ask, and he just laughed.

~

On to Penzance. The website of their Literary Festival describes it as 'the friendliest in the UK.' They have a process of selection I haven't seen anywhere else. They allocate places by competitive entry, which makes them open to lesser-known writers. Perhaps they set that up because there are so many local writers who would love a slot, and they need to be transparent about their decisions? Whatever the reason, anyone can apply, so I did my 250-word piece explaining why I thought an audience in Penzance might be interested in my book, and I got through the hoop.

The Festival has a packed four-day programme, sometimes with four or five simultaneous events. As a rule they don't pay author's fees. They have a minimal grant to cover costs and aim to keep ticket prices as low as possible, but a few of the writers are well-known enough for me to wonder whether a bit of the budget goes on them. For writers from outside Cornwall they offer hospitality in the homes of some of the organisers, which is where Robert and I are staying, a lot more comfortable and interesting than a hotel would have been.

I get up early before the house is awake, and walk down the hill towards the sea. The sound of my footsteps on the cobble. The mewing of seagulls. At the seafront I stand against the railing, looking out. The sea is almost motionless, long lines of shifting shades of grey and blue in the filtered light of dawn. Then the first streaks of orange light edge the horizon. Then more, then more, till it is on fire.

I love this place ... Memories of all the years when the ferry port was our departure point, and we would arrive to spend the night here beforehand ... Bed-and-breakfast places, or a couple of times the Youth Hostel ... The morning rush to join the queue down at the pier with our piles of luggage, swimming gear, blow-up dinghy, rain gear ... Always with children, creating life, creating chaos, and sometimes with adults tense from the stress of trying to detach from daily life.

It's a treat to be here on my own before the day starts.

~

My session today. Robert has opted to go to a different one. Good for both of us. I can't quite lose the awareness of him there, and I want to be free to focus on everyone else.

There's one person there when I arrive. A few others drift in slowly. It's a gloomy room, a bar-basement below an arts centre.

In mid-winter it might be cosy and atmospheric but today we all know it's high summer outside, and here we are in the half-light. I move about, saying hello, but they're shy and I don't get much response.

Gareth, the man who is going to chair the session, arrives. We got to meet a few weeks ago because he lives mostly in London, though some of the time here in Penzance. A comfortable feeling to have one known person. There are chairs set up for him and me on a stage with lighting, which is a disaster given the size of the group. I suggest we could just make a small circle so we could chat naturally, but a lighting man has come specially and Gareth doesn't feel he can change things. A young woman from the local independent bookshop has set up her stall, with piles of my books. I joke with her about the fact that there are at least six copies per person in the audience. She says, 'Well, we never know, so we have to come prepared for whatever.'

Someone else I recognise arrives. Tim Hannigan interviewed the writer at the opening event last night, and I was impressed. He had clearly read the book with great attention and asked sensitive, opening-up kinds of questions. Afterwards I checked him out in the programme. He writes about Indonesia where he has had a long connection. I feel supported that he is here, someone for whom the international context of *Uncertain Light* will resonate.

By now there is an audience of about ten, time is ticking by, and Gareth says 'Let's start.' He prompts me with some questions, and then opens it to others. There are a couple of questions about how I first started writing, about how to get a publisher (I wish I knew). Talking to a group that hasn't read the book is so different from the experience in St Ives a few days ago, and I'm thinking I haven't done it well enough to engage them. I'll have to think about that before I do another talk of this kind.

A woman asks about the hostage-taking with which the story begins. With the stage light in my eyes I can't see her very well, and she's talking quietly, so I'm straining forward to hear. She's asking if it is based on real events? I say yes, and tell her a bit about it. But I have a feeling there's another question lurking behind the one she has asked. It comes. 'When you were working in Save the Children, did you hear about a hostage-taking in a civil war in west Africa? Also in the 1990s?'

I have to think a bit, then I remember, yes I did, but I didn't have any direct connection to it . But of course she's not actually wanting to know if I did or didn't; there's something she wants to tell me about it. And she does, quietly, her voice shaking slightly. Her son was in the British army, in a unit seconded to be part of a UN peacekeeping force there. He was one of those taken hostage.

The feeling in the room is palpable. We are stilled by the weight of her memory, her courage in sharing it.

When the session is over she is waiting to talk to me, and I can ask what happened to her son. He was released, after some days. But it was an agonising time.

She is Sara MacDonald. She's a novelist, a popular one, and successful in all the ways I am not. She came to my session because the blurb mentioned hostages.

My fiction, her reality.

~ 18 ~

Director's Choice

October 2015, Beverley, East Yorkshire

Early morning. I have slipped out of my hotel before anyone is about, to look for Beverley Minster. A short walk along old streets and here it is, a magnificent 13th century church. First light, not a soul around in the precinct that surrounds it. The stillness seeps into me, my steps become a kind of meditation. A notice board tells me it won't open until ten, but the outside is enough to take in. I stand at the massive door staring up at the intricate stone-carved figures that surround it. All this artistry, and the craftsmen's names are lost to us. All those stories that we will never know.

I was an adult before I saw a medieval cathedral, but I have a special feeling of connection that goes back to childhood, when my mother directed Dorothy Sayer's play *The Zeal of Thy House*. It is set in Canterbury in the 12th century and based on a real happening.

A section of the cathedral had been destroyed by fire and was being rebuilt. The architect fell from the scaffolding, was crippled and could never work again. Mom's production was staged in the cathedral in our home town, Bloemfontein, a late 19th century brick building. I was part of a crowd scene of pilgrims. My brother Brian had the enviable role of incense bearer to the Archangel Gabriel, wore a long robe and walked before him swinging a thurible. I watched in some awe as his face turned gently green and he almost fainted from inhaling too much of it. He even had a line to speak. 'Why did God make people in two sorts, if it causes so much trouble?'

The 'trouble', which I couldn't take my eyes off in rehearsals, was embodied by the central actors. The architect, William of Sens, a tall, commanding figure with dark curly hair, and Lady Ursula, a wealthy widow, benefactor to the cathedral — these two people whom I knew in daily life to be completely different people stood close together, she looking up at his face intently as his words soared, describing the magnificence of what he was causing to be created. The chemistry between them was palpable. I wondered how they could each go back to homes with their real spouses after a scene like that.

When my mother was in her eighties and came from South Africa to spend time with us, we took her to Canterbury. At first she wanted just to stand and stare, eyes lifted towards that extraordinary, soaring stonework. Then she and I slowly moved up the nave with the shoals of tourists. It was as if she had become part of the crowd scene in her own production. When we got to the rebuilt choir, she stopped. We looked up. Just beyond where we could see, William of Sens was falling from the scaffolding, and the Angel Gabriel, magnificently judgemental with giant feathered wings, stretched out his arms, while a child in the crowd of pilgrims cried out, *Look at the angel, the terrible angel.*

All of it, that old story, recorded by the monk Gervaise, who saw the hand of God in it. A punishment for the architect's excessive pride, he thought.

Even as a child I was indignant. Why should he not, like God, look upon his work and see that it was good?

Stories upon stories, moving through the years.

I turn to walk back, and see, coming through the old stone entrance to the precinct, an unusually tall black man whom I recognise from the literary festival programme as one of the writers. Kwasi Kwarteng. He is surprised to meet someone here at this hour. Perhaps like me he had hoped to be alone. The programme said 'Born in London to Ghanaian parents, Conservative MP, a leading historian and social commentator.' The Wikipedia entry added to his CV Eton and Cambridge. He is here because he has written a book on Margaret Thatcher. We are possibly the only two people with an African background in this town today, but politically we could not be further apart.

He, naturally, has no idea who I am or what I think about anything. Yet for this moment, in an irony that only I appreciate, we meet on common ground, each having chosen to use our quiet morning time to see this extraordinary building.

Our differences are a measure of how complex a matter identity is. He might look more of an outsider than I do, but politically he's a better fit with attitudes here and in the countryside around. They've had a Conservative MP for decades.

Why I thought it worth putting in a proposal for the Beverley Literature Festival I can't remember. It's a historic market town for the fertile areas of the East Yorkshire Wolds (otherwise, hills) and the year's calendar is full of festivals. A food festival, a jazz festival, an early music festival. Small wonder that the literature festival attracts big names. Sarah Waters and Jane Gardam have been here recently. But how's this for a gift from the gods? I got a personal response from the festival director, Dorcas Taylor. Years ago, she said, she was working part-time in a bookshop and saw a book called *A Shield of Coolest Air*. She remembers being captivated by the title and that drew her to the book. She loved it, recommended it to friends, still has it on her shelf.

So here I am, having through this delightful coincidence slipped onto the festival programme. Since no one will have heard of me, she has found a clever way to bill me. I am listed in the programme as 'Director's Choice.'

Since they are paying for my fare and a night in an elegant small hotel, I am making the most of it and arrived yesterday to give myself time to be a tourist. The hotel opens onto a square that for centuries has held an open market place. Bordering the square are attractive period buildings and cobbled streets. Canals lead east to the port at Hull, once used for serious trading traffic, now with colourful painted canal boats. It was colder than I had expected and I began to feel insecure about what I had brought to wear for my session. Perhaps I might need another layer? I examined all the clothes stalls in the market, couldn't find anything that felt suitable, then plumped for a colourful scarf. Irrational, because it won't keep me warm, but I was pleased at having treated myself. By then dusk was coming on, the stalls were shutting up, so I went back to the hotel and spent a while going through the festival programme and googling to find out something about the other writers. It was all a touch intimidating, but I selected a couple of sessions to go to. I had a meal as soon as they started serving. The only other person in the dining room at that hour was an elderly woman on her own at the next table. I had to remind myself that I too am now an Elderly Woman. I don't feel like one, but then probably she doesn't either.

We got talking. In her retirement she has become an artist, and was here on an etching course. She lives in Hebden Bridge, where my daughter lives. She invited me to visit her studio next time I was there. I invited her to come to my session. She said she would think about it.

Enough sociability for one evening, so I went to my room early.

Day 2: Before my session I listen to Lisa Jewell, whom the programme says is one of the queens of women's fiction. She's about the age of my older daughter. Her first novel was a best-seller and since then she has written 13 in the time it has taken me to write two. But it's her main job. She is a tad irritated with questions about her writing process. The general tenor of her answers is that it's a lot more difficult than people think, having to keep feeding that publisher's deadline monster. I can well imagine. I don't for a second begrudge her her success.

Then it's me. I'm full of admiration for Dorcas, the festival director, for her ingenuity in billing me as 'Director's Choice' has drawn at least 40 people. Three friends-of-friends who live within reach have made the journey to hear me, and the artist from the hotel is there. Dorcas's questions range over all my writing years and the parts of my life that provided the spark for each book, which succeeds in making me sound like a significant writer. People queue up to get their copies of *Uncertain Light* signed. Many of them hang around till the queue is done because they have things they want to tell me about aspects of their own lives that connect with themes in my books.

And now, a writer I am so happy to be meeting, Marina Lewycka. Like Kwasi Kwarteng she is the child of immigrant parents, but there's no Eton and Cambridge in her story. She was born in a refugee camp in Germany after World War II and brought to the UK as an infant. Her book *A Short History of Tractors in Ukrainian,* published when she was 60, won and was short-listed for any number of prizes. It was both funny and touching, an art in itself, and one I admire particularly, not being able to do it. I love her attitude to her success. She said in an interview, 'I've been a 'successful' writer for almost five years now, but I never forget that I was an unsuccessful writer for more than 50. It helps to keep things in perspective.'

We're having tea and crumpets in a café after her session, and there's an immediate sense of familiarity. She tells me she recognised my name when she saw it in the programme, nothing to do with my books, she hadn't known that I wrote. But she used to teach English as a second language, and she once heard me talk at a conference. I tell her how much I like her second novel, *Two Caravans*. It didn't get quite the fame of *Tractors* but is more powerful in its empathy.

It describes the lives of East European migrant farm workers in Kent, and has an extraordinarily sustained dark-humorous passage about working with factory-farmed chickens. I can't image anyone who has read it being able to face cheap chicken meals again.

She talks about the pressure from her publishers to be funny. That's how she made her name, that's what they expect of her. She herself is moving in other directions, but if she goes too far, it'll make it hard to market her books.

There are definitely advantages to not having made the breakthrough into mainstream publishing.

Day 3: Early morning. I have spent the night in the home of friends who live a little out of town, in the middle of fields. Warm company, interesting talk, a lovely vegan meal. Now I'm out on my own again, letting the stimulus of the last days fall away from me, finding my own stillness. There's a magical mist as I walk along the canal. Cows materialise out of nowhere. I am almost level with an owl perched on a fence pole before we see each other. I stop, not to disturb it. It eyes me solemnly, then in unhurried movement spreads its wide wings, lifts its weight off the pole and heaves off, flap, flap, till it disappears in the mist.

As I walk back I'm thinking of another comment of Marina's in that interview I found. She was asked, 'What drives you to write?' She said, 'A sense of urgency, of time running out. So many things I want to say, stories to tell, techniques and ideas to experiment with, even to make mistakes and learn from them; and so few not-completely-gaga years left in which to do it all.'

I like the impulse. But right now I feel more like the owl, unhurried.

INSPIRATIONS
ALONG THE WAY

~ 19 ~

Migrations

November 2015

The days are drawing in. I look up to see geese outlined against the fading light. Each heart pumping energy but the whole creating an effect of apparently effortless grace. The *lightness* of flight.

Migration is awe-inspiring. The geese are powerful, I can imagine them travelling long distances, but it confounds imagination to think of small birds covering thousands of miles twice a year. The endurance, the eerie inner knowledge of where they are heading for. Hard to believe that the garden I grew up in on a dry plateau in the middle of South Africa was home every summer to birds that would return to where I now live, 6,000 miles further north.

Human migrations happen all the time, but so slow, so ponderous. Too much baggage. Even Somali nomads with their camels or Central Asian herders who move with their sheep for better grazing must take days packing up their clobber.

The only thing approaching it in human experience is sound. Music. Song. Words. Only they can move on the wind, cross continents, fly between us. Thoughts spoken, words sung, live for a moment, then waft away. Yet write them down, and a continuing life becomes possible.

A friend has recommended *Uncertain Light* to Anna Dreda, who runs an independent bookshop in Shropshire. Anna sends me a message. She loves the book, will stock it in her shop. She is sending it to a friend in the Outer Hebrides.

The Hebrides, in case you've never heard of them, are islands off the west coast of Scotland. The one where her friend lives is North Uist, with a population of about 1,300, the majority of whom are Gaelic speakers. It has miles of sandy beaches, amazing bird life, bracing walks, wild Atlantic weather — and a small arts centre. On a day that Anna and her partner were on holiday there, the arts centre was holding an exhibition of sea-scape paintings by a local artist; and also poems.

Anna asked the artist who the poet was. 'Me,' she said.

Her name: Pauline Prior-Pitt.

It's not a name you forget. I am flipped back 30 years, to Coventry, a city in the English Midlands —

I'm here for a conference on language teaching, browsing the bookstall at lunchtime. Among the worthy but unexciting textbooks I notice a slim volume of poetry, a wild flower in a field of wheat. It's called *Waiting Women*, which for some reason makes me laugh. What is it doing here? The woman in charge of the stall tells me the poet is local, and they're helping distribute it. I flip the pages, stop at a poem, and am caught.

I buy it and read it right through on the train journey home, laughing in the way you do when someone has captured exactly what you have felt, but so lightly. A butterfly landing, a moment of recognition, then taking off again.

After the conference I order another copy and give it to my daughter. 30 years ago, all that.

And now, where the sea marks the western border of the British Isles, Pauline Prior-Pitt is reading my book.

Never have messages by internet seemed more miraculous.

'It's my book of the year!' Pauline emails, and she moves on to reading all my others.

I tell her I have loved her poems for 30 years. She has kept writing all this time. There are *six* slim volumes waiting for me catch up on! She posts them to me. Elliptically her poems capture moments in a woman's life — a lover, a friend, a mother, a grandmother; someone who holds on to those she loves, and who faces loss. She sees it all with the sharpest, but also the most loving, eyes. And because she has fashioned those moments into words, and put them on paper, they are there still to be shared.

The printed word too is a miracle. Maybe a bigger one.

~

I discover that Anna, who sent *Uncertain Light* to Pauline, is the mover behind an annual poetry festival, hosted by her bookshop in the small town of Much Wenlock. She loves the Urdu and Persian poetry that weaves like tendrils through the story. She emails, 'Maybe we should get you to the Festival, to talk about Urdu poetry?'

I'm sure she can't mean it, but before she can change her mind I say, 'Yes please!'

Many other readers have commented on the effect of the poetry in *Uncertain Light,* and unlike Anna, some were not already poetry-lovers. Here's a sample:

'I have to confess that I have never much liked poetry. The way it was taught at my school made it feel totally baffling and unreachable. Reading the inspiring poetry in *Uncertain Light* has made me want to explore more. Maybe I was just starting with the wrong poets?'

'I was well put off poetry by having to study Milton's minor poems for O-level, and have never recovered. But the Urdu poetry in the story brought me into a world I have never explored.'

'I can't remember reading any poetry at school, and if I did, it made no impression. But I loved the examples in the story.'

How is it that poetry from a different culture can touch a nerve of recognition in people who have not responded to poems in their own language? Perhaps it is *because* it's different? They come to it lighter, without unhelpful baggage?

There are plenty of English readers who after leaving school have never voluntarily read a poem. My friend Jonty Driver, a poet himself, says, 'The headmaster of my first school thought nothing had ever been said in poetry that couldn't be better said in prose. But then I had the good fortune to be taught by a tough-minded old widow who brought poems alive. I suspect the passion for poetry which has stayed with me for the rest of my days was there in me already; she merely helped it to evince itself, as well as giving it a critical focus. I don't like all poems; I like only some poems. She was the first person I showed my early attempts to, and I shall be grateful to her forever for her generous response to what were pretty feeble efforts.'

My schooling wasn't that different. I don't remember ever being invited to compose a poem. My mother was probably the strongest reason why I took to poetry naturally, though I'm not sure any of my brothers did. Inside the door of her wardrobe she had pasted quotations she liked, and gradually I came to realise she had a huge store of them in her mind. Her growing up years were spent largely in the home of her uncle, a self-educated man with a Victorian-style library of classics. She spent hours reading 19th century novels, and absorbed swathes of poetry at an age when I, a generation later, was just emerging from *The Famous Five*. She didn't regard her knowledge as anything special. Occasionally she would quote fragments, sparked off by something that was going on, so I came naturally to the idea that a line of poetry could be the most succinct way of saying something of value. Before we read any Shakespeare at school I had a part as a page in *As You Like It,* directed by my mother. I don't remember finding the language difficult, just delighting in the atmosphere that words can conjure — word-music, multiple forms of sound-patterning. Not just rhyme, but the rhythm of words that in itself suggests movement:

> Everyone suddenly burst out singing,
> and I was filled with such delight
> as prisoned birds must find in freedom
> winging wildly across the white
> orchards and dark green fields; on – on – and out of sight.

Those lines are for me still a perfect example of the relevance, and irrelevance, of understanding the context of a poem. When you know what Siegfried Sassoon and others had been going through in the trenches of a World War, the image of prisoned birds winging in freedom has immense power. If you're 12, as I was when I first read it, and can't begin to imagine any of that, it still communicates something that touches a deep human instinct.

~ 20 ~

Moving Across Cultures

I had some of my early lessons on how poetry moves across cultures when I was teaching in a girls school in Zambia. It was soon after the country had become became independent and the curriculum was still entirely British-culture-centred. I searched for stories and poetry that would resonate with the rapidly changing world these girls were inhabiting. They were growing up in a city but many had had their early years in small villages, and even if they were town-born, most had village relatives with whom they spent time.

Literacy featured little in those daily lives, but there's a lively oral culture, so I was looking for words to be spoken to an audience, not read in private. I coached a group to take part in a choral-verse competition led by an inspiring lecturer at the new university. Our entry was by a Malawian poet, vivid with the sounds and images of a tropical rainstorm. But we crossed borders too, in a production of *Under Milk Wood*. The sea-struck Welsh village could not have been more different from the land-locked ones they knew, and almost every sensual image had to be explained, yet the gossipy small-village-ness made sense to them, and Dylan Thomas's unexpected poet's use of words was a game they enjoyed being part of —

> *It is Spring, moonless night in the small town, starless and bible-black, the cobblestreets silent and the hunched, courters'-and-rabbits' wood limping invisible down to the sloeblack, slow, black, crowblack, fishingboatbobbing sea.*

One of those girls, Anita Salim, now a woman of 60, traces her first love of theatre to that production. She is from an Indian family that was in Zambia for a few years. She's now a theatre director in Mumbai, working with children and college students in workshops that draw on Indian sources. A long line of cross-cultural influence that delights me.

~

Encountering the poetry of another language through translations is a different matter. Poetry by its nature is notoriously difficult to translate, some would say, impossible. For the reader there's a suspicion that you're not getting the real thing, and of course you're not. You're getting what the translator is able to show you. I see often on social media quotes supposedly from the 13th century Persian poet and mystic, Rumi. I doubt the authenticity of many of them. They seem too soft and woolly, which Rumi never was. And none of them say which of his works they come from or who translated them.

Only if you know both languages can you tell the quality of a translation. I do know that about Ralph's translations, fragments of which form a thread through *Uncertain Light.* They are faithful to the original, meaning that nothing has been added that isn't inherent in the connotations of the Urdu words, nothing left out, and there is no attempt to make it 'poetic' with flowery language if it's not there in the original. Unlike many other Ghalib translations I have seen, they respect the form. Much of Ghalib's poetry is in a classical, but still very popular, form called the *ghazal,* which values conciseness above all things. Each ghazal consists of a series of couplets, linked by rhyme and metre, but each couplet is independent in meaning, complete in itself. That makes for an extremely condensed form of expression, capturing in two lines a thought or feeling that might take a paragraph to express in prose. Add to that a love of wordplays and nuances created by words that carry strong cultural references, and you have something that seems almost impossible to fit into just two lines in the translation. But that's how ghazal poetry works, so that's what translators have to attempt to do.

Ideally they also need to suggest the metre, the key thing that distinguishes poetry from prose. Metres in Urdu poetry are complex, impossible to replicate in natural English, but Ralph used lines with a similar number of syllables, and a rhythm as near that of the original as he could, but always one that sits naturally with spoken English.

To people who like the poetry in *Uncertain Light* and ask for more, I recommend the new edition of Ralph's writing on Ghalib, which I edited. A lot of it had appeared in scattered articles, and had not been published alongside his interpretations of the poetry. In the years before his death he knew he would not have the energy to put it all together, and we agreed that I would. It was a joy to be able to do it, a way of sharing the exceptional privilege I had had of being able to study Ghalib's poetry in one-to-one lessons with Ralph.

The title he had chosen for an earlier edition was *The Famous Ghalib* – a quotation from one of Ghalib's own verses. Ghalib was many things, but not modest, and he was strong on irony.

He didn't think most of those to whom he was famous actually understood what he was saying in his poems. He was probably correct, yet his fame has lasted undimmed in the 150 years since his death. I am provided with a neat example of this, when, sitting in my study in London, I am interviewed about the book by video-link from Mumbai. It's for an on-line literary festival, LitfestX. Over ten days, 80 writers are being interviewed by Skype, and the interviews go up instantly on YouTube. When it's my turn I am astonished to discover that the entrepreneur who set it up is doing *all* 80 interviews himself. What an endurance test! How can he possibly have read all those books? He says calmly that he doesn't attempt to. He puts himself in the position of his viewers, who will know nothing about the book. It is up to each writer to get them interested.

The response to our session is amazing. By the time the interviews have been up on line a week, over 5,000 people have viewed it. There are 80 writer interviews to choose from, and they don't all get 5,000 viewers. I am unknown in India, so it certainly isn't my name that draws them. 'Ghalib' in the title is enough.

Would the translations work for English speakers, who have little knowledge of Urdu or its culture? It was certainly Ralph's intention that they should, and the response to the fragments in *Uncertain Light* makes me hopeful. To people outside the culture the forms of poetry may seem odd, the meanings too deeply embedded in a different world-view, the symbolic language opaque. These are challenges, but they do not make communication impossible. There is enough in Ralph's sensitive translations, and his introductions to the cultural context, to enable connections in meaning to traverse centuries and languages, and speak to us directly.

~ 21 ~

Like People Journeying

I watch as my book travels, reaching people I have never met, will never meet. Thoughts that started in my mind are intertwining with theirs. I feel alongside it the flights of my other books, the currents of air that have carried me with them, to places I have never been, ways of being I have never experienced —

> Like people journeying while moving camp
> like a well which has broken its sides
> or like the bees entering their hive
> or food crackling in the frying ...

The voice of a Somali poet, Raage Ugaas, words composed over 200 years ago and circulating still, not through being written, but memorised by listeners, passed down the generations. Versions have been collected in many different parts of Somalia, and there is almost no variation between them.

I first learnt about the extraordinary oral poetry of Somalis when I was responsible for organising English classes for adults in a part of South London. Towards the end of the 1980s we started getting increasing numbers of asylum seekers. Each new arrival reflected some disaster in the world beyond. There were Kurds fleeing chemical weapons being used against them by Saddam Hussein in Northern Iraq. Afghans were escaping from decades of civil war fuelled by both Russian and American arms. African villagers were fleeing rebel armies in the Congo and Sudan. There were Tamils from Sri Lanka, Ahmadiyas from Pakistan, and people fleeing a civil war in Somalia.

In 1988 the dictator Siad Barre had ordered the bombing of Hargeisa, the main town in Northern Somalia. It was home to the Isaaq clan, many of whom had opposed his rise. Half a million people fled across the border into Ethiopia, where vast refugee camps grew up in the desert. I went once to listen to a doctor who had worked in those camps, talking about conditions that had led to such a high death rate of people who had been healthy when they fled. Gradually small numbers of them managed to move on, and arrived in countries in Europe where they applied for asylum. And a few got to our English classes.

The classes created a small mutually supportive community, where gradually, through halting English or through interpreters, people began to share their stories. It was impossible not to be moved by them. It was also striking that, wherever they were from, whatever disaster they were fleeing, once in the UK they were in the same situation. Their lives were all now dominated by having to negotiate permission to stay. Whatever level of society they had come from, here they were all dealing with sudden poverty, loss of family, place, role.

I called together the teachers who were getting to know asylum seekers and we set up a community support group. I did the rounds of organisations with longer experience of all this. We pressed the local authority for funding to employ an advice worker. She found interpreters, and from a small office in our adult education centre she dealt with a trail of crises. She steered confused people through bureaucratic hoops to access the basic support the state provided, helped children get into schools, connected them to legal advisers, transported donated furniture and winter clothes to those in need.

I don't remember consciously making a decision, it just became clear to me that I needed to share some of what all this was teaching me — what it was like to have your life so dramatically cut across by a political situation not of your own making, and if you did manage to get away, the new sets of crises you landed in.

Gradually a story took shape.

A Shield of Coolest Air is an entirely fictional story, told through the eyes of two people who get to know a woman who has fled from war, and try to help her bring her children to join her. Early on I realised that for a reader new to all this I would need to choose one backstory to focus on, the reason why this person had fled. That story became Somalia. But I was just at the start of what I would need to learn if I were to do it justice, and with the ongoing war, there was no way I could have got myself to Somalia, even if I had been free from work and family responsibilities. So I would have to learn what I could here, in Britain.

~

I visited Somali community centres, talked to people. I read whatever I could, the limited amount that was then available in English. I kept hearing about a professor of the Somali language at SOAS, the School of Oriental and African Studies in London. Somalis regarded him as a phenomenon. 'He is a European but he speaks our language perfectly,' they said. 'If you hear him without seeing him, you couldn't believe he's not a Somali.'

So I approached him, and asked if he would be willing to help me make sense of what I was learning, and take me beyond, to things I needed to know.

B.W. Andrzejewski — Goosh to all who knew him — was Polish, and how he got to be a Somali specialist is a story in itself. He too had had to flee from a war. When he was 17 and at school in Warsaw, the Nazis invaded. He escaped, and through a series of dramatic adventures managed to join the Free Polish Forces abroad. His training took place in Palestine, where his facility with languages first became evident. He was simultaneously learning English, Arabic and Hebrew. As he also knew German, he was given a job as an interpreter accompanying prisoners of war who were being moved from one place to another. After the war he put himself through British university entrance exams, studied English literature at Oxford, and then linguistics at SOAS. He was by now also a poet in Polish.

At that time the British government was looking for a linguist to work in Somaliland, the northern part of Somalia which had come under their administration after the defeat of the Italians. The country is mostly desert. Camel-herding and trading was how most people survived. There had never been an agreed script for the language. They had little need to read and write; the only reason was religious, to read the Quran, but that was in Arabic. A small minority had gone to schools where they learnt to read the languages of the colonial powers that had divided the country, but they all shared their spoken language. The colonial officials wanted a linguist to develop a script so that it could be used for administration and communication. So Goosh was sent to do a linguistic analysis of a language he had yet to learn. He spent the rest of his life studying it, and living it.

He entered into the spirit of my attempt to evoke in my fictional story aspects of a way of life that he knew well but that I had never been part of. A busy man and a tired one (he already had cancer), he generously gave me time. He guided my reading, and talked about things he had learnt through years of living in Somalia. He read each stage of my book in draft, and commented in detail on anything that reflected the Somali context. When I said that I wondered if I was stepping too far beyond my own experience, he dismissed this vigorously, and said something which has stuck with me ever since. 'One of the most powerful novels about the inner life of a woman,' he said, 'is *Anna Karenina,* and it was written by a man. The whole point of fiction is to imagine lives we have never lived.'

I told him that even Somali refugees in my classes had heard about the excellence of his Somali. He smiled and said it was simply that so few outsiders had ever learnt the language, so to Somalis, hearing him was like hearing a cat speak.

Those conversations with Goosh started me off on an extraordinary journey, discovering things about my Somali friends, and the culture they had grown up with, that I might possibly never have learnt otherwise. And one of the most significant was the role of poetry.

Goosh had discovered very early on in his time there that they were great orators, and adept at learning things by heart. He described to me how he had first become aware of how important poetry was in Somali society. He was working with a Somali colleague, Muusa Galaal. When he asked Muusa for an example of how a particular word was used in different contexts, the examples Muusa gave were always spoken in a metre which suggested that they were quotations from poetry. Goosh began to realise that Muusa's mind carried a vast store of poems, and as the language was not yet written, they had been memorised simply by listening to the words being recited.

To people who have always relied on the written word it is astonishing to discover that generations of illiterate camel herders had memorised long, complex poems, which told the history of their people. Someone who memorised a poem had an important role as culture-carrier, and was expected to get it 100% correct. There was a deep respect for the actual words chosen by the poet . Each carries verbal richness beyond the basic sense, in subtle word play, images with double meanings, metaphors reflecting cultural references.

If you live under a dictatorial regime, there is a particular value in being among people who are adept at memorising. The poet Hadraawi spent five years in prison because of his poetry's outspoken references to the dictator, Siad Barre. When he was released, he continued composing poems without committing them to writing. They were recited in secret, memorised, and passed on, to circulate, unstoppably.

Alerted by what I was learning from Goosh, I started asking my Somali friends about all this. They had never mentioned that their heads were full of poems, but why would they bother to tell someone who didn't know the language? They found my questions mildly perplexing. Why wouldn't they love poetry? Surely everyone does? Nor did they have any feeling that by fleeing Somalia they were now cut off from their poetic roots. They are historically a nomadic people, and poetry travels with them. Those in exile were composing poems about what they were experiencing, and sharing them with others who had landed up in other countries. They recorded them onto cassettes and posted them to each other, so it was still primarily oral poetry.

The deeper I got into my novel, the clearer it became that poetry was going to have to be part of it.

~

In the translations that Goosh had given me, there was a great deal that I couldn't connect with. Extravagant praise of war-like leaders, decrying one's opponents. I could see that this was powerful oratory, not unlike passages in Shakespeare's history plays:

> But when the blast of war blows in our ears,
> Then imitate the action of the tiger;
> Stiffen the sinews, summon up the blood ...

Spurring people on to kill others isn't something I go for, in any language. But there are also poems expressing the despair of those trapped by a dictatorial society. Written more than a century ago, they speak to people today, like this one by Raage Ugaas:

> When men closed their doors
> before the awful darkness of the night
> There emerged from the depths
> of my tormented being a deep groan
> like the rumbling thunder of a gloomy rain
> or the roar of a prowling, hungry lion –

That translation is by a Somali, Said Samatar. Other poems that appealed to me had been translated by Margaret Lawrence, a Canadian novelist who lived there at the time Goosh was doing his analysis of the Somali language. Her translations were made from literal versions Somalis had given her. Goosh was, understandably, a linguistic purist, and said she sometimes departed from the literal meaning. But it's a method others have resorted to with the poetry of other cultures, and it has the virtue of sidestepping any barriers to appreciation, because what she produces are good English poems. I'm grateful to her for them.

Moments of lyricism give us glimpses of a way of life, in a harsh landscape where young men are away from home for months at a time, moving with their camels and goats to find fresh grass; where a nomadic family will move house by packing all they own onto the back of a camel; where, in a drought-stricken land, rain acts as an image for the unexpected joy of finding love:

> *You are like a place with fresh grass after a downpour of rain*
> *on which the sun now shines*

The imagery is vivid because it is so specific; but the poets know that the thoughts and feelings they express are common to us all:

> For of course that life is sweet I grant you
> And where terror dwells, are not all men the same?

That commonality was at the heart of my story.

The title of my book came from a poem by the early 20th century poet, Sayyid Mohammed Abdille Hasan, in Margaret Lawrence's translation. It's a poem of farewell, to someone who is setting out on a long and hazardous journey:

Now you depart – And though your way may lead
through airless forests, thick with *hagar* trees,
through places steeped in heat, stifling and dry,
where breath comes hard, and no fresh breeze can reach,
Yet may God place a shield of coolest air
between your body and the assailant sun ...

The novel was rejected by more publishers than I can remember. When I had published it myself, it got seven reviews in national and regional newspapers and many radio interviews. I remember the sense of shock when I saw the review in The Scotsman, which filled half a page. I had sent it out to journals that looked as if they might have an interest in asylum seekers, Somalis, or just humanity generally, and reviews kept coming in, for almost a year. In the end there were over 30 of them. Scores of letters arrived from readers unknown to me.

One reviewer said, 'It affirms the triumph of the human spirit in the face of adversity and honours the power of love. It is moving and beautiful. And if that sounds corny, I don't care.' The story had touched something that connects many of us. I wouldn't like to try to put words around it because they would sound too profound, and what I mean is something quite basic. There's a sense of it in a comment by a reviewer that I have always valued, perhaps more than any other. 'She writes with great simplicity about ordinary people, yet that ordinariness is universal.'

~ 22 ~

If You Can Walk, You Can Dance

I am boarding a small plane in the UN base in Lokichogio, northern Kenya, to fly into a remote area of South Sudan. It is in the midst of a civil war that has dragged on for decades, and seems likely to continue for decades more. Our destination is a settlement called Mapel, a base from which Save the Children's team supports local people to keep life going during these troubled and dangerous times. Mapel is about as near the middle of Africa as you can get. Put a pin in the centre of the widest part on the map, and you're almost there. Far from cities or any sign of economic development, it has become a gathering point for people who have fled marauding armies. We fly over an apparently empty savannah landscape, over dry river beds and occasional collections of mud and thatch huts. It is difficult to get a sense of what people down there must be dealing with, or what I might encounter when we land.

A small airstrip comes in sight. The plane gets lower, lands, taxis to a halt. I step out. It takes a moment to adjust. So many physical sensations ... the feeling of feet on the earth again ... the glare of sun from a punishing, cloudless sky ... the limitless sense of space, with low trees fringing the edge of the airstrip ... And —

Music! Loud, energetic, and right here, the voices of a large group of people clapping, moving their bodies, singing to welcome us. For a few minutes more I stand, amazed, till the rhythms take over and I dump my small case and move to join in. The nearest women catch my hands and draw me in, laughing as they sing. The call-and-response lines pull my voice along with theirs. It doesn't matter that I have no words, my hands clap and my feet move with the beat, because that's what music does to a human body. All anxiety I might have felt about coming here has gone. I am an outsider, unaffected by the war that has devastated their community, and I move freely through the world while they are trapped in one small corner of it, but for this moment the music makes us one.

That is music's unique power. But this is also a specifically African use of music. I had grown up in Africa, my bare feet on the same soil. As a white child in South Africa the music I heard came mostly from the music of Europe and America, yet one of my earliest memories is of being enchanted by the deep, effortless harmonising when African voices sang. Hymns were what I mainly heard, and the harmonising itself a cross-cultural fusion. I was an adult before I began to discover the range and special qualities of African music, when my brother Colin gave me a recording made by the ethno-musicologist, Hugh Tracey — Mozambican xylophones, with gourds as sounding boxes and extraordinarily complex rhythmic patterns. In the years of living in Zambia my response to that kind of music shifted. It was no longer someone else's music, it was simply *music*, something anyone can connect with, but expressed in this way through this particular culture.

Much later, in travels across the continent, my African colleagues would take me to local markets, wanting me to take something of their culture back to share with the outside world. It was always a musical instrument that I chose. They are with me still, a deep throated *djembe* drum from Mali, a *kora* from Burkina Faso, a stringed instrument called a *kirar* from Ethiopia, a small wooden box with metal struts, the *mbira* from Zimbabwe, a child-size *timbila* xylophone from Mozambique, that my grandchildren played on until the strings that held it together gave way. I have been greeted by singing, clapping groups of women in Zimbabwe, where Save the Children supported farm workers to negotiate with farm owners to build preschools for their children; in Mali, where they sang to educate their communities about how to protect against the spread of HIV, using traditional work songs to face new challenges. Across the African continent people with different histories and social systems sing in totally unrelated languages, moving their bodies to rhythm in the same way, to use music as part of everyday life.

That flight into Mapel happened after I had just finished writing *If You Can Walk, You Can Dance,* but it captured for me something of the spirit that had inspired it.

~

Shortly before I had started work on the book, I had begun learning to play the violin. Music has been part of me for as long as I can remember, and like many people in the West I had dabbled in making music. I sang in choirs, taught myself the recorder when my children were young, had a few piano lessons, got excited by the simplest chords, but it never went further. When I was in my late forties and my daughters were learning to play instruments I got the idea that I'd like to play the violin. It is hard to think of a less suitable choice. It is such a difficult instrument, and starting in mid-life doubly so. But I discovered a Late Starters Orchestra, and I was away, with the joy of making music with others, and also of noticing the stages by which it happened.

All learning processes interest me. I have worked in education of one kind or another all my adult life, with adults and children, with the highly educated and those who have never had the chance to become literate, in materially privileged societies and in the most deprived. Starting late in life to learn something that is most easily learnt as a child is a stimulus to observing in yourself some of these processes. I was lucky to be doing this in the company of others similarly inspired to try something new. We were taught by sympathetic professional musicians, and one in particular was extraordinarily skilled. Wendy Giles, a brilliant young violinist, treated each of us not as struggling beginners, but as potentially as musical as she was. She gave us precise, simple steps that made it possible for us to get nearer producing the sounds we could hear in our minds but could not yet produce.

For me the decade of the 1990s happened to the accompaniment of that almost magical process. It was also the years when I was writing *If You Can Walk, You Can Dance,* so it's hardly surprising that music runs through the novel. I drew on sources beyond the particular kind of music I was learning to play, inspired by the extraordinary variety of musical expression across human cultures, and discovering the underlying similarities of the way music works on us.

~

If you can walk, you can dance is a story with many themes, each of which had its own genesis. It starts in a politically charged time in South Africa in the 1960s — the time when I was coming to adulthood. It was the height of the apartheid era, when the daily lives of different racial groups were so rigidly separated that a child growing up in the 'white' part of town would only encounter Africans or people of mixed race as domestic servants or other manual workers. I was unusually fortunate in being part of a family where some of the adults crossed those barriers, but even for us there was zero opportunity to meet African children our age, or to get to know people of different racial backgrounds on anything like an equal basis. Then I moved to university in Cape Town, where for the first time I had friends of other races. Together a group of us travelled out to the poor parts of town where Africans lived, to teach in a night school for adults. I taught basic Maths to men and women who had never had the chance of a school education. Most were old enough to be my parents. Tired from a long day's manual work, they still turned up each week and tried to concentrate. It was utterly humbling. I got involved in the national students' organisation, NUSAS — I had a minor role but collectively we were part of the growing groundswell of opposition to each new disastrous law of the apartheid government. It was a dangerous time to make any political stand, and we all knew that. The political police, the 'Special Branch', were at our meetings. We were organising demos at which there were scary encounters with police. Some of the organisers got arrested, and were held in prison without trial. To my considerable surprise I had been elected onto the national executive, and decisions were having to be made about how best to protest unjust laws in a context where more and more NUSAS activists were being imprisoned. Robert and I visited one, once his interrogators had decided they had nothing on him — a scary experience. People we knew would suddenly disappear, trying to get across the border to escape arrest. Others were on trial for their (non-NUSAS) activities.

Going to lectures & writing essays happened in between all that.

Those were my only years of adulthood in South Africa, for I left straight after graduating.

In the decades afterwards, my energies were focused on a new life elsewhere, and it never occurred to me to write about those times. It wasn't my story to tell. So much had moved on in South Africa, both in the extremity of oppression and the forms of resistance. But with the huge political changes of the early 1990s that feeling began to change. The lifting of official apartheid was only the start of the transitions, but it changed lives fundamentally, and not just for those in South Africa. For those who had taken a stand and then left, it changed the nature of our exile.

I began to meet young people the age of my daughters, late teens, early twenties, who had no idea of what had been going on in South Africa. It dawned on me that its history, like every traumatic history, was going to need restating for each new generation, and that it was not only one kind of story. It would be a huge jigsaw made up of many different stories; and among them were stories of exile. Some of those who had left had suffered devastating personal damage which would mark the rest of their lives. Some had joined liberation movements, taken up arms; when they returned, those who had stayed could hardly value anything they had experienced. Those like us, who had left young enough to restart life in less oppressive circumstances, were the fortunate ones, but even our less dramatic stories were formed by the experience …

A story began growing in my mind of a young woman who had to leave suddenly, and make the transition into adulthood in a new place, learning to survive without any of the privileges or emotional security she had grown up with. It was not my own story, but an imaginative amalgam, stimulated by stories of exiles from the many other situations I had come across in the life I had found after leaving. Through the slow process of exploring what might have happened to that young woman, it became clear to me that underpinning the story of sudden exile was something quieter I wanted to capture, about the inner resilience that comes from a childhood made secure by loving and open-minded adults. The simplest way to convey this was to give to the fictional central character, Jennie, my own childhood home. My parents were no longer here, but I doubt they would have minded, for I was honouring what they had given us. And why invent new people, when nothing could have been more suited to the story than their real selves?

The interaction between real life and the fiction that grows out of it is difficult to describe. I like what the Lithuanian writer, Sigitas Parulskis, said about it in an interview. "My experience, transformed, is my writing. Writing is amazing because you are the God of your own universe, you are creator and creation at the same time."

Of all my novels, this is the one for which I most often get letters from strangers. People write to tell me how much they have been affected by it, and then they tell me their own life stories, often at length. A few have said it was 'life-changing'. For some it's the musical theme that makes the powerful connection, for others it's the largely African setting. But Jennie's journey through her twenties seems to reach beyond, to people who have never been to Africa, nor explored their own response to music. For there is one central binding theme that has universal resonance. Exile is not just the exile of those who flee from politically dangerous situations. It is also about leaving behind the home of childhood, which has formed you, and to which you can never return in the same way.

Above all, I was telling a story about the possibility of unexpected growth when we find ourselves in new and challenging situations — among people who are different from us, different in race, class, language, culture, assumptions, in the things they enjoy, or make happen, or that inspire them. We have the choice to close up against difference, or to be open to learning from it, and be changed by it.

Those layers of being were reflected on that airstrip in South Sudan. I was clapping and moving my feet with people whose life experience had been so different from mine, had been devastated by war and human cruelty, yet who could still sing with vigour, and through the joy in singing could draw me in to be part of them for those few days.

TRAVELLING WITH A BOOK

~ 23 ~

The Reluctant Nomad

December 2015

Christmas with my family, then it's time to start packing.

There's something so irrevocable about airports. My friends think I am a seasoned international traveller because I did so much of it for Save the Children. What they don't know is that I have to gear myself up to each journey. Packing takes me days. I make lists, lose them, make others, rediscover the first ones. My medicine bag grows, fending off all possible emergencies. Chemists exist where I'm going, but I want to be free of such worries when I'm there. People in my stories move with ease through climates and cultures, but when it's me, I can't work out if I have the right clothes. I lose a sense of scale when I have to translate currencies. I am hopeless about large numbers, and many of the currencies I have had to deal with start in the thousands.

And then, passports, visas, the whole business of having the right papers to allow me to cross borders, all of that makes me tense. Partly that's the old paranoia about moving between Zambia and South Africa in apartheid times. To get to see my parents I had to go through two hostile immigration control posts. Nothing ever happened to me but too many people I knew had got into real difficulties. Before my first Save the Children visit, to Kathmandu, I confessed my nervousness to a woman colleague (it didn't seem possible to do so to the nothing-daunts-me men who flew in and out of war zones). She assured me this would be completely different. Anywhere I went I would be met at the airport by a local driver and I could just leave everything to him. He would be holding a sign with our logo, a red circle with a child-figure inside it. But the man with the logo who scooped me and my luggage up and drove me off handed me a folder with someone else's name on it. Turned out he worked for the US branch of Save the Children (same logo) and was expecting to meet someone from Indonesia. We had almost no words in common so I couldn't get him to understand the error, and by then he was caught in traffic and driving me to the Save US office, which (I later discovered) was in the opposite direction from the one I should have been headed for. It seemed to take forever, a surreal journey, the kind you could only have in a nightmare. It was late afternoon when we finally arrived and the office was being locked up. The driver was all for leaving me on the doorstep with my suitcase, but luckily one of those locking explained to him, and he reluctantly let me back into the car to drive me to where I should have been. I was inordinately grateful to be finally in the care of someone who knew who I was and what I was here for.

Then there was the time I got stuck in a hotel in Chengdu in China, when my onward flight into Tibet was cancelled. Neither I nor my colleagues making the travel arrangements in our regional office in Bangkok had realised it was the fifth anniversary of Tiananmen Square, and the authorities weren't keen to have foreigners watching whatever might happen. Trapped, I stood on a balcony of the top floor of the hotel, watching hundreds of cyclists stopping at a traffic light below, and thought about China's rapid economic progress, and how sometime too soon that might be hundreds of cars adding to the CO_2 levels we're all pumping out. Daily the hotel bills mounted, and the manager made clear they weren't going to let me out till I had paid, which I couldn't do because I had too little cash. Normally we were advised not to take much, but use the organisation's credit card. China was different, foreign credit cards not accepted. The regional office staff must have known that but had neglected to tell me. The charming young man who had met me at the airport (a stringer for Save the Children's travel arrangements into and out of Tibet) said he couldn't see any way out of the problem, and disappeared. When he didn't reappear I phoned the regional office in Bangkok. I got someone who spoke only Thai but managed to convey that everyone else was away at a conference. I phoned Save the Children's office in Beijing but couldn't get through. I discovered later all the phone numbers had just changed, adding another digit. I phoned our London office — night time, office closed. I tried to keep sane by doing yoga and playing my recorder. Then it all got on top of me and I felt I was about to have a panic attack. I phoned the home number of the programme officer in London responsible for our work in China, waking her at 3 a.m. She was remarkably patient, said she was sure something would be sorted out. And next day it was. The young man appeared with an air ticket to get me back to Bangkok. I never discovered how he got the hotel to release me.

These things make good stories after you're safely back home. Even I can see that.

Besides, I am not sure going to India with my book is a sensible idea. It's a country of 1.3 billion people, with 22 official regional languages, each with a lively literature of its own. At the last official count only 5% of men and 3% of women were said to speak English fluently. OK, that's 52 million people but how many of them read novels? And if they do, there is a flourishing world of Indian novelists writing in English, so really, how likely is it anyone will be interested in mine?

I have no one to blame but myself. It was I who came up with the idea, excited to have an Indian edition of *Uncertain Light* coming out. When the publisher said they'd love to have me come for a launch but couldn't pay the fare, I decided I wanted to do it anyway.

~

Flight to New Delhi.

As the plane comes down we seem to be descending into a thin brown soup.

I wait, as instructed, for the driver who is to meet me. He never appears. I don't have an Indian sim card for my phone, so I can't call the publisher. Eventually I get a taxi. It is, of course, so easy that I am embarrassed that I ever thought of asking to be met. When I arrive at the home of a friend where I will spend the first night I hear that the publisher has been phoning frantically: Author disappears on flight from London to Delhi. There *was* a driver. He must have waited at one exit, I at another.

~ 24 ~

Dropping into a Maelstrom

January, 2016

It's over ten years since I was last here, and each time arriving feels like dropping into a maelstrom. It is vaster, busier, more confusing than I had remembered.

I try to imagine what it is like to have to live here, daily breathing this almost brown air. Delhi ranks 11th worst of the cities in the world for air pollution. I bought a mask after I read that but I couldn't find it when I was packing, and anyway, what is the point? It would be like expecting an umbrella to be of some use in a hurricane.

On every journey we are stuck in humongous traffic jams. *Just Chill* says the sign painted on the back of a *tuk tuk* just ahead of us, a rattly motorised three-wheeler. Difficult to do as you clatter along the Outer Ring Road with honking traffic eight cars deep. Delhi's administration is running a two-week experiment to cut down private car use. 'Odd-Even' it's called. Cars with registration numbers that end in an odd number may only be used on odd number dates, and similar for even numbers. Theoretically this should cut the numbers of vehicles to half, but there are lots of permitted exceptions. If what's on the road at the moment is just over half the number of private cars, I can't bear to think what it's going to be like when the experiment comes to an end.

The friend I am staying with lives in a gracious colonial-style house in a part of New Delhi that dates back to the last days of the Raj. It is set in a huge garden with lush vegetation, and after the press of the streets it is blissfully calm. We have tea under the trees. Meals materialise, drivers are right there when one needs to go somewhere, someone is setting out fresh towels in my bathroom. A highly competent man who seems to be a general manager of the household is allocated the task of sorting me out with a sim-card. Apparently you can't just buy one, it involves layers of bureaucracy. He drives me to the market and does everything. I just hand over my passport when required, and pull out rupees when the task is done. I am infinitely grateful.

I'm going to have to learn all over again how to get about independently in this city. I travelled here with a backpack 30 years ago — what has happened to my confidence? What has happened is that I'm 70 now. Learning the systems in a new place is no longer an adventure, it's an anxious necessity. Everyone I interact with employs a driver who is summoned when they need to go anywhere. He waits off-stage till the meeting is over, then reappears in answer to a phone call. Drivers, house servants, street sellers, they all now have mobiles. My Indian sim-card appears only to do local calls and has no data to get on the internet when I'm out, so until some clever person can help me sort that out, I can't even call an Uber.

~

I have moved, and am now in the apartment of my friend Shireen from Save the Children days. Opposite the apartment is a park where I take my early morning walk. At the entrance a fruit-seller arranges fruit on his cart. A barber has set up shop with a chair on the broken pavement and shaves his first morning client. Next to them piles of decaying refuse spill out from the municipality's uncleared bins. Just inside the park is a large blue notice: DON'T DO THE FOLLOWINGS. An intriguing list, so I stop to study it. Then I move on, pausing to watch a lively cricket match .(Number 4: 'Don't play cricket, football or cycling.') A ruined mosque emerges through the trees , in current use as a place to hang clothes out to dry. (Number 7: 'Don't washing cloth.') In the park's central covered area Hindu *bhajan* (hymn) singers have gathered, loudspeaker turned aggressively to max. (Number 11: 'Don't putting up loudspeakers.')

There's an echo of a moment in *Uncertain Light*. Rahul Khan's father wakes to the sound of bhajan singers who have positioned themselves strategically, aggressively, opposite the local mosque. It was an image from the time I was first in India, the 1980s, when communal tensions simmered, exploded, simmered again. They never go away.

~

I have now found the answer to getting around this city: the Metro. I am astonished that the people who spend time in traffic jams hardly seem to consider it a viable option. It was Shireen's driver who suggested I try it, instructed me on the route to the station and how the ticket system works. It's efficient, quick, safe. You go through airport-type security, with a separate queue for women which is far shorter than the men's. Amazing, a public facility that privileges women. The first time I tried it I hadn't paid enough attention to the route to the station, and by the time I got out of the Metro coming home, it was dark and everything looked different. I walked for a long way on a busy street with shops without recognising anything, realised I must have come out at the wrong exit, backtracked and tried again. No better. There are no street names, only suburb 'block' names, like Green Park Block C, and no one seems to know blocks beyond their own. Each time I asked the way I got sent in a different direction. I was by now getting strange looks — a white woman out alone at night? Walking? Where's her driver? I do now have a phone that works but Shireen is out of town. I might disappear and who would know? I might become another newspaper story.

Finally I recognised a building and limped home, more shaken than I can remember being for a long time. This kind of thing does not happen to me in Britain. I have a good sense of direction and don't get stressed about finding my way around new places.

Next morning I told the driver. He was shocked. 'Why didn't you phone me?' Because he lives far away. 'But I could have told you on the phone where to go!' So disoriented was I, it didn't occur to me. I am touched. Independence is all very well but I'll swop it happily for the knowledge that someone's looking out for me.

~ 25 ~

History Can Be Dangerous

Shireen and I are stuck in an eight-lane traffic jam, on our way to a meal with the eminent historian, Romila Thapar. She's 84 and you'd think she'd be taking life quietly, but history here has suddenly become hugely controversial, and she is right up-front, critiquing the government on what's going on politically.

While the world's press has been focussing on Islamic fundamentalism, here it's Hindu fundamentalism that's the really worrying trend. Modi's ruling BJP party and their associated cultural groups have been pushing the concept of *Hindutva*, that India is a Hindu nation and everyone else, apparently, an outsider. In total contravention of India's constitution. You can't open a newspaper without seeing Modi looking fatherly and pious, but he says nothing when violent attacks against Muslims are whipped up by members of his ruling party. One of the worst in recent years happened in Gujarat state while he was Chief Minister there.

History has become a battleground. Anything that doesn't fit Hindutva theories is getting airbrushed out. Road names that reflect the Mughal (Muslim) rulers are being changed. Rightwing Hindu groups have been targeting journalists who report things they don't like to hear. They've been getting schools and colleges to remove books which they claim give negative interpretations of Hinduism, and substituting their own versions of history. Ten years ago around 150 Hindu militants broke into a research institute in Pune, overturned library shelves and damaged many books, and some ancient Sanskrit manuscripts. Why? A book by a researcher at the Institute years earlier had quoted something which they thought brought disrespect on the Hindu hero, Shivaji. The book's publisher had been intimidated into withdrawing the book, but that was not enough to save the Institute from being trashed.

And against this background a highly respected retired professor of history steps out to challenge. YouTube has interview after interview with her. She is an authority on India's earliest history, all so long ago you'd think it would be safe ground, but far from it. 'Every time you write a textbook that the right wing Hindu extremists don't like,' she said in an interview, 'they call it anti-national and anti-Indian. The historian is then attacked.'

I am reflecting on how privileged we are to be invited to a meal with her. Months before I knew I was coming to India I happened to see on FaceBook a video of a TV interview she had given, that really impressed me. Her face was very familiar. Had I perhaps met her, all those years ago on my first visit to India? Did someone give me a contact? I did a bit more googling and found that she and Ralph shared a publisher at one time. I sent an email via her publisher, to say I admired what she was doing. 'You won't remember,' I said, 'but I think we might have met.'

She replied, 'Of course I remember you. When you're next in Delhi, come to dinner.'

The traffic hardly moves, and we are horrendously late for the meal, but Romila and the cook have graciously waited. 'This is Delhi,' Romila says calmly.

Over the meal I ask about her current role. She talks about how the Hindutva outlook is based on fundamentally unhistorical assumptions. Over the millennia, among people who consider themselves Hindu, there have been many styles of worship, sects revering different gods, differences of philosophy, and all of these have evolved over time. There are innumerable written sources in Sanskrit but no single 'Holy Book', no agreed theological set of positions. Yet the Hindutva interpretation attempts to hold people to a 'correct' version, and one which also happens to be socially conservative. Romila's contention is that by viewing history as a conflict between fixed religious groupings, they have bought in to a rigid colonial classification of the stages of India's history, which described a Hindu period, followed by a Muslim one, followed by a British one. Her own scholarship and those of many others show that the historical reality was always much more complex.

When we leave we exchange copies of our books. The one she gives me is called *The Past as Present: Forging Contemporary Identities Through History*.

~

I make my way (independently, by metro) to Pragati Maidan, a vast expo centre (150 acres) where 18 exhibition halls are filled with publishers' stands. It's the New Delhi World Book Fair, and I am somewhat overwhelmed. I had not expected such throngs of ordinary people and I am being carried along by the crowd streaming in. It's clearly a day out for families, young, old. A chance to buy books at discount prices.

I eventually locate the hall where Speaking Tiger Books have their stand. It's my first chance to meet most of them, these lovely people who made my book happen in India. They have been going only a year but already their stand is filled with an impressive list of books. My editor, Renuka, who I have met earlier, introduces me to Ravi Singh, one of the co-founders. He's a man I have read about, for Speaking Tiger was set up in the wake of a publishing controversy, around a large book prominently displayed on their stand here, *The Hindus: An Alternative History*. It is 800 pages long, so not, you would think, a book for the faint-hearted, but it's written in a lively way with unquestionable scholarship, and became a best seller almost instantly. It's by Wendy Doniger, an eminent 75 year old scholar who has spent her working life studying Sanskrit sources and is in a position to challenge myths. Her book queries interpretations of history that are current in Hindu extremist circles but have no foundation in, or are directly contradicted by, Sanskrit sources. It was loudly condemned by people who almost certainly hadn't read it. A Hindutva campaigner filed a lawsuit against Penguin, the publishers, claiming that the book was a 'deliberate and malicious act intended to outrage religious feelings.' Penguin agreed to pulp the remaining copies. He then threatened to do the same against another publisher, Aleph, that had published an earlier book of Doniger's. They announced that it was out of print and that they would not be republishing it. Ravi Singh was at the time a senior editor in Aleph, and resigned at what he thought was their unnecessary cowardice. He co-founded Speaking Tiger Books, they took Wendy Doniger with them, and here is *The Hindus: An Alternative History,* once again in bookstores, and no action has been taken against them.

I buy a copy, to pack in my suitcase alongside Romila Thapar's. I'm going to be a whole lot better informed by the time I've read them both.

Back home I'm packing again, just a weekend case, but I'm changing climate zones. I'm leaving Delhi in winter for Hyderabad, 1,000 miles further south, so that means different clothes. Or does it? My publishers have got me into a couple of literature festivals and I'm going to be listening to Indian writers about whom I at the moment know nothing, so the unexpected awaits. There's also a definite excitement about scale. The best known of the festivals, Jaipur, set the style by securing funding from large corporations so that they don't have to charge for entry, and free entry has massive implications in a country like this. There are 37 million students in higher education, few of whom would be able to afford to buy tickets. Most festivals last a weekend and thousands of people come each day. Audiences of hundreds for each event.

There's also, always, politics. Life is controversial. What people write is controversial. Which writers get invited is controversial. I'm going through the programmes of the ones I'm heading for, trying to get a sense of what, if anything, each of the writers represent, and who is on which side of current political fault-lines.

I'm up early next morning to get the plane. The driver is waiting, but hardly visible through the fog. The car crawls towards the airport through fog so thick that the driver is virtually sightless. Terrifying. I am convinced we will land in a ditch, and certainly there is no way we can get there in time.

But we do.

Inside the airport building it's a heaving mass of people. A tannoy voice announces each delayed departure as if it were a surprise. I make several attempts to get hold of the people who are expecting me, and then give up. By now I have developed a certain fatalism, which seems the only way to survive when systems we have got used to relying on give up.

It's late afternoon by the time we arrive, five of us coming off different planes. After the delay I hadn't expect to be met but there are a couple of student volunteers waiting to bring us to our hotel. We are in gorgeous winter sunlight, looking out on an avenue of palm trees against a clear sky. I am enchanted and stop to take a photo, to the amazement of the students who can see nothing particularly interesting about a line of trees at the airport.

~ 26 ~

Hyderabad

I've been in this city twice before, each time memorable. The last time was a year after Ralph's death, when the University of Hyderabad ran a three day international seminar to celebrate his life and work. It was punishingly hot, the air like a blanket you were trying to breathe through, but the seminar was in the grounds of the university and between sessions we sat under trees, carefully positioning ourselves to get maximum shade. My memories of those days are a blur of warm people, stimulating company. It started from the moment I arrived at the airport, to be met by a smiling man who turned out to be the head of the Urdu department. Almost anyone else in his position would have sent a driver — Ralph would have loved his disregard for status. He identified himself by holding up a copy of the second part of

Ralph's autobiography, which I had edited but not yet seen, for it had just been published in India. 'I thought this was the best way of welcoming you!' he said.

The other time was soon after I had joined Save the Children, when I was brought to Hyderabad by a young colleague to meet people in a local organisation we were supporting. They were to take us to the remote places in Andhra Pradesh where they were working with indigenous communities, running clinics and pre-school centres, but there was some delay in setting off so they spent a day taking us around Hyderabad. Travelling out to Golconda, to the remains of a massive fort-city built on a granite hill, you see everywhere the geology of the Deccan Plateau, low hills, rocky outcrops, huge granite boulders lying scattered around. History is everywhere here. There's a series of artificial lakes created by dams on the river that were built 450 years ago. The largest, Hussain Sagar ('sagar' means 'sea') is right near the city centre. For over 400 years the city and its surrounding country formed India's biggest and wealthiest princely state, ruled by the Nizam, a Mughal ruler, and the city is full of their architectural heritage — tombs, mosques, palaces — as well as Hindu temples and shrines. The patronage of successive vastly wealthy Nizams led to a distinctive culture of painting, clothing, handicraft, literature. Urdu was the language of the court, and developed its own distinctive literature.

~

Luckily none of us coming for the literature festival on delayed flights have missed our sessions, but we did miss the opening address by Nyantara Sahgal, an 88 year old writer in English, widely known as a niece of Nehru. She is prominent in a current literary controversy about the threat of Hindu extremism. Bertolt Brecht said in 1933, 'Where you burn books, you ultimately burn people,' and now there are frightening signs that it's beginning to happen. Several writers and intellectuals known for their rationalist views, who have written against the caste system and caste-related violence, have been murdered in recent months by hit-and-run gunmen on motorbikes. No charges have been brought. No one has any doubt that the murderers were Hindu extremists. One of those murdered had been a recipient of a prestigious award from the Sahitya Akademi, a government supported institution which gives awards for outstanding literary work in any of India's many languages, and other writers expected the Akademi to at least issue a statement condemning his assassination. When days went by and they had said nothing, a Hindi writer publicly returned his own Sahitya Akademi award. His gesture sparked into action the latent anxiety of other writers. Within a month 40 had returned their awards, a snowballing that the press now refers to as the *Wapesi* movement; the word means 'returning'. From across all India's languages they made statements echoing a deep concern about the direction of government, and the responsibility of writers to speak out. One quoted Premchand, the best known early 20th century novelist and short story writer, who wrote in both Urdu and Hindi and populated his stories with Hindus and Muslims living side by side. 'Literature,' he said, 'is not something which follows politics. It should lead like a torch.'

Nyantara Sahgal was one of the first to return her award. She sent an open letter to the government, saying, 'India's culture of diversity and debate is now under vicious assault.'

Now, in the hotel where writers for the festival are staying, I come down to breakfast to discover that yesterday's opening address is front page news. The governor of the province, the official guest of honour, became increasingly angry at her outspokenness, abandoned his prepared speech and slammed into her. The event turned into an acrimonious public confrontation.

There is no sign of tension when we arrive at the festival venue. It's in the grounds of a pre-Independence era public school. Not posh, but spacious grounds, a peaceful haven in this crowded city. This is my first experience of an Indian literary festival, and they do it with flair. Most events are outside, in colourful marquees or under trees, and its own small rise in the ground covered with granite boulders. The place is buzzing with people of all ages. There are some well known people appearing, prominent in Indian fiction, politics, journalism, alongside new writers finding their first major audience. With free entry, young people are streaming in. You get used to large numbers here. Hyderabad is the fourth largest city in India with over 14 million people. At a conservative estimate there are 20 universities in this city. If you include other higher education institutions and private engineering colleges, the list scrolls down almost indefinitely.

The delegates are looked after by an enthusiastic team of university student volunteers. The ones I chat to are not studying literature, they're doing engineering & IT and anything you care to name. The language used in most events, as of much intellectual life in India, is English, but the festival takes care also to highlight writing in India's regional languages, a different one each year. This year it is Marathi, official language of Maharashtra state and a dominant language in Mumbai. There are sessions on Marathi art, music, drama, film, creativity of all kinds, too many even to dip into. The place is teeming with children. There are workshops under the trees on storytelling, animal rights, art, drama, making toys out of cow dung. One workshop leader tells me they were told to expect 30 children and at the last minute were told it would be 50. They took it in their stride.

Everyone mills about relaxedly between times. Sheltering from the heat under a tree there's a 'Meet the Author' space for people who want to ask more questions than there has been time for in the sessions, and inside there's a quiet space for participants to retire to if they have had an over-dose of sociability.

I am taking part in two sessions here. For the one on *Uncertain Light* I share a platform with an Indian novelist. We are interviewed by a young journalist who tells me she has just got married, and read our books on her honeymoon. The session is called 'Love across cultures'. The name attracts a lot of the student volunteers.

It's the older people in the audience who ask questions publicly but several groups of young women come to find me quietly later.

For the other, in one of the largest marquees, I am to talk about Ralph's book on Ghalib that I edited. Alongside me is a man who has written a book on the philosopher/poet Iqbal, and such is the passion for poetry that there must be 150 people waiting to hear what we will say. It's tough on him to have to share the session with Ghalib. In Pakistan Iqbal's status is almost sacrosanct; in India he is less popular, for his long philosophical poems are mostly addressed to Muslims. Ghalib, writing 70 years earlier, was a man and poet of a different kind and his ghazals are recited, sung and appreciated by people all over India, whatever their language or religion. The Sufi mysticism that informs the ghazal is strongly anti-fundamentalist, inclusive of people of all religions.

Mostly what this audience is intrigued to hear is how it happened that an Englishman came to devote much of his life to translating & interpreting Ghalib's poetry. So I tell the story, how as a young conscript during World War II Ralph was sent to India, where Urdu was the language of communication in the Indian army ... How, unusually for an English officer, he applied himself seriously to learning it because he wanted to be able to speak to the men in his unit. The story could have ended there, but after the war he wanted to keep his links with India, and got a scholarship to study Urdu literature ... And became not just a scholar but a pre-eminent interpreter of Ghalib.

Two distinguished physicists, one Indian, one Pakistani, are in the audience, both keen Ghalib-lovers. Later I listen to their session, a conversation that for me is the highlight of the festival. As young men both were studying in Massachusetts. Far from both their homes, they became friends. Now, 45 years later, they are both deeply concerned about the rise of religious fundamentalism in each of their countries, Hindu in one, Muslim in the other. Political tension between their governments makes it very difficult for people to move across borders, so this is a rare meeting.

The visiting Pakistani physicist is Pervez Hoodbhoy. I know about him already because years ago Robert, at Zed Books, published his first book to tackle these issues. He hasn't let himself be deterred by populist attacks. He keeps writing, and speaking — clearly, calmly. It feels an exceptional privilege to be here listening to them both. Humane thinkers, speaking quiet sense against all the dangerous, divisive noise going on beyond.

Back outside, browsing at the bookstall, I get talking to a man about my age and discover that he has written a memoir about cricket. He was one of the Hyderabad City team's best known players.

'Are you interested in cricket?' he asks, expecting the answer No.

'I grew up with it,' I say, and I tell him that as a small child I used to play at the edges of the cricket field in the Ramblers Club in my home town, for my father was a cricket commentator, and president of the South African cricket board in the early 1950s. We settle down to chat. This man knows stories of South African cricket in considerably more detail than I do. In the late 1960s he followed the D'Oliveira affair, about whether the England team touring South Africa would include a player who was a South African of mixed race ancestry who had left the country because of the restrictions of apartheid. There is a delightfully bizarre quality about the exchange. Here, in India, I am sitting under a tree with this charming man who shared so many interests with my father, thousands of miles away.

~ 27 ~

Ghalib's Delhi

Now that I have oriented myself, I am beginning to enjoy aspects of Delhi. It's a city where ancient monuments spring up like surprises, history always present, mostly ignored. In the park where I do my early morning walk is a ruined mosque, probably 15th century, the signboard says. Apart from that, little is known about it. It would have been 400 years old already in the time of the poet Ghalib.

Old Delhi was Ghalib's city. It's a challenge now to imagine it as it was in his time, but there are moments when it comes suddenly near. When we pass any of the prime tourist sights we are treading on his memory. The Red Fort, where he recited his ghazals in the court of the last Mughal emperor. Opposite it, the Jama Masjid, India's biggest mosque with its vast forecourt area where thousands still gather on special days, as they did in Ghalib's time. The purest

Urdu, I remember Ralph telling me, was said to be that spoken on the steps of the Jama Masjid. The language of the greatest poets was the language of the ordinary people of Delhi. The crowded lanes around the Chandni Chowk bazaar, where Ghalib would have walked to enter one of the old houses, and through into the hidden courtyard, to sit and talk with a friend and fellow poet.

Awesome thought, that we can still, over 150 years after his death, know anything about him — and only because he put his thoughts into scratched marks of ink on paper. 'Writing,' said the 14th century Persian, Muhammad ibn Mahmud al Amuli, 'is the offspring of thought, the lamp of remembrance, the tongue of those who are far off, the life of those whose age has been blotted out.'

At several removes I am a privileged custodian of a fragment of that lamp of remembrance, through being the literary executor for Ralph's work on Ghalib. I have people to meet who knew Ralph. They want to talk about him, and what his influence meant to them. I am taken out to meals, to places they think will interest me — and they do. I'm being absorbed in the wonderful embrace of Indian hospitality.

Roli Books, the publishers of Ralph's book on Ghalib, are taking advantage of my being here to arrange an event to promote it. A young woman arrives to collect me in a taxi. We're heading for the Oxford Bookstore on one of the city's central shopping streets. Though it's a short distance she has come an hour early, appropriately, for we spend most of an hour stuck in the usual traffic jam. She's understandably anxious that we will be late. When we arrive rows of chairs are set out in a space where they have events, and it's already filling up.

I have a few minutes to meet the woman who is going to chair the proceedings. Rakhshanda Jalil is a literary historian, critic and translator and runs a monthly series of events in which she interviews poets and writers. She calls it *Hindustani Awaaz,* the voice of Hindustani, reviving an old name for the areas of common culture of both Hindi and Urdu speakers. The audience are Urdu literature enthusiasts, and all of them are likely to know a lot of Ghalib's poetry by heart. A trifle intimidating — but I remember how Ralph dismissed my anxieties when he urged me and other of his more advanced students to help teach beginner Urdu courses. 'Just stick to what's in my course book and you'll be fine.' I'm on safe ground now if I stick to what's in his book on Ghalib, and if anyone asks anything beyond my knowledge, I pass the question over to Rakhshanda. There are people in the audience who can complete almost any couplet of Ghalib's that I refer to.

I like Rakhshanda's directness. When I learn that her grandfather was an Urdu scholar, I ask if he and Ralph knew each other. 'Yes they did,' she says, 'and Ralph wrote critically of him.' That's a jolt. I run quickly in memory through his published essays, wondering what he said, what his reasons would have been. He was on warm terms with almost all the Urdu scholars he knew and always made clear how much he learnt from them, but he did love a controversy and there were occasions when he lambasted someone in a review or an article. A pity that one of them was Rakhshanda's grandfather!

I'm impressed that she is nevertheless willing to chair the event. She doesn't see why it should be a problem. She has read Ralph's books, knows the respect in which his work is held, and is positive about anything that engages a wider audience for Urdu literature. Before she discovered her talent for translation, she taught English and edited books, among other things — until she realised that these are things thousands of highly educated Indians can do, but few can make Urdu literature available to a wider readership in the way she, through her home exposure and her later study, is able to.

She and Ralph are so alike, in their directness, and in their dedicated work as translators and literary historians. I think, What a pity they never met. I can just picture their animated conversations.

~

For the official launch of *Uncertain Light* the publishers have booked a room in the Indian International Centre. It's a pleasant set of buildings dating from the 1960s, light and airy. Visiting politicians, cultural figures, scholars, celebrities, can stay here when in Delhi; but mostly those who use it are local, the highly educated and well-off. It has a library, restaurants, concert venues, meeting rooms, and it's on the edge of the Lodhi Gardens. They too were created by Mughal emperors, and the gardens still house examples of their architecture. It's a favourite place for many to walk, with trees, cool open spaces in the midst of often punishing heat. I have come here often with friends, and once with Ralph, when we happened to be in Delhi at the same time.

And here, I imagined, Rahul in my story walked with a friend at a critical juncture in his life, talking about the transitions he faced.

Now I am here in real life again, meeting my editor, Renuka, to discuss the Delhi launch of *Uncertain Light*. My friend Manju Kapur will interview me. We first met at the Commonwealth Writers Prize awards. She was there with her first novel, *Difficult Daughters*. She has since gone on to become well known, especially for her sensitive portrayal of the dynamics in Indian families. Her novel *Custody* has been used as the basis for a popular TV series. But I can't see that either her presence or Renuka's publicity is likely to produce much of an audience. Why should it? There is so much cultural happening in this city, and only my handful of friends here have ever heard of me.

~ 28 ~

Negotiating with Rebels

We wait, Renuka, Manju and I, hoping there will be an audience. They trickle in. I talk to each as they come.

A young woman comes up to introduce herself. She heard about the launch, she says, from a friend who once worked in Save the Children. She turns to the man who has come with her, slightly-built, blond (Nordic?), I would guess in his early forties. 'He used to work in Tajikistan,' she says.

I ask what he was doing there.

He says, 'Negotiating with rebel leaders, in the mountains around Gharm.'

I have to ask him to repeat. It seems incredible. Gharm is the small town in the mountains of eastern Tajikistan where *Uncertain Light* begins, from where a convoy of UN vehicles sets off to negotiate with rebel leaders. He is the first person I have encountered outside of Tajikistan who has even heard of it. But there is no time to ask any more. Renuka is calling me, time to begin.

I have difficulty changing gear. All the time I am talking to the small audience and answering their questions, it is, unavoidably, his eyes that I keep connecting with. What is he thinking as he listens?

Meeting over, people crowd round me, asking questions. In my peripheral vision I see that he too is waiting, and I am urgent for him not to leave before I can get to speak to him. The moment I am free to move, I ask if we can meet again, for me to hear his story.

~

He has suggested we meet in the Habitat Centre, near his office. Another large cultural-cum-office complex. In the American Diner, he says. To get there I walk through beautifully laid out grounds, past palm trees and fountains, where people are setting up for an outdoor classical music concert — sitars, tabla, beautiful cloths spread on the podium, men in white garments and women in highly coloured saris moving about arranging things. Once inside the Diner I am surrounded by images on the walls of the American West, cowboys and hamburgers. The contrast is bizarre, and all of it worlds removed from the high, remote mountain valleys where the man I am waiting to meet once worked.

He arrives. He is warm, thoughtful, and quietly extraordinary. For a start, he is one of those rare fortunate people to whom language learning comes easily. In this way too he is like Rahul in my story, and I wish I could exhibit him to those readers who think such people don't exist. As a young man he was interested in India so he thought it would be useful to know some Hindi. Then he got interested in poetry and someone told him in that case he should learn Urdu. Then he found out that Urdu poetry derived from Persian so he went on to that, which meant that when he got to Tajikistan he already had a basic knowledge of the language. Why and how he got to Tajikistan is another story, not mine to tell, but he stayed long enough to become fluent and get a job as an interpreter for people working in international agencies. The quiet way he says it all, he could be describing a commuter journey in a big city. Get this train, then that bus.

By now I know I'm going to have to write about him and ask if he minds. He doesn't, but asks me not to use his real name. Further down the story there are people who might mind. So I'm calling him Olaf.

The UN staff and aid workers were the ones supposedly negotiating with rebel leaders, he says, 'But they couldn't do anything without us, the interpreters. We were the ones actually doing the talking.'

And there weren't many prepared to do it.

'So why were you?'

He smiles, looking suddenly like a much younger self. 'I had to find a way to stay in Tajikistan.' He pauses, then decides there's no point keeping this back. 'I had met the woman I wanted to marry. It was taking a long time for her family to accept me, and I wasn't leaving till they did.'

What was he negotiating about? Well, the organisation he worked for was trying to resettle refugees, and they needed to find out in the mountain villages which people had fled, and make notes about houses destroyed or taken over by others. Then they would match the details with the names of people who had turned up in refugee camps. But they couldn't risk going into an area until they had negotiated access from the local rebel commander. Though it is almost 20 years since he was there, he remembers the name of every village along their route. He picks up a paper napkin and starts to sketch a map, conjuring the landscape that I have imagined so intensely, how the road winds up a ravine with steep mountains on either side. As he names places I have the sensation of hearing echoes, for these were exactly the roads that in my imagination Rahul travelled, and at precisely that time, talking to the same rebel leaders —

This is the story of *Uncertain Light*, coming back to me, but this time for real.

On his hand-drawn map he circles the area controlled by each commander, and writes their names, describes personalities. The dominant commander of that area was a charismatic bearded man, a renowned fighter, always accompanied by a quiet man with whom they sat and drank tea. Another founded an Islamic revivalist movement in Uzbekistan which the authorities viciously suppressed. He escaped by taking his followers across the border into the mountains of Tajikistan, from where he later staged raids back across the border into Uzbekistan —

That piece of history is in my story too.

I can see it's all becoming vivid again for him too. 'It was an extraordinary job. We got to hike in mountains, we were welcomed into homes. Constantly fed.'

'So they had food enough?'

'Sure. Those valleys are fertile, and those who are better off have land, goats, sheep. And there's wild game. And you know about Tajik hospitality. Even during a war.'

He talks about how different it felt being up there from what happened in the offices back in the city. How news spreads in the mountains ... Once he and his colleague were summoned by radio to return to the capital, Dushanbe — there had been a security alert. Two humanitarian workers travelling that road had been shot at on a stretch of no-man's land between two checkpoints. As Olaf and his colleague drove back down, they paused in the villages they were passing through and tried to find out what had happened. Back in Dushanbe he reported to his manager what people had told him. It wasn't hostility to the aid workers as such, but a cultural misunderstanding. The people who had been shot at had stopped their vehicle because they needed to relieve themselves. The man had peed behind a rock on this side of the road, the woman on the other side, both unaware that they were defiling rocks that served as shrines. Suddenly shots were being fired into the air around them. They scrambled back to their car and retreated out of range.

Olaf's manager said, 'I know you like to find cultural explanations, but there are limits.'

He shakes his head. 'She lived in a different world.'

'And for yourself, weren't you scared?'

'All the time. Yes seriously, all the time.'

He is laughing now, and so am I. What else to do? 'But you get high on it too,' he says.

'You travelled unarmed?'

'Of course – with our role, how could we have weapons?'

A couple of times he had near misses. Once their job was to check that men who had been captured as prisoners of war were not being ill-treated. He and his colleague took permission from the commander to go through to the village. It was very isolated, up a narrow defile. There was a road, but as far as they knew no one from outside had been there. They arrived, equipped with this letter from the commander, but didn't get near enough to show it, for they were met with aggressive hostility. This had never happened before.

They retreated to the car, trying to work out what was going on. Suddenly bullets were whizzing past his ears, shattering the car windows. The noise was deafening, they were stunned by the suddenness. Miraculously un-hit, they managed to get into the car. By now they were shaking with delayed shock. They were trapped on the upper side of the valley and to get out of it, they had to drive back down, back past the men who were shooting. To stay where they were would have been even more dangerous. His companion reared the car back, turned, and down the road as fast as possible — and they got through, the shooting following them as they sped round a terrifying corner, and on to another village where they were known.

'One of those commanders,' he says, 'was mad. Really off his head. Rezvon Sadirov.'

I know him, the hostage-taker of my story. I don't have to tell Olaf because he was there in Dushanbe when news came that a group of UN military advisers had journeyed into territory controlled by Sadirov and been taken hostage. But he can tell me details I didn't know about what really happened. The government sent in the army. As it approached, Sadirov made all the hostages lie face down in the snow, with guns pointed at their heads, and radioed to the government forces that if they advanced one step further, he would give the order to shoot.

'And he would have.'

His manager said she herself would go to negotiate the release of the hostages.

'I told her, that's really not a good idea, the man is mad. She insisted, and expected me to come to interpret. But I refused.'

He had reached his own limit. He was married now, and his wife was about to have a child. It was not a time to be taking extreme risks.

His manager ignored his advice. She took a Tajik to interpret. They were both instantly taken hostage. Olaf had to break the news to the family of the interpreter. When the hostages were finally released, it was he who had to go in the car that was fetching his manager.

'She was treated as a hero. To me that was crazy. She had acted irresponsibly, putting herself and her colleague at unnecessary risk, and for zero tactical gain.'

Sadirov escaped and lived to take more hostages. A year later, in a shoot out with government forces, a French aid worker was killed. Olaf had known her. She was a friend.

~

For days afterwards I am thinking about his story. It is an echo not just of my story, but of things that happen all the time, in other dangerous places. Each year, worldwide, there are several hundred deaths of aid workers and of local journalists reporting on things their governments do not want known. Just two weeks after we launched *Uncertain Light* in London, nine Afghans in northern Afghanistan were attacked as they slept, murdered by an unknown armed group. They were working for an organisation that had been in the area more than 10 years, delivering health, education and agriculture support in that starkly beautiful but implacably dry area. I feel humble thinking about the special kind of courage it takes to keep working in these situations.

For every one of these courageous people, and for all those close to them, there is a story that will probably never be told.

But we can imagine it. Just.

~ 29 ~

Who Reads Novels?

Delhi events now, a run of them. In among the crowded publishers' stands in the World Book Fair is a space called the Authors' Corner with a rolling programme of talks. Renuka has booked a slot for me to talk about *Uncertain Light*. We arrange the podium, a table with books, set out chairs. But with the buzz of crowds and blaring tannoy announcements, will anyone want to attend a talk, or be able to hear?

Before my session is due to start there are maybe 70 people sitting there, people who know nothing about me or my book. What has brought them? Are they tired of standing about and the chairs looked inviting? They are waiting hopefully, for — ?

A well known professor of literature was to have interviewed me. But he has called in to say he is ill and can't do it, so we have been phoning my friend Shireen, currently working in Mumbai. She rises beautifully to the challenge. She'll come straight off her flight to join us.

'It'll be OK,' the others say. No problem.

Shireen arrives. She has a highly responsible job in a development agency, but it's the first time she's done anything like this. 'What do you want me to ask you?' she asks.

'Anything,' I say. 'You'll be fine.'

It feels a bit of a joke, both of us unprepared.

Adrenalin kicks in. Shireen does an excellent job, and all I have to do is answer her questions. The audience is so attentive I forget the tannoy announcements. Scores of books are sold.

I sign one to the youngest reader I've ever had – she's 13 and writing already. I wish her luck with it. I had no concept that my book might be read by a 13 year old. I wonder – what will she make of it?

Now I'm in the office of a group of social activists who work on education. A friend fixed this event up for me and I am regretting that I accepted. I have no idea what the people I will be talking to think they will be hearing from me. It's 13 years since I worked in education and produced my last book on the subject for Save the Children. Do they actually know this is a *novel* I'm touring with?

When I arrive there are just three young men to make up an audience – the organisers. Did they advertise the event, I wonder? While we wait to see if anyone else will come I ask about their work. Indian law guarantees free education, but everyone knows there are millions of children who miss out. This group co-ordinates local organisations across many states to deliver statistical reports on the numbers of children who are not getting schooling, the most marginalised — Dalits, oppressed minorities, and that vast group of children who can't be at school because they have to work. One of these young men works with children who are rag-pickers. That is about as near bare-survival as you get. These are the kind of people I used to work with in Save the Children, and if I were here to learn about their experiences that would be fine, but to talk about my book —? Nothing about our conversation so far suggests that they might read novels.

They have work to do. Perhaps no one else will come and we can call it off?

But no, a couple more have arrived. We chat, waiting in case there will be more. It is now 20 minutes after starting time. I am finding it difficult to follow some of their accents in English, so presumably they are finding it equally difficult to follow mine. A young man arrives with a large box, and begins piling books out of it, copies of my book. He is from the publisher, it turns out, and he is disappointed that I did not immediately recognise him. Apparently he was there at the event at the Book Fair (among the hundreds of strangers I was surrounded by.) He's a cheerful young man, and I like his confident assumption that he should have made an impression. The pile of books is embarrassingly large.

A few more people drift in, including a woman who is introduced as the CEO of the host organisation for this building. I suspect she and the other newcomers have been summoned out of their offices to save my face, to make up an audience for this visiting foreigner. I'm thinking that I could perhaps make this work if we could sit in a comfortable circle and I could get them talking, but the room itself imposes formality. We are seated around a heavy, immovable table.

The convenor says we should start. No help for it, we all have to somehow get through this. I talk briefly about what led me to write this book, then try to encourage questions. Someone asks about my background in apartheid South Africa — great, that's a lead. I abandon *Uncertain Light* and talk instead about *If You Can Walk, You Can Dance*, which starts with anti-apartheid activists having to flee. By now they're looking positively engaged. I tell them about the music in the story, different in each culture, but people everywhere respond to music. On a sudden inspiration I abandon caution and sing the African song that appears in the book. It's sung by a woman calling from a distant hill-top, loud and uninhibited. The young men are looking stunned. One is grinning awkwardly, but it has jolted them out of reserve. 'In India,' one says, 'we have something worse than apartheid. Caste. Maybe you can write a story challenging caste issues?'

'Not me,' I say, 'I don't have the experience, but maybe *you* could.' And I tell them that there are stories being written by Dalits and Adivasis themselves, and Speaking Tiger is publishing some.

It's time to end. The CEO woman astonishes me by announcing that they will buy four copies of my book for their library. Four of the men buy their own copies. That's eight, which at least makes me feel less guilty about the cheerful young man from Speaking Tiger having lugged that heavy box all the way here. I am not sure whether those who bought copies are just doing it to boost my morale, but I feel absurdly pleased at having sung to them – some light relief in their report-writing-computer-dominated day.

One of those who bought a copy comes up quietly to say that if he likes it he might translate it into Hindi. So much for my assumption that they are unlikely to read novels.

Now to Miranda House, Delhi university's oldest and most prestigious women's college. A friend of a friend teaches here, and is hosting my talk for students who are members of the Literary Society. She herself writes short stories, which she's hoping will come out in book form soon. The students coming to listen are mostly doing degrees in English Literature, so they can be assumed to be interested in novels.

I order a taxi. The driver has never heard of Miranda House. Shireen's driver, who is still looking after me, instructs him, then turns to me and says, 'Why you not go by Metro?' I can't imagine why. For a moment I must have slipped back into the habits of those around me and assumed a car would get me there quicker. Big mistake. But now I have engaged this taxi driver I can't turn him off.

The journey takes forever – I am afraid we are leaving the city and will never arrive. When I think we must be nearly there the driver stops to ask people at the roadside – '*Miranda House kahan hai?*' – Where is Miranda House? No one has any idea. We try again a little further on – Delhi University? – Miranda House? Women's college? No idea. We turn a corner – and here it is, right here,

50 yards from all those people who had never heard of it. It's an impressive heritage building with large gates and the name written up. Every day the passers-by must see hundreds of young women coming towards it, going away. Well, that puts things usefully in perspective – just how peripheral university-educated people and writers and books are in the lives of most people.

The woman organising the event meets me at the gate and we walk across a courtyard to the room where young women are already assembling. While we wait for others to come I ask them what writers they are studying. Every English writer from Chaucer on, it seems, in a syllabus so packed I wonder how they ever get time to read books being written now. Their lecturer says, 'They don't.'

By the time we get going there must be about 80 young women in the lecture room. They're listening rather too respectfully, and I am feeling for clues as to what might interest them. Do they themselves write, or aim to write? (Who chooses to study literature without at least a secret fantasy of writing?) Someone asks about how easy it was to get a publisher. That makes me laugh, which is not the reaction they expect, so I begin telling them about the decades of rejections and resorting to self-publishing. They love every story of going-it-alone, of literary prizes that proved those rejections wrong. Their laughter eggs me on and it turns into a hilarious session.

Despite the heavy weight of Chaucer and the rest of the literary canon, all the copies of *Uncertain Light* that the publisher has sent disappear. It's the same cheerful young man who has brought them, and luckily this time I remember him. A small group of students stays on to chat, the laughter still on their faces when someone says, 'We need a photo.' They're all still laughing and relaxed as it is taken. It will remind me of the moment when I ceased to be the successful author they thought they had come to hear, and became instead a person like them, who writes for the love of it.

~ 30 ~

Jaipur

Now to Rajasthan, and the country's (possibly the world's) most prestigious literary festival, Jaipur. I join a friend who is driving there from Delhi. It's a long, tiring journey, the last part desert, with as many camels as lorries on the roads.

The festival is based in the grounds and buildings of a 'heritage hotel', a luxurious mid-19th century home of the ruling family of a small principality. Last year 35,000 people came over the course of a weekend, and young people make up about 80% of those who stream in constantly. It's a celebration of colour and Rajasthani artistry. Overhead float handmade puppets in brightest colours. The marquees are festooned, the buildings themselves an architectural experience, all the festival signs and banners are done with flair. In the spaces between the event venues are pop-up food stalls and craft stalls, with the tantalising smells of spices and sounds of traditional musical instruments. There are guides and support staff everywhere, young people courteous and helpful, perfectly inducted into their roles. Even the refuse collection works.

The crowds never seemed to thin, 700 people fill the largest marquees to hear the more famous writers. There was threatened crisis because the Jaipur police said they couldn't guarantee security with such a crowd pushing into a venue designed to hold 2,000. They were persuaded to change their minds, but nevertheless there are airport-like security precautions in place.

Ten separate platforms run simultaneously, with over 350 writers and others taking part — the biggest names in Indian writing and Bollywood films, celebrity poets, TV current affairs hosts, journalists, politicians who have written memoirs, and scores more besides. There's a staggering array of internationally known writers, more best-selling authors and Booker Prize winners than you could count, leading travel writers, political thinkers, TV stars. My publisher has been angling for months to get me a slot. Now I've seen the programme I'm surprised they bothered. I decided to come anyway, just for the experience. Then as I was setting off I got a message — someone has dropped out from one of the panels on fiction. Do I want the place? Unbelievable.

I am duly grateful, but I feel (and am) an appendage. The programmes have already been printed so I am not on them. But I get to be an inside observer, watching the world of writers.

I slip in at the back of sessions, dipping in and out, hearing a bit of them all. A couple of times I queue to get a book signed by a writer I admire, and have a few words with them. In the festival bookshop I am momentarily adopted by Jerry Pinto when we discover our books are both published by Speaking Tiger. He's an astonishing man, large, funny, serious, a novelist and translator from Marathi. I buy a copy of his latest book and he signs it to 'The Speaking Tigress'. He has set up a pop-up stall to tell people about his book. I am bowled over by his *chutzpah*. He is without fear as he performs for this ad hoc audience, and it works, for several of them go off to buy his book. Then he thrusts me up in front of them, 'Your turn,' he says, 'Tell them about your book.' I don't have time to think, but what I come out with has no punch, and I give up quickly.

Later that night I start reading his book, *Em and the Big Hoom*, a semi-autobiographical novel about growing up with a manic depressive mother they all love, but who repeatedly breaks their hearts. It's as extraordinary as he is.

~

This festival is not uncontroversial. It must cost the earth, and to keep it free to all comers, it requires a massive input of sponsorship. For the last couple of years its chief sponsor has been ZEE, Zee Entertainment Enterprises, a media corporation that includes Zee News television, considered by some to be inflammatory in their reporting of communal tensions. The festival organisers say ZEE has never interfered with the programming. The event has become not just a place where books are discussed, but a series of platforms for political and intellectual debates, inviting controversy. There's a session discussing intolerance in India, where a Bollywood director and TV talk show host says, 'Freedom of expression is the biggest joke in India. Democracy is the second-biggest joke.' His autobiography is cleverly entitled *An Unsuitable Boy*. He's gay, still now, in 2016, a criminal offence in India.

The best part about having slipped onto the programme is that I have a red lanyard with a name badge that lets me in to the Authors' Lounge. It is elegant, spacious, with armchairs and tea laid on — and most precious asset of all, peaceful. A retreat when the pressure of crowds gets too much. The atmosphere is relaxed and I chat to a couple of people, but mostly I simply observe others moving in and out. You can tell by the body language those who have done this many times before, and for whom it has the ambiance of an Old Boys Reunion, and those who need to be ingratiating themselves with the more famous. I find I'm thinking irreverently of a couplet of Ghalib's:

I dress myself in beggar's clothing
And watch the way the bountiful behave.

For my event I share a platform with an Assamese novelist, and interviewing us is a Bengali woman writer. None of us have heard of each other until this event, but surprisingly we find our books have one thing in common, a civil war setting. Over 150 people have assembled to hear us. Looking down, I get the impression that the great majority are young women. They listen as attentively as students to an eminent professor, and their serious eyes looking up at us evokes in me that responsibility I always feel when people are open to hearing what I might have to say. The questions are thoughtful, and soon we get onto issues about language. The writer appearing with me is widely read in Assam, but unknown beyond. It's an issue for all those who write in any of India's languages — how to reach a wider audience? Without thinking of an international audience, even just in India, translation into English is the only option. So he decided to write this novel in English. His situation is quite different from those of English-medium-educated writers, for whom English is now the language in which they can best express themselves. His spoken English is competent but it has taken me a while to tune in to his accent, which suggests that he didn't hear it often as a child. It's unlikely that his writing in English will have the natural idiomatic force it would have in his own mother tongue. I have worked closely with people who are having to write in a learnt language, and have seen how frustrating it is.

How lucky I am that I face no such dilemmas, having been born with a world language as my mother tongue. But I tell the audience that I know it's also a limitation. There is a whole different perspective on life that comes through each language culture, and I've gained hugely by having a taste of it through learning Urdu. After the session there is a little crowd around each of us, wanting to keep the conversations going. I had had no expectations of eliciting any response in an event so over-crowded with celebrity writers, and am touched. I ask the young women around me about themselves. Several of them are writing.

Suddenly tired, I make my way to the courtyard area where meals are being served for participants — organisers, speakers, VIP guests, hundreds of us, a small festival-worth crowd on our own, each with our name-badges swinging from separately coloured ribbons round our necks. I join my friends from Delhi, am introduced to others and then lose them again as we each get carried along in the queues that move slowly along the serving tables, behind which rows of white-clad chefs stir cauldrons of food. I slip out of the line to watch, mesmerised, the perfect body-dance of an assembly line of people producing fresh chapatis. They sit, men and women, cross-legged on a platform where one kneads dough then presses it into small spheres, passes them to another who rolls them out into perfect flat discs and throws them onto a large hot cooking surface, where another deftly flips them over and out onto waiting trays, piles and piles of fresh *roti* that get lifted almost instantly onto the plates of the people in the slowly passing queue, plates already piled with an assortment of deliciously spiced dishes, then move further on to stand in little groups talking vigorously as their hands carry food up to their mouths and back again. The sound of hundreds of voices blends into its own kind of accompanying music, heads moving side to side in that specifically Indian nod of agreement, the vibrant constantly moving colours of saris and shalwars and shawls…

I summon the effort to talk to someone new. Move on to the next thing. But I carry with me for a long time the picture of those cross-legged men and women creating a constant flow of chapatis, to keep us all going.

~

Delhi again, Tuesday 26th January 2016
Republic Day in India, a holiday. There will be vast crowds in the city centre, parades of all kinds, celebrations. I'm staying clear,

inside in the quiet of Shireen's home. We have a last walk and chat in the park together. For the rest of the time I'm sorting out the piles of books and papers I have accumulated, and packing for my flight home tomorrow, trying to gather up the multiple strands of what this month has been. What started as a personal journey, me with my book, has become absorbed in a swirl of wider issues.

I'm returning to face again the world out there that continues on its tension-filled, deeply divided way. Paging through the newspapers to catch up ... The headline news from Hyderabad since I was there is that a university student has committed suicide. He was a Dalit, someone who would once have been called 'untouchable'. He left notes making it clear that his life had been made intolerable by the aggressive behaviour of right-wing Hindu groups on campus ...

In Pakistan and Afghanistan there have been more suicide bomb attacks by the Taliban. ISIS has extended its control over new areas. Saudi Arabian bombs are destroying Yemen, and Britain sells them arms. The Syrian conflict, now four years old, continues to escalate, as does the migrant crisis in neighbouring countries and into Europe. And that's not even mentioning extreme climate events, and what they portend about the ticking time-bomb of climate change. Britain is having its hottest January ever while the US is in the grip of blizzards and 11 states have declared a state of emergency.

It's difficult to keep any sense of perspective.

Do I write fiction to escape the helplessness the world induces? Go to a place where I have some potential control?

Control? Here's Ghalib:

I have not ceased to struggle; I am like the captive bird
Who in the cage still gathers straws with which to build his nest.

I think I'm tired. I'll be glad to get home.

~ 31 ~

Lahore

February 2016

Two weeks' break to catch up with home and family. One book group, one library event. Now I'm heading back to the airport again, this time to fly to Lahore, Pakistan.

'Are you sure you want to go?' Robert asked.

It's an understandable question. Pakistan straddles a dangerous geopolitical fault line, with Afghanistan on its border where the US has for decades armed radical insurgents. It has one of the highest levels of sectarian violence in the world. But yes, I want to go. Millions of Pakistanis live with all that daily, and I'm not going to be personally in any danger. Besides, I trust the judgement of the Literature Festival organisers that it will be safe.

I've only once had the chance to visit Lahore, an extraordinary journey among children who were stitching footballs for premier league matches internationally, and impressive small organisations that were trying to do make sure that working children also got an education. But it's a city with an absorbing cultural and political history, and I had too little time to experience anything beyond my work. The festival programme looks amazing. It is not just about books, more a celebration of all that books open up to us. Debates will range from political issues to novels about personal relationships, from innovation in art to the need to preserve Lahore's architectural heritage. There will be film actors, museum curators, a drama production and an evening of Sufi-inspired music, a tradition that goes back 700 years. They're expecting 100,000 people.

~

And here I am, arriving at Lahore airport a couple of hours after midnight.

There is no one to meet me.

Still half asleep I watch the swirl of people around me, wondering what's gone wrong. I guess it's not so surprising, for participants for the festival will be flying in from 40 countries. My mobile rings. The organisers, with profuse apologies. They were let down by a taxi company and have had to rush around finding a substitute. I wait where I have been told to, at the entrance to the car park, along with a companion so elderly that he can hardly stand. I find a luggage trolley and up-end it for him to sit on. As car lights flash past in the dark it feels like the start of a *film noir*. I try to distract my companion by asking him about himself. He is a notable Pakistani artist, has lived in New York for many years, and this is the first flight he has made in ten years. He is so frail I wonder if he will make it through the festival.

A car pulls up. Thank goodness, it's for us. We are driven through the night and dropped off at a hotel that looks totally closed up. *Film noir* still spooling. It's 2 a.m, there's one sleepy man at the desk who gives us keys, tells us that our rooms are in an annexe at the far end of the grounds, but he has to stay at the desk so can't help my companion with his luggage. The driver is about to go. There are people still waiting at the airport, he says. With some difficulty I persuade him to stay and bring the luggage while I take the elderly artist's arm and we walk slowly, slowly, along a dark path that seems endless. Then up even more endless steps to his room. Open the door for him, take him in, sit him on a chair. And now? He needs care, this man, he shouldn't be travelling. Shakily he assures me he will manage. I tip the driver, then to my room.

After a few hours' groggy half-sleep I wake, wash, and make my way across the garden to the main building. At reception I discover that this hotel is overflow. We are far from where the other festival participants are staying. I get on my mobile. The organisers are charming and full of apologies for the mess-up last night. I tell them that whatever it takes they have to get the elderly artist into the already-fully-booked hotel where the other participants are staying, and that he will need a dedicated volunteer to take him about. And while I have no special claim, I'd be most grateful if they could get me in there too, because it doesn't feel like I'm going to be part of anything here.

Don't know how they find the extra rooms, but it happens. Once I've seen the artist handed over to someone who can take proper care of him, I begin to be ready to enjoy myself. We have half a day before the festival opening session.

~

It now becomes clear that the organisers are dealing with a crisis. Two days ago, with the first participants already arriving, the government of the Punjab (the province of which Lahore is the capital) withdrew permission for the festival to happen. Speakers who had not yet set out were asked to cancel flights. The reason? 'We cannot guarantee security.'

Well, no one doubts that Pakistan has security issues but they didn't suddenly arise two days ago. It's hard not to believe there are other agendas here. Political differences? Personal jealousies? Gradually we pick up hints as to other layers of intrigue … The festival organisers come from influential families and have secured wide sponsorship from businesses, media corporations, some international cultural sources. The arts need patrons — they always have done — and you don't run a free-to-all festival without someone having to pick up the bill. Many who have helped inspire the festival are active citizens also in other ways that might have got under the skin of the authorities, like protesting the bulldozing of heritage buildings to make way for a new metro line. Is this a ploy to demonstrate who really holds power?

Hours later a compromise has been reached. Permission has been granted for a reduced festival: two days instead of three, and they will have to find a new venue. This is bizarre. If security cover can be provided for two days, why not three? And why in a new venue, which turns out to be a hotel just across the road from the Arts Centre where it was planned to be?

Mohammed Hanif, author of the biting political-satirical novel, *A Case of Exploding Mangoes*, says, 'To be a satirist in this country you don't have to make anything up. You just tell it straight.'

Meanwhile, who can complain at having a brief unplanned holiday in an interesting city and in excellent company? Gradually a group assembles, people I had never imagined I would spend a companionable day with. A petite, lively woman in her 80s appears. It's Madhur Jaffrey. In her early life a famous actress, the programme now describes her as 'The Woman Who Took Curry Global.' With her is a tall, quiet American, her husband. I wonder if he is slightly overwhelmed by being with so many chatty women? As we wait to set off I ask about his own line of work. He says, self-deprecating, 'I guess you could say I spent a lot of my life trying to master the violin.'

I sympathise – I'm a late starter on the violin and it is the most difficult instrument. I discover later that his name is Sanford Allen. He was in the New York Philharmonic, its first full-time African-American violinist.

Cars and drivers arrive. My guide-companion is a slim, elegant young woman who grew up in Lahore and is now a professor of art in Dubai. She came back for the festival to see friends and family, and now finds herself unexpectedly co-opted to keep the visiting speakers occupied. She is an excellent guide. We pass the Art College where she studied. She tells us it is one of the few places where they teach the skill of miniature painting, techniques developed centuries ago to achieve incredibly fine detail. 'You start by catching a squirrel,' she says. I think she's joking, but no, you lay out a few hairs from its tail in length order, to end up with a one-hair fine brush. Later when I see examples of her art work the connection becomes clear. She creates exquisite, immensely detailed land- and city-scapes.

We wander around the Shahi Qila, a vast fort-cum-Mughal palace, moving along cobbled streets and into different sections of the palace, views framed by 500 year old stone arches. She looks regretfully at the decaying tile-work and murals. 'There's no culture of preservation here,' she says. Her love for this city is so obvious that I imagine it must feel like exile living in Dubai. On the way back in the car I ask how often she gets back. Quietly she says it's been a year since she was last here, and this is an emotional return. A year ago her brother was murdered here, yet another victim of religious intolerance. They are Shia, a minority here; the Taliban target them.

Day 2:
The logistical miracle has been achieved. The venue is ready to receive tens of thousands of people. The programme for the truncated festival is set. Of the planned 99 sessions, 45 are no longer there. I was down to take part in three panel discussions — none have made it into the new programme. A stab of disappointment, but the feeling is momentary. How gutted the organisers must be feeling at watching their months of preparation unravel. My own loss seems not particularly consequential. At least I am here.

There's a heavily armed soldier in the mini-bus that collects us to take us to the hotel, where people are already streaming in. More soldiers stand around the entrance, looking, frankly, bored. We pass through x-ray portals. The women in the security teams staffing them all wear headscarfs, which few of the women in the crowds do, different strands of this polarised community. Through the security checks they come, a constant stream of people, flourishes of colour from elegant women's dress, people calling to friends, crowding the foyers and grounds. People browse bookstalls, families sit on the grass, young friends meet. Volunteers from local schools are in T-shirts with the festival logo, guiding people, offering help. The festival team are everywhere, welcoming, making sure everything happens according to the constantly having-to-be-revised plan. You would hardly know they have had a fraught time and are sleep-deprived.

Pakistan has one of the lowest literacy rates in the world but all those with positions of influence are fluent in English, and probably a high proportion of the people milling about here have had their education through English-medium. The conversations I overhear among the young are in a lively mixture – English with Urdu words thrown in, Urdu with English words. It's pleasurable just moving around the crowds, listening in.

Lahore lies close to the border with India, and during the Partition in 1947 – within living memory of the oldest people here – it was the setting for a tragic history of mass migration and communal killing. There are sessions here that open up that painful history. Older people are being interviewed, remembering those times. Others critically re-examine the hopes with which Pakistan was founded. Several high-profile participants are Indians who have achieved eminence in different cultural spheres, invited here to celebrate the culture that Pakistan and India share. The biggest marquee is packed with over 1,000 people to hear the Indian actress, Sharmila Tagore. At 71, looking still serenely beautiful, she gives a thoughtful retrospect of her career, starting with the independent 'art' films of Satyajit Ray, then going mainstream to become Bollywood's most loved heroine. One expects crowds for film stars, but there are as many crowding in to listen to the art historian, B N Goswamy. Now in his 80s, he was born in a town west of Lahore and was a boy at the time of Partition when the family migrated across to the Indian Punjab. There is an atmosphere of total absorption as the audience listens to him share his insights from a lifetime of studying miniature paintings, part of the joint Indian-Pakistani heritage. He says he must have scrutinised about 150,000 paintings, and can clearly recall more than a thousand. The diligence is awe-inspiring. 'You need to absorb a painting,' he says, 'the way you absorb a poem,' and all the way through he keeps quoting poetry. The sounds circle around me, and I wish I could follow the sense. Afterwards I buy his beautiful book, *The Spirit of Indian Painting: Close Encounters with 101 Great Works*. Studying it will last me a life-time.

That evening when I am sitting next to him in the mini-bus going back to our hotel he tells me of his youthful passion for Faiz's poems. Once as a young man he saw on a bookstall a magazine with a new poem by Faiz. He had no money to buy the magazine so he pretended to be browsing until he had memorised the poem, then he put it back.

The Urdu poets belong equally to all, Indians and Pakistanis. There is such a crowd wanting to hear TV personality Zia Mohyeddin reciting from Ghalib that security guards have to handle potentially unruly young men, desperate because they can't get in. The organisers look worried. 'You should celebrate,' I say. 'In how many countries do young men almost cause a riot because they can't get to hear a poetry recital?'

~

Day 3:
I take my place on the platform in the largest marquee, for a session called 'The Passion for Love Literature'. I am with two other novelists, both much better known than me. I look out over the faces in the audience – maybe 700 people? A buzz of animated

talk, waiting for things to begin. I feel the weight of this moment, being given the chance to share thoughts with all these people. At one point the woman interviewing us asks if 'transgressive' love is a theme in our novels, the tension between the power of individual love and the constraints of society. Yes, it's there in *Uncertain Light,* the central love story raises moral issues that it does not resolve. But it's as much about loss, for in loving we make ourselves vulnerable.

How best to talk about this, here, with this audience? The love poetry everyone here has grown up with reflects a kind of love that was almost always frowned on by society. It is about feelings that won't be neatly packaged, longing that cannot be realised. I quote Ghalib:

hazaron khahishen aisi ki har khahish pe dam nikle
bahut nikle mere arman lekin phir bhi kam nikle

Pleasure ripples like warmth across the hundreds of people in the marquee, and many of them are reciting with me after they hear the first two words. For those who have flown in from elsewhere and who don't know Urdu, I give Ralph's translation:

Desires in thousands, each so strong it takes away my breath
    anew
Many longings have been fulfilled; many, but even so, too few.

Everything comes together. Ghalib, *Uncertain Light,* this audience.

When the session is over, I go to the bookstall to sign copies. Within a short time it has sold out of both my novel, and Ralph's on Ghalib.

~ 32 ~

And After

March 2016

Back home again; but nothing stops. Yesterday, Easter Sunday, a series of bombs exploded in one of Lahore's main parks, where families were out for the day. Killing, maiming. Yet again. Beyond Pakistan, I wonder how many people have noticed. The world has become numb to this kind of news.

I see them all now, that other crowd so peacefully moving about, picnicking, browsing the bookstall, meeting friends. I feel so far away. I scroll through the Facebook posts of some of the people I got to know there. With all the downsides of social media,

I am grateful for this continuing link. A young woman who came running up to get me to sign her copy of my book is visiting children in hospital, who struggle for their lives. She is giving them toys that her friends have donated; hugs and smiles amidst the suffering. Another posts a photo of young men crowding a hospital entrance, wanting to give blood. 'Pray for Lahore,' several of them say.

One says, 'Don't pray. Fight against hateful religious ideology.' Another quotes Faiz:

Our world knows other torments than of love
Dark curse of countless ages, savagery.

IN QUIET PLACES

~ 33 ~

It's an Umbrella

April 2016

Home. I am grateful to be in a quiet place, where nothing dramatic is happening. Catching up with family, ordinary life. It's spring, and nature calls. I'm going to see friends who have no connection with my writing. Spend time with my grandchildren.

~

I'm in a Puppet Theatre with Zander, two-and-a-half years old. It's dark all around us. He is moulded into my lap, his body stilled by concentration as he watches the extraordinary goings on at the other end of the room. A young woman swings her puppet in the air, pretending to fly him over painted-cardboard-mountains and cotton-wool-clouds amidst birds that suddenly appear on sticks.

In the seats in front of us children call out and wave their arms as if they too could fly. The toddler next to us is a groupie in the making, jerking excitedly as her mother holds her up to almost-stand on her lap. But Zander is stolidly silent, staring ahead.

I whisper encouragement. 'Look, he's going over the mountain!' A slight tightening of small leg muscles on mine is the only sign I get that he has heard. Now the flying puppet has landed in a bunch of twigs at the top of a pole. With her free hand the young woman brings out a closed umbrella, points it at us rather than up to the sky, and flicks it open to reveal scores of green leaves pasted on it. It's the best moment in the show so far — the pole has become a tree, with the puppet in his nest at the top. I whisper to my silent Zander, 'See, it's a tree!'

He says, loudly, his first words, 'It's an umbrella.'

Well, you have to give it to him. It's an umbrella, with leaves stuck on it. That's all it is. We expect children to be so gullible. We create for them stories that can't possibly be true — Father Christmas, Peter Pan, Harry Potter. Most children are at home in fantasy, and through it they practise that capacity to lose yourself in another reality which we call imagination, but they also have moments when they want to be clear about what is fantasy and what is real, and it is an instinct just as valuable as imagination. It is after all what enabled a child to challenge complicit adult society and say, 'The emperor has no clothes.'

And what do we know, anyway, about what gets through and what doesn't? A week later Zander's brother and cousin, aged seven and nine, present us with a Magic Show. Once again he is in an audience, on my lap. The magicians wear special hats, the chairs are set out in a row, so he understands what kind of event this is going to be. While we wait for it to begin he moves his hands in the air, flying his imaginary puppet.

~

Fantasy probably makes as much sense to children as any of the other things that happen around them and which no one thinks to explain. There must be many moments when they are confronted with stories that cannot be reconciled with their developing understanding of what is real or possible. Each religion has its own. Virgin birth, reincarnation, rewards in paradise. The media and celebrity culture propagate equally unquestioned beliefs, for instance that you'll be happier if you buy lots of things, or are rich and famous.

Fiction is strikingly more honest: it comes with a label on the tin, 'This is only a pretend tree.' This puts the reader, child or adult, in the right frame of mind for fairy tales, adventure stories, science fiction or thrillers. There's more confusion in the kind of fiction that aims to reflect real life. I am regularly asked questions that try to sort out the umbrella from the tree, like, have I ever been to Tajikistan? That one still surprises me. How could I possibly evoke the atmosphere of the place otherwise? But perhaps the question simply reflects how sceptical we have learned to be in a world where we are overloaded with information, much of it fake. We need to know if we can trust our source.

With personal stories, 'true' has another meaning. We don't need to know that it literally happened, only that it could have. For me, writing fiction creates the freedom to get closer to an emotional truth not tied to specific people. It's perhaps one of the reasons I don't ever start with a plot. I start with people, in a situation. After that it's free fall, letting them react as those particular people would react — as true to life as my understanding allows.

~

My grandchildren have all loved being read to when little, but the particular ways they latch on to what books offer are quite different. Zahira is practical, a realist. She goes for stories about children who could easily be real. Zeph soaks up serious factual stuff about the world. For a while it was fossils, currently it's ancient China, but he also goes for implausible quests after dragons. Isla is a story-monster. Any kind of story. She can never get enough of them. From earliest childhood she has been able to disappear for amazing amounts of time into her own story-world, arranging things in a doll's house or recreating daily-life-stories peopled with Sylvanians. (For the uninitiated, these are small dressed animals that come in families.) She does all the voices, adults, children, interaction. Omni never did anything like that. Her imagination has a zany quality, skipping with élan around chocolate machines on other planets. The answerphone message on her mobile says she can't take the call because she is sitting on a rainbow. Theo by the age of three had mastered the London underground system and could tell anyone which line to take and where to change to get from any station to any other station. He likes systems and facts (who scored in World Cup matches, the Guinness Book of Records, technology.) Contrary to popular belief, it takes considerable imagination to be able to relate to information that you haven't experienced, or to take in abstract concepts. It's just not of the story-making kind.

Zander, the youngest, is his own person, following no one else's pattern. What's going on in the moments when he slips into his own private world? He talks to his trains as he pushes them about, an almost inaudible monologue. Perhaps it's a slowly evolving story about where they are going and why? I don't ask, because it's clear that an audience would be an intrusion.

It could be an umbrella, or it could be a tree. Perhaps both.

~ 34 ~

A Community of Poets

April 2016, Shropshire

I'm in Shropshire, a few miles from the unmarked border that separates England from Wales. Tourist information describes this small town of Much Wenlock as 'quintessentially English', and it certainly has a picture-history-book look. My morning walks follow paths people have taken for centuries, green lanes where trees meet overhead, across fields where sheep turn momentarily to stare, then return to the more important task of grazing. I stop every now and then to look back at the still-sleeping town, with its tiled roofs and the ruins of Wenlock Priory rising above ancient oak trees.

I wander through the cobbled town square and along a street where timber-framed Elizabethan buildings stand alongside medieval stone ones, and Victorian shop fronts like illustrations from *A Christmas Carol*. But these are not museum pieces. The bookshop is busy. People are arriving from all over Shropshire and beyond, and the cafés and Deli are filling up. Poets are being met off trains from Birmingham, Manchester, London, and are checking in at the hotel in town. Wandering through the town, I meet poets at every turn — 67 of the species, famous poets, local poets, award winners and newcomers, old and young. The Pottery has pushed its pots and work tables to one side to make a space that will hold 50. I go to check it out, because that's where I will be doing my session. In a café facing the town square a Poetry Breakfast is happening. Bring a poem you'd like to share, and read to each other over coffee and croissants. In the church grounds bunting loops through the yew trees, and in a marquee a lively young woman is getting children to write poems. Local not-yet-published poets take turns at an Open Mic session. In another marquee a BBC interviewer talks to well-known poets about their lives and work. In a decommissioned ambulance an Emergency Poet dispenses poetic remedies for whatever inner ailments you bring.

I told any friends who I thought might be within reach, and the idea of a small town poetry festival was intriguing enough that several have made journeys to be here. It makes the town feel homey. We bump into each other, then each go off to different events we have chosen. Some I am touched to see, one from Wales, still in crutches after an operation on her foot; one from London, recently bereaved, and a friend has brought her. Another is elderly, and can hear very little. It will be the last time I see her.

And I finally get to meet Pauline Prior-Pitt, whose poems I first encountered 30 years ago. There is an immediate feeling that we already know each other.

~

A festival with as many local participants as this doesn't spring out of nowhere. It draws on a thriving community of everyday-poets, several of whom read their poems alongside the well known poets at the opening event. I had no idea there was such a lively culture of contemporary English poetry-writing anywhere, and, it seems, a mutually supportive one too. There are monthly public readings together in several small towns. People of all ages are discovering talents they didn't know they had, or perhaps knew, but had never earlier had the time to develop. Their poems are beginning to be published by local presses, or one poem at a time in poetry magazines. On the first night, where several well-known guest poets perform to a packed auditorium, it is a local poet whose words move me most. Carol Caffrey is Irish but has lived in Shropshire for years. The short selection of poems she reads includes a range from light-delightful, serious-thoughtful, hilarious. One remembers her sister, no longer alive, simple images, deeply personal yet they let us feel the experience as if it were ours. Afterwards I look for her to tell her. She was earlier an actress and now that her children are grown she has begun returning to it, acting in local professional theatre when opportunities arise; and on her own she does a short one-woman play by the Irish writer, Paula Meehan, which she launched at the Edinburgh Festival. So much talent and energy in this quiet place.

But it is not, in fact, quite the rural backwater it may seem to an outside visitor. Hardly 25 miles to the east is Wolverhampton and the other Black Country towns, and just beyond them Birmingham, places that were at the heart of Britain's rapid industrial growth in the 18th and 19th centuries. These towns, now grown into a megalopolis, were 100 years ago centres of coal mining and steel production. The name 'Black Country' is thought to come from the open cast mines, or the black soot deposited everywhere by the factories making locks, cars, motorcycles, bicycles. In the last half century these towns have suffered in successive recessions and they now show obvious signs of industrial decline. Outsiders may fail to see their appeal, but the area continues to generate strong local loyalties; it has universities and arts centres which run courses that several of those performing at this festival have been on.

The nearby industrial cities are vibrantly multi-cultural, multi-class, while the residents of Much Wenlock and surrounding small towns are the opposite. In the square in the centre of the village today almost the only black or Asian people I see are one of my friends, and two of the invited poets, Daljit Nagra and Lemn Sissay. Lemn in particular stands out, He is tall, gangly, very dark, with a mass of Afro hair, but it is his personality which claims attention wherever he goes. Watching him perform, the impact is almost unnerving. I marvel at the journey of the child who became this man. Born in Britain to an Ethiopian mother who returned to her country before he got to know her, he was moved between foster-carers with never a sense of being valued for himself. Words became his weapons in fighting back. He wrote on walls, poems to tell the world what it's like to be a child rejected, his troubled vision of what life could yet be. He almost overbalances his listeners with the torrent of words, lurching along an emotional tight-rope, exposing himself and us to danger, then pulling back just in time. As the power and chaos subsides I am left feeling deeply sad. No words will ever fill the gap of insecurity of an unloved childhood. Yet later as we sit talking in the town square and he is calm, I think of how much he has made of his life. And of one of his short poems, as quiet as last night's performance was dramatic:

How do you do it? said night
How do you wake and shine?
I keep it simple, said light
One day at a time.

~

This is the year, the month, the actual day of the 400th anniversary of Shakespeare's death, and the festival is staging an all-day reading of his sonnets. There are 154 sonnets, so this is some Big Read. I didn't get round to reading them until a couple of years ago, when I had a binge-read, stimulated indirectly by the actor Mark Rylance who had come up with the idea of the Sonnet Walks. You join a group on a short walk around parts of London that Shakespeare knew, ending up at the Globe Theatre, rebuilt on the place where it operated in Shakespeare's time, and every now and then along your route an actor pops up and recites a sonnet to you. Would I ever have gone looking for such a thing for myself? Who knows, but luckily my brother and his wife were going and suggested I join them. It was bizarre, entertaining, and wonderful. Having spent the best part of a Saturday doing that, it seemed a pity not to go the whole hog, so for some weeks afterwards I worked my way through all the sonnets. Some I wouldn't bother to revisit but there were so many tantalising lines that I went over them all again and pulled out the ones I thought I'd like to learn. When the total came to 50 I realised that perhaps life wasn't long enough, so I did another filter and got it down to an irreducible eight that I want to be able to carry in my mind as a resource. I typed them up, printed them out on separate sheets and for the next many weeks took one on my morning walk each day. As I walked along I recited to the surprised crows and morning dog-walkers. It was salutary discovering how long it took me to get even one sonnet word-perfect, leaving me with an even deeper respect for actors who regularly learn whole parts, or Muslim children who learn to recite the Quran in Arabic (often without understanding it, which is even more of a memory feat.)

When I learnt that Wenlock was staging a marathon Sonnet Read-in, I asked if I could read one. My wish was granted. I chose the one that begins

O never say that I was false of heart

which has lines that are quoted in *Uncertain Light,* because they so fitted the story:

As easy might I from myself depart
As from my soul which in thy breast doth lie ...

The readings take place in a church hall, a little away from the other venues. There are teams of readers, morning and afternoon. People drift in to listen for a while, then out again. It doesn't feel like a performance. It has more the quality of ritual, something you do because you know it has spiritual value aside from whether anyone else is listening. We're telling the poet, here we are 400 years on, and we still read your words. They still speak to us.

My own task is to introduce people to the Urdu and Persian poetry that sifts its way through *Uncertain Light*. I start by explaining Ghalib's chosen form, the ghazal. Once you know there's a whole poem-thought in each couplet you can dip into them randomly. Almost any Ghalib couplet will give an idea of the man's subtle mind. Some are obscure until you become familiar with the poetic imagery that Urdu speakers have grown up with, but there are enough to choose from that can be understood anywhere ... On what makes life worth living:

> Love furnishes the pride of those whose hearts are truly humble
> Makes every grain of sand a desert, every drop a sea

His experience of love as both joy and suffering:

> Love taught my nature what it is to know the zest of life
> I found a cure for sorrow in a sorrow without cure

His commitment:

> All that gives radiance to life comes from the love that ruins your
> home
> Only the lightning that destroys the crops lights up this gathering.

Something about his ability to weave complex thought into a few words connects in my mind with Shakespeare's sonnets. Good to have had them both here, at the same event.

~ 35 ~

A Magic Mirror

There are moments when something a reader says make me realise that what I've written is no longer just my book. It has taken on life of its own, means something to someone else that I will never experience in the same way. As if it holds up a magic mirror that reflects someone else's confusions or certainties.

It has happened a few times when I have been invited to talk to members of a book group who have been reading *Uncertain Light*. Groups that meet in people's homes are so personal that this feels a bit like being invited to join someone else's family for Christmas.

Some have been meeting since they all had small children and were baby-sitting for each other. They have seen each other through life crises. Over years of reading and discussing their reactions to the other-lives that books introduce them to, they have got to know each other at a level beyond what chatting in daily life provides. Of course, when I come into a group the very presence of an outsider makes it a different kind of session, so I never experience what it's like for the regular members, and I'm sure not all groups work in that way. Being unstructured, they're also vulnerable to becoming unbalanced, with one or two dominant personalities grating on the others. But the ones that last do seem to me a wonderful resource.

Library-based groups are more like adult education classes where you can if you choose remain slightly anonymous. They have the advantage of being open to anyone, including people who might never have the social confidence or the range of friends to be in a personally set-up group; and to some people, having the discussion led by a librarian feels more satisfying.

Today's group is unusual. It has a fluctuating membership, for it is open to any parents whose children go to an international school in London. As we go round the room and each person says where they were from we get to 15 countries, culturally far removed from each other — Japan, India, Iran, Eastern Europe, Australia. They are an appreciative group, and connect in interestingly different ways with the story.

As we are coming towards the end of the session an American woman suddenly starts saying what has clearly been bothering her. She is quite worked up about the central relationship portrayed in the story, about its morality. Perhaps she had been waiting to see if others would raise it, and as no one has, she has to get it out. Once I understand the question I turn it to the others. What do they think? Most of them can't see her problem, but she isn't going to be fobbed off. She comes back to me, needing to pin *me* down as to what *I* think. It was I, after all, who chose to put it in the book.

Afterwards we have a quiet word together. She needs to have it explained that I wasn't taking a moral stand about it, but portraying a personal situation that could happen, something I have seen happen to people, and not necessarily out of choice. The question then is how those concerned handle it.

She seems mollified, and thanks me for explaining that. She says she feels better about it now.

I am touched, but it doesn't feel as if it is something I have done. Unknowingly my story was channelling something that got under her skin.

People have used many different words to say what, for them, *Uncertain Light* is about. Love, but of many kinds. Grief, and the need to get beyond it. Courage. Compassion. Poetry, and the everyday-ness of life. Last week I had a letter from a friend who can look back over 80 years and more of life. He said that on reading it for the second time he realised 'that it is above all a book about complex families, about deep, deep friendships, about managing overwhelming love; about my life in other words.'

~ 36 ~

Unrecorded Lives

May 2016, Scotland

I'm in a train, heading for another unmarked border, this one into
Scotland. It's a personal journey as well as a book-related one, for
in the witches' brew of my genetic inheritance I'm more Scots than
anything. My grandfather grew up in Auchtermuchty. His father had
died before he was born, leaving his mother to raise six children on
almost no income. They all had to leave school aged ten to help earn,
the boys by working in the fields, the girls taking in weaving work
to do at home. As adults the sisters lived in adjacent cottages. I have
a postcard from 1904, the year my mother was born, and the old
lady who gave it to me assured me that the women standing outside
their front doors are my great aunts. It looks picturesque enough in

summer, but my mother was there in winter and remembered it as punishingly cold, with a family of eight living in two small rooms.

Her father defied the odds by emerging from that hard, manual-working childhood passionate about books. He educated himself at night school and got a job as a publisher's assistant. His abiding desire was to run a bookshop. He did, for a short while, but unsuccessfully.

My mother had no memory of her mother. She died of TB when the child had just turned three. Her father, afraid he would lose her too to the cold and damp, took her to the Cape. Somewhere warmer, he said.

There's Scots family too on my father's side, but much further back. A great-great-something grandfather was a son of a miller in a village in Aberdeenshire. His father, too, died young. He was educated by an uncle, and went to the Cape as a minister of the church.

They were all part of a trend. Already by the mid 1800s there were two emigration offices in Cupar alone. You only have to track town names in Canada, Australia, New Zealand, South Africa, to get a sense of it. Canada alone has over 200 towns named after the ones their Scots settlers came from. The reason for the emigration in the vast majority of cases was economic — sometimes real poverty, often just hoping for better opportunities in an era of repeated economic recessions. 'Economic migrants' is often a pejorative term when used about people from poorer countries looking for better opportunities in Europe or America. It's useful to remember that for centuries most economic migration went the other way.

All those stories, those fragments of unrecorded lives, swirl around me, part of me as I watch the shifting landscape through the windows of the train. I am moved by the thread that runs through them. Books, education, and the things that reading opens up to us. How lucky I am that I didn't have to struggle to get there as they did.

~

When we pass Gretna Green I know we are in Scotland. Two years ago this invisible border narrowly escaped becoming a definitive one, when a referendum was held on whether the Scots wanted to stay part of the United Kingdom. The issue evoked intense emotions on both sides of the border. As my train travels north to Glasgow, I still live in the country that Scotland is part of. But the times are volatile, and nothing is immutable.

Industrial growth made Glasgow one of the first cities in Europe to reach a population of a million. Shipbuilding on the River Clyde produced half the country's ships. Its manufacturing produced a quarter of all locomotives in the world. More than half the country's imported tobacco arrived through its port. Economic decline in the last century led to closure of much of its manufacturing and has left it with large areas of endemic poverty, alongside the wealth made during its boom period. But there's been a major renaissance, and Glasgow for many decades now has been home to a vigorous cultural life of all kinds. It also has an unusual resource — a Women's Library. And that's where I am headed.

There are only two Women's Libraries in the UK. This one is housed in a 19th century library building, sensitively converted. It has an extensive collection of books, by women, about women, and archives reflecting their roles in society, lives that would otherwise have been unrecorded surviving inside all those pages. The collection has been built up almost entirely out of donations and is constantly used by researchers. There's a programme of events to tempt readers to learn about women's history, and signs everywhere of the creativity that goes on here, much of it run by volunteers. Once a week they have a session called Story Café, where women come to chat over tea and cake, and Wendy Kirk, the young organiser, reads to them from something different each time. It's the Story Café readers that I will be talking to.

When I arrive there is a table with copies of *Uncertain Light* on display, and women are beginning to drift in, greeting, chatting, putting out cake and sandwiches on the table. The urn is on, the café part gets going. I talk to a few as they come in, catching a quick glimpse of what they get out of this group. It's been going for four years, and it's fuelled, Wendy says, by kindness, openness and the sharing of stories. Because it's a morning event, the majority are older women but there are younger ones too, unemployed, free-lance, young mums. Wendy herself has young children, works part time, and says it's a privilege to be doing this. 'Reading (and reading aloud) are beautifully creative endeavours but sometimes aren't thought of as being 'creative' in the same way as writing. But as we read our minds are constantly creating and imagining different worlds, and that's incredibly creative!' Looking for a wide range of things to share has challenged her own reading, and she now reads much more widely than she used to.

By the time we start there is, as Wendy says, 'a great wee turnout'. Delightfully, there are two women I know, colleagues from Save the Children days. They were working in Africa and we met only occasionally, but they are now back in Glasgow, and here they are, making the far-away-ness of *Uncertain Light* seem less exotic for the others here. It's about people like my friends here, I say, who happen to work for an international charity.

Wendy's warmth brings it back home. She says her mum had gone off reading for a while, and but this book has reawakened the joy of reading for her. 'She literally couldn't stop reading it, it was so compelling.'

The copies fly from the display table.

~

I'm staying in the home of Anne, another friend from Save the Children days. She has got her book group to read *Uncertain Light,* and I join them as they discuss it. Anne and her family moved to Glasgow a couple of years ago, and are a microcosm of internationalism. She is Irish. Her husband is Scots. He grew up here and speaks the Glaswegian of his childhood. (The accent is pretty distinctive. Ken Loach's award winning film, *My Name is Joe*, set on a Glasgow council housing estate, had to have subtitles when shown to US audiences.) They met working in East Africa and have adopted twin girls who are Chinese. As infants they had been in an orphanage, and at 17 months when she and her husband received them they were not even walking. They are now the brightest, most talented and secure young girls, growing up Scots, with cousins here and in Ireland, but also with a clear awareness of their Chinese heritage, which Anne has worked hard to give them. She is so modest about it all, but it's a huge achievement.

We talk about our times in Save the Children. No one is the model for the characters in *Uncertain Light* who work for international aid agencies, but I learnt from many people like her what the challenges of that work can be. When I hear people say they want to give money to a charity but they want their donation to go directly to support projects, not to 'administration', I think about what actually makes good things happen. 'Administration' means putting in place and running all the systems that enable the visible parts of projects. Raising the money. Recruiting suitable people to manage the process. Supporting those who work in extremely difficult situations. Without their skilled judgment, and capacity for making and carrying out difficult decisions, any money spent on the projects might as well have been thrown away.

~

Diane, one of the friends who came to my talk, takes me to a country park. Huge — 360 acres of open land, only a few miles south of the city centre, and in the middle is an extraordinary art collection that connects me back unexpectedly to Central Asia. William Burrell, a Glaswegian who made a fortune in shipping, spent much of it buying up art from all over the world, which he bequeathed to the city. A competition was run to find an architect to design a building appropriate to house the collection. You enter through a 16th century stone archway, and move through rooms of different periods that have been lifted from other buildings but put together here in a way that lets in light everywhere. The

eclectic collection ranges from stone carvings from the empire of
Ashurbanipal (7th century BC), through ancient Greece, Egypt,
China, Islamic art, medieval European stained glass windows, all
the way to French impressionist paintings. And suddenly we find
ourselves in a Central Asian room. Persian carpets, Tajik and Uzbek
embroidered cloths, pottery and wall hangings from Bukhara. In
imagination I see men and women of each of those cultures across
the world, across time, chipping stone, working glass, making
pots, weaving carpets. So much skill, so much artistry. So many
unrecorded, creative lives.

~ 37 ~

Summer Moments

Late May 2016, Cornwall

It's half term for the children and we are off, the whole family, for a holiday to the Scilly Isles. From Yorkshire, London, and Copenhagen, we all converge on Penzance. One night bed-and-breakfast, and in the morning we'll cross over to the islands, some by ferry, some by small plane. Either way, it's 30 miles across the sea and when you get there you feel you have entered another world. Three of our grandchildren have never been and the others are excited to share it with them. While our own children were young the islands provided a magic holiday retreat, idyllic, safe for children, removed from the pressures of our usual lives. On our last day we would fantasise about a storm blowing up that would make it impossible for us to return. The place worked away in my imagination. What would it be like to live there all the time? What would draw people from elsewhere to choose to do that? Gradually these imaginary lives began to inhabit my mind, and now the islands are part of my writing life too, through *Somewhere More Simple.*

It's too early for the Penzance Literature Festival, but the organisers I met a year ago have arranged a one-off event for me, so while the family have gone off to get fish and chips, I am back in the same venue. The man interviewing me is Tim Hannigan, whose chairing of another writer's session I admired last year. He has suggested that this time we focus on *Somewhere More Simple,* but refer also to *Uncertain Light.* He starts by getting me to talk about the differences between the two novels, one set in a small community on the islands, the other among people whose lives span continents. We are clearly on a similar wave length and I am totally relaxed. Then he moves on to saying something about the striking similarities of theme. I don't know what he means — there's almost no overlap.

He says, 'It's that they both deal with death.'

Am I surprised? I can't be. There's nothing in the stories that I didn't put there.

'Well, of course,' I say, 'death is part of life.' And I start talking about my other books. Now I come to think of it, there's a death in each one.

I realise I am shivering, violently, and uncontrollably. And icy cold.

The room is dark. As I try to control my shaking, I am thinking, I hope the audience can't see this. But Tim certainly can, he is sitting right next to me. Quietly he keeps me talking through it. I am trying to keep going and say something that will make sense, yet all the time still trying to understand what has happened to me. Why is my body doing this? There's nothing shocking in what he has just faced me with —

But it seems there is. In each book, whatever else the story is about, I have also been learning, without consciously choosing to do so, how to accept the death of someone close. In one book it's a father. In another an aunt. A lover. A close friend. A child. Even someone whose life just brushed past yet left an inexplicable hole. I can name the people in my own life through whom I have had to learn what loss means. The close friends whose children have died, some through suicide, leaving a lifelong pain I can only barely imagine. My brother, who died at too young an age. My father, who died when I had been away for too long, and hardly had any adult time with him. My mother, with whom I had 13 more years after Dad died, but separated by thousands of miles. We spent time together once a year, getting closer all the time, yet I was not able to be with her as she declined. Ralph, the only one of them all that I was near enough to care for in his last years. The exile, and the absences, and the impotence. The gap in the earth we tread on that will never be filled.

The session comes to an end, somehow. The lights go up. Tim is still there, quietly supportive. He holds out a hand to help me down the steps of the platform, and I need it, so unsteady am I. I move over to the book stall. Though the shivering is quieter it is still unstoppable, and my hands are so cold I am clumsy signing my name. All the time I am grateful for Tim's calm presence and acceptance. If *I* don't understand why I reacted so, how can he? But he saw it, and helps me normalise it.

People leave, we say goodbye. Someone, maybe Tim, says, 'Will you be OK getting back?'

'I'll be fine,' I say.

But I am still still shivering on that warm night as I walk in the dark back to the place we are staying. The others aren't back yet. I am glad. I get into bed and curl up under the duvet, tight. Gradually, very gradually, the shivering subsides.

When they get back Robert asks, 'How did it go? Was there an audience?'

'Yes, but something odd happened.'

How to describe it? Something Tim asked me touched a nerve, and I got the shivers. Which nerve? It doesn't have a name. Maybe the recognition of my own unknowingness.

~

I wake feeling normal. I am ready to forget about writing or the bits of me that go into it. Looking forward to just being with family, going somewhere we all love.

Star and her family are going by ferry, which is what we usually do, but this time Robert and I are treating ourselves to going by plane, and May's family have opted to do that too. We arrive at the airport at Lands End, surely the smallest in the country. It's a foggy morning and the flights are delayed. Nothing unusual in that, but the fog doesn't clear. Flight after flight gets cancelled, and the airport lounge fills up. It has one small café, but clearly a point will come where they're not going to cope. Stressed parents, bored children, each in their own small family cluster. May is trying to break the invisible barriers, to draw her children into chatting to others they don't know. She admires the soft toys they're holding on to, and the blow-up boats they're waiting to use when they get there. Suddenly I see she is standing up and announcing, with a clarion voice that reaches to the far corner of the small airport lounge, that there are children's games being organised outside the building.

There aren't yet, but she's about to. Everyone is dazed at this un-British lack of inhibition. (Not her family, we are used to it.) Shyly, children nudge their parents. Parents cautiously go with them, to find out whether this is for real. May, who in her day job runs an outdoor school, within minutes has them all sitting in a circle on a bare stretch of concrete while she explains the first game. Now they are pairing up and running around, discarding all shyness, while their parents stand at the edge, bemused, admiring. Any of them could have done it, but only May did.

I get talking to the young woman next to me, one of mums. We exchange names. She says, watching May, 'She's amazing.' I agree.

About an hour later the airport officials announce that there will be no flights today. The games instantly cease as parents summon their children and scramble into emergency action. We will now all have to find somewhere to spend the night, and an alternative way to get to the islands. A throng forms around the officials, asking for information. Tomorrow's flights, if they happen, are already fully booked. It's a Saturday, the ferry has already left, and there isn't one on Sundays. Insurance refunds will be no compensation for missing the children's long-planned holiday.

Taxis are summoned, buses arrive to take us back to Penzance. Eventually we get a message: a special ferry has been laid on for tomorrow morning.

Sunday morning. We get there early, join the queue that already stretches half a mile back from the pier. We're all elated, relieved. We'll get there after all! The children are recognising others in the queue that they were playing games with yesterday. The young woman I chatted to is there. She tells me she went on the internet last night to check out my name, and see if I was the person she thought I was …

Almost 20 years ago, when she was working as a volunteer in Mozambique, she and her friends were reading my first novel, *A Shield of Coolest Air*. 'We were passing it around between us,' she says. 'It was my favourite novel.'

Mozambique in the 1990s. How did a copy even get there?

Life is full of coincidences, but if I had put that in a novel, people would say, 'Too far-fetched.'

~

St Mary's, Isles of Scilly
We arrive, settle in to our tent-homes, take the children exploring — are caught anew, as we are each time, by the shapes and colours of sea, sky, rock formations, headlands. The rest of the world falls away.

~ 38 ~

Who Is 'We'?

June 2016

Yesterday was Referendum day in the UK. While people queued outside polling stations to vote, our home was a campaign hub for Remain, those who want Britain to stay part of the European Union. From early morning volunteers were arriving at our door to collect stickers and leaflets. I greeted the first ones in my dressing gown. By the time we'd had breakfast we just left the door open. Through the day they kept on coming. They came to refuel, to take the weight off their feet for a short while, then out again. I found my vocation as a tea/coffee lady, and I loved the vibe, all of us energised by the set of shared values that grows out of the kind of society we were voting to keep, broad-minded, outward-looking, tolerant, interested in others, confident in our shared humanity. By the time polls closed there had been over 50 people in and out, of all ages, backgrounds, political affiliations.

I listened to the stories they brought back. A couple of young women had been accosted by heavies as 'traitors'.

To value being part of a wider community means you're a traitor?

'We want our country back,' the Leave slogan said.

Who exactly is 'we'?

This morning, walking on Wandsworth Common in early morning light, in this place I love and that for 40 years has been my home, I am facing up to the fact that just over half those who voted are celebrating the result. They're not the half I know or whose judgement I can trust the future to, and that says something about how divided we are.

It's depressingly obvious that the leaders of the Leave campaign lied consistently, deliberately misled the voters, and had no idea what would happen if they won. A million words have documented this. Now while they squabble about who is going to take the flak for the mess we are in, the immediate outcome is a sudden rise in openly expressed hostility to anyone seen as 'other'. It's a no-brainer what the connection is. 'Leave' to their supporters meant that immigrants should leave. School children taunt a Polish child. Hate messages are scrawled on doors. Teenagers tell a black man on the metro to go back to Africa.

'Immigrant' means anyone who is different. The 'not us'. London, wonderful multi-cultural London with its 120 mother tongues, is foreign territory. The mayor, Sadiq Khan, is the son of an immigrant bus driver. He became a lawyer, an MP, and is now mayor of one of the world's biggest cities. He posts on social media a photo of sharing his meal at the end of a day of Ramadan fast with a crowd of every religion and ethnic group, including the Archbishop of Canterbury and London's chief Rabbi. Our 'we' embraces anyone who lives in the UK, but it goes way beyond that. We remain, whether officially or not, part of Europe, and in today's globally connected world, we use things made by our fellows in countries we've never even visited. Having a multiple identity is normal, one reason why the 'traitor' label is so slippery. Each of us is defined by layers of belonging which may or may not overlap. Family, friendship group, workplace, town, language, economic class, ethnicity, religion. History.

Once we have classified people as 'not us', we block off empathy, accepting as inevitable that they are enduring levels of suffering that would be intolerable if they happened to those we think of as our own. A recent foreign minister of Pakistan (the first woman and youngest person to hold the post) said that Pakistan's children have been taught for 60 years that 'national identity is to hate someone.' The same is true now of children who have been fed the Hindu chauvinist view of history in India, which fuels them to regard Muslims as intrinsically anti-national. Hate is poisonous, the ultimate form of rejecting another's humanity. Hate leads to killing. Terrorists of all ideologies only kill people they have defined as 'not us.'

I too am an immigrant. Given what's happening now, it's important for anyone who has moved countries to make that statement. I am the child of a long line of immigrants from Europe to the southern tip of Africa, some of whom have then emigrated back. Between them, the different strands of my family exemplify all the possible reasons people might have for moving to a new country. My father's ancestors fled religious persecution in France, and wars in Germany. They found passage on ships across a dangerous ocean to an unknown, far-away land. It doesn't take much for me to imagine what it's like doing this from Syria or Afghanistan or Libya. One of my distant ancestors was a freed slave, originally from Indonesia, her own mother taken by force across the sea into who knows what situation. The genealogical records gave her no name.

The privations of war were responsible for the early death of my father's father. That was the Boer War. The British military burnt farms to starve the Boers into submission, and herded women and children into concentration camps. My grandmother and her sisters got access to those camps, trying to keep women and children alive. I think of them all when I see photos of the devastation of wars today, and vast camps of refugees.

All the time I have been travelling with my book, my small portable inner life, hundreds of thousands of people have been making a traumatic journey, getting into small boats to cross dangerous seas, desperate to reach somewhere safe. The UN's High Commissioner for Refugees estimates that last year 3,550 lives were lost during the crossing. The depth of individual trauma behind each of those stories got through to people in a new way when a photo went viral on social media, the body of a three year old Syrian child washed up on a beach in Turkey. What had it taken for those parents to risk their lives and their children's in this way? The father's story came out. They had fled the bombing, arrived in a vast refugee camp. Turkey already had two million in camps. With little hope for the future there, he had applied for visas to Canada where he had an aunt who was willing to sponsor him and his family. The application was turned down. He had twice paid smugglers to get his family on boats to Greece, hoping to apply for asylum there. Nothing came of it. So he and others got hold of a boat themselves. It was unseaworthy. Too many desperate people packed into it. When it started to take in water they panicked and stood up, destabilising it. The boat capsized, at night, and most couldn't swim. The life-jackets they had been sold didn't work.

In the depression caused by so much horrific news, I take courage from examples that have come my way of people who think of themselves as 'ordinary' but do extraordinary things. While Hungary puts up a militarised fence to keep refugees out, tens of thousands of people in cities across Europe demonstrate to urge their governments to support refugees. People arrive at railway stations to provide food and blankets for those in transit. For them to take that step, to set aside the demands of their own daily lives and respond to the exceptional needs of people they don't know, the first essential is that they feel their common humanity — are able to imagine what it feels like to be in that situation. Only then does the truth shine that we belong to each other, as people in a small boat out at sea belong. Whatever mess the world is in, we're in it together. The wider we can stretch our definition of our own identity, the safer we will all be.

If there is one thing that links everything I have ever written, this is it. Each time I find someone willing to travel those roads with the people in my stories I feel elated, because in their identification with someone different from themselves, the total store of empathy in the world has been increased.

~ 39 ~

Border Crossings

Up on my Facebook screen pops a photo of a friend cooking in a makeshift shelter. Liza Lort-Phillips, I discover, is in Lesbos. She has taken four weeks out of her life to go and help receive refugees arriving in boats on the island.

I don't know Liza well — we were once briefly colleagues — but well enough to be interested in what she's up to, and bowled over by what she is now doing. She has worked for international development agencies and doesn't have a simplistic idea that individual efforts alone can change the world, but there are moments when the immediate pressure of someone else's need pushes other considerations aside, and you just do what's in front of you to do.

For the next four weeks I follow her at an admiring distance. Up to 6,000 people are arriving each day. Liza and hundreds like her are providing them with food and warm clothing, and then taking them on to reception camps. Without these volunteers, many would not survive.

And here's another story. In a London theatre Benedict Cumberbatch is playing Hamlet. He has celebrity status for his TV roles, and performances have sold out many months ahead. Young people who have never been to a Shakespeare play compete for tickets. After the show he comes out in front of the curtain and tells the audience that the cast will be collecting money for Save the Children to use in supporting Syrian refugee children. He quotes these lines:

> No one leaves home unless home is the mouth of a shark
> No one puts their children in a boat unless the water is safer than
>   the land.

Few people in that highly literate audience have ever heard of the poet, a young British-Somali woman, Warsan Shire. She was a child of two when her family arrived in Britain, fleeing civil war. Too young to remember it, but close enough to feel an empathy for refugees anywhere.

There are stories like that everywhere, stories about people doing the small thing they are able to do, but which collectively add up to something big. Here's one from 77 years ago that is still having an impact, right here where I live.

In December 1938 a 29 year old in London, Nicholas (Nicky) Winton, was about to join a friend in taking a group of schoolboys on a skiing holiday in Switzerland. A telegram arrived cancelling the trip – the friend was in Prague and said, 'Come and see what I'm up to.' He had joined a group of British volunteers helping those who had fled the Sudetenland after Hitler had taken over.

So instead of skiing Nicky spent his holiday helping in their make-shift office and visiting the temporary camps crowded with refugees. With Hitler poised to invade the whole country, desperate Jewish parents asked if he couldn't do something to at least get their children to safety. He talked to the organisers, and offered that on his return to London he would contact the Home Office, would communicate the urgency of the situation, and hope to get official agreement to allow the children in. The agreement was given, with conditions: refugee children under 17 could be admitted provided they had a place to stay and £50 was deposited for each. A young British teacher whom Nicky had met in Prague gave up his job to organise things from the Prague end. Nicky's mother in London set up another impromptu organisation from her home to raise money and find homes for children with families or in hostels. Volunteers accompanied the children, who were put on trains by parents who knew they would almost certainly never see them again, to travel across Europe to an unknown future. It would become known as the Kindertransport. The last train left in September 1939, just before war was declared. Another was ready, but was not allowed to leave.

Winton went back to ordinary life. 50 years later a notebook came to light with the names of the children, their parents, and families in Britain that were willing to take them. His efforts and those of the other volunteers had saved the lives of 669 Czech children. The television programme 'That's Life' tracked as many of those now-grown-children as they could, and brought them together to meet him. Winton, now an 80 year old, said he didn't feel he deserved special recognition. He had done what anyone might have done. He had not been in personal danger, because he had left before the Nazi troops arrived. Other volunteers had kept going to and fro to accompany the children, at considerable personal risk.

One of those children on the Kindertransport trains was a six year old called Alfred, child of a Jewish father and a non-Jewish mother. His father had left Prague the day after the Nazis arrived, and got to the UK. Alfred's mother put him on the first Kindertransport train, giving him a food pack which he did not touch for the two days of that train journey. He was luckier than most, for he had a father there to meet him. His mother was at first refused an exit visa, but eventually was able to join them; his father died soon after. She was now alone with the child in a strange country, but safe.

Almost all the Jews they had known who had stayed in Prague were murdered in the concentration camps. You can meditate on the unspeakable enormity of it in the small synagogue in the old part of Prague, surrounded by the names of those lost lives, every one of them written on the walls, floor to ceiling, room after room.

That child, Alf Dubs, later became the Member of Parliament for Battersea, the part of London I live in. Until that television programme he had had no idea to whom he owed the fact that his life had been saved. Now they got to know each other. Alf described Nicholas Winton as 'a phenomenal individual, one of the really great human beings.'

For me Alf himself is one of the people whose existence makes me rejoice. He was a model of a hardworking constituency MP. He said that he went into politics because he realised that if it could be a force for evil it could also be a force for good. Later he was director of the UK's Refugee Council. For years now he has been back in Parliament, in the House of Lords, and is a leading campaigner for Britain to accept child refugees. For that campaign to succeed, public opinion needs to move, as it started to do with a jolt after people saw the shocking photo of the Syrian child.

Public opinion is us. My friend Liza and all those like her who have given up their leave to volunteer at refugee reception centres in Greece. Cumberbatch, those who hold the collecting tins, and all those who put money in them. The journalists, activists, novelists, poets and playwrights who write to share the refugee experience. People who write to their elected politicians to urge them not to build walls against refugees. People who are upset at what they see and hear and talk to others about it. You and me.

TRANSITIONS

~ 40 ~

Interlude

Late July 2016
It's the middle of the night, the ward is quiet. There's a dim light from the corridor, which casts strange shadows when the nurse on duty walks past.

I'm in a hospital bed, shifting gingerly so as not to disturb the new hip that I've been fitted with. I'm tanked up on something which is keeping pain at bay.

early August
Learning to walk again. A different kind of journey — the unavoidable demands of the slowly healing body, the necessary

quietening of the spirit in response. Stretches in a tunnel, then emerging to greet the early morning sun once again. It casts long shadows of my still-stumbling legs and crutches on the dew-covered grass of the common. I am aware in a new way of how fortunate I am to be able to walk at all.

Being reminded in this small way that health and mobility do not last forever. Our days are not infinite. Use the time while we have it.

~ 41 ~

It's My Job

I'm sitting on the stage of the Queen Elizabeth Hall, part of London's South Bank Centre, watching the profile of the man next to me. I feel sure I have seen him somewhere.

We are rehearsing for an event to pay tribute to Nelson Mandela, while 6,000 miles away the man himself is so frail that it will not be long till he is gone —

Which tells you that this isn't now.

I look around the other participants. We're in a semi-circle, 23 of us altogether, writers and performers. We each have three minutes to read, recite, sing, anything of our choice. I wonder about the journeys that have brought each of us here. Our origins, or those of our parents, are in South Africa and Jamaica, Nigeria and Guyana, Zimbabwe and St Lucia, Ethiopia, Eritrea, Malawi. A microcosm of those who have lived with the experience of racism and challenged it, and for whom the world is different because of how Mandela lived his life. Choosing, at every point, and never the easy choices.

Framing our personal tributes, two British actors take it in turns to read extracts from Mandela's autobiography; both black. One in his mid 20s, the one sitting next to me perhaps 50. We have never met but I am certain I know his face. Where have I seen it? His is no easy task, for Mandela's prose, like his spoken delivery, is pedestrian. It was always striking when he spoke in public that for a man of such magnetic qualities his voice had a flat intonation that in anyone else would have been boring. He held his audiences entirely by the moral authority of what he said. How can anyone else convey through those plain words the spirit that inspired millions? Yet this man next to me does it, quietly, and with no superimposed drama. It's all in the timing, I think. He has found the significant word in each phrase, to drop into a waiting space.

Suddenly memory breaks through. In a rehearsal pause I turn to him and say, 'Are you Brutus?' Yes, he is! A year ago I had watched him in a Royal Shakespeare Company production of *Julius Caesar*, set in Africa, with an all black cast. I had not focused until then on the fact that it is above all Brutus's play, and it's this man who brought it home to me. He *was* Brutus — his intensity, his inner vacillation, the compulsion of emotion that drove him. Now that skill, that human understanding, will bring Mandela's voice to an audience of 900.

His name is Paterson Joseph. Anyone in the UK who watches TV more than I do would have had no difficulty recognising him. Even I should have known, for I have seen him in other stunning lead roles in theatre. He was Atahualpa, Inca king-god in Peter Shaffer's *The Royal Hunt of the Sun*, and in Eugene O'Neill's *Emperor Jones*, he was the escaped prisoner who set himself up as dictator of a small Caribbean island. Paterson is one of Britain's outstandingly talented actors, an achievement even more remarkable given his background, a child of working class Caribbean immigrants.

When I tell him I was touched by his reading he says, with a slight shrug, 'It's my job.'

It's the perfect answer. No false modesty. He knows he's good, why wouldn't he? But it speaks also of what goes into producing such unobtrusive skill. It's his job. It's what he has chosen to do with his life, and he makes sure he does it well.

After the rehearsal we all gather for a group photo under the huge bust of Mandela just outside the Royal Festival Hall. The photo is a collection of people celebrating. Each of us delighted to be there, held in the brief companionship of strangers, lit by the privilege of being part of this.

Perhaps some of us are feeling we haven't really earned our place here. It's easy to be intimidated by the stature of those who have emerged as real leaders, who have shown the kind of courage we know we could never rise to. But in the quietest life there are issues to be faced, campaigns to be waged, practical tasks to be done. There are values that we share by living them, that we pass on to our children, who may in their turn make things around them a little better.

We each do different things.

What a great actor like Paterson does, is to allow us to feel inside the people whose life he inhabits. That's his job; and through it, like any great artist, he helps us grow, become more human.

What do I do? Some days it feels, not much.

I used to say, 'I work for Save the Children.' And before that, 'I work in adult education.' I've been a teacher. I'm a mother, a grandmother, and when this hip works properly and I can get down on the floor again I'll get back to being an active one. They're all valuable things, but like everything, it's how you do them that matters.

Funny, I've been writing for 40 years but it's only since I stopped earning an income at something else that I've felt able to say, 'I'm a writer'. But this journey has helped me become clearer that it matters. I have discovered that I can tell stories in a way that helps those who read them empathise with situations other than their own.

So that's what I do; that's my job.

~ 42 ~

A Better Place?

September 2016

Emerging from retreat, I am alarmed to be reminded by my diary of what lies ahead. I am to be a keynote speaker at a conference in a month's time. Then there's a London launch of Ralph's book, and because the publisher is in India I'm doing most of the arrangements. Straight after that a literature festival, and in between a couple of book groups. And this was the time I was going to do less running around so I could get back some consistent time for writing. Something went wrong with my planning.

The most alarming bit is the conference. The organisation is called National Women's Register. This is a regional conference in Salisbury. They are expecting 200 women. It's the theme that's the problem — 'Making the World a Better Place.'

My first reaction was, 'You're asking *me?*'

That we urgently need to find ways to make the world a better place is obvious. It feels at times that we are living in a dark age. But what can I possibly say to 200 well-read women about how to do it?

I suggested two other women who would be a better choice. The organisers were politely grateful, but said they would like me. One of them, Caroline Worsley, heard me talk at the Mere Literature Festival last year. Since then she has read all my books. She was sure I'd have something useful to say.

That conversation was months ago, before my hip put me out of action. It's only now that it's almost upon me that I am giving it proper thought.

The National Women's Register is a nationwide network of local discussion groups. It started 60 years ago after an article in the Women's Page of The Guardian, about intelligent housewives stuck at home. It was followed by a letter from a young woman suggesting that a national register could be set up for women who wanted to meet others to discuss things beyond domestic and family. The response was overwhelming, and soon groups were meeting all over the country. Today they have upwards of 6,000 members. Their website describes their purpose as 'Connecting women who are interested in everything, and talk about anything.' For many of the women, the NWR group has been part of their lives for decades. They joined when they were young, have moved many times and each time found new friends quickly through the local group. Today there are different pressures on young women who juggle work and family. The 'housebound' bit doesn't apply, but doubly-stressed, it's just as hard for them to take an evening off just for themselves.

I am getting nowhere in thinking about what I can say. This is not like preparing for a talk about my books. What *is* it that I have to offer?

I am not by nature an activist. I have had to learn, slowly, how to react to things that I see going on that I know are wrong ... I'm remembering an incident from early on in my time in Britain. I was on my way to a meeting when I saw racist graffiti scrawled on a street sign. Several of my Indian friends lived in that street. I thought of them having to walk past those signs of hate every day, and I knew I'd feel pathetic if I didn't make some kind of protest about it. Before I had time to think about what would be a sensible action I had turned around, abandoning the idea of getting to my meeting on time. I went back to the High Street to look for a DIY shop, bought a small pot of paint and a brush, and forced myself to say to the shopkeeper, 'I'm going to paint out some racist graffiti.' I was trembling, expecting — what? Everyone in the shop to attack me? They just looked at me as if I were slightly mad. I went back to the graffiti and painted it out.

That was all. Such a small act of defiance, yet my heart was thumping as I did it, as if I were a criminal who might be caught in the act, just for stepping that tiny pace beyond convention. And what did I achieve? Nothing. I doubt if anyone living on that street even noticed.

But then something else happened. Now that it was over, I talked about it in the adult education centre where I worked, laughing at my own nervousness. One of my colleagues, someone a lot more practical than me and untroubled by what anyone else would think, decided this needed doing properly. She started harrying the local authority to get them to systematically remove all the racist graffiti in our part of town. And they did it.

That incident crept into the stories that became *A Language in Common*. I guess the point of it was that even though my small action was pathetic, it gave someone else the idea.

~ 43 ~

Ruth Warren's Notebook

I owed my job to an extraordinary elderly American woman, Ruth Warren. She walked with a stick, lopsided, but determinedly getting about. She had spent most of her adult life as a missionary in India, married an English missionary, retired with him to Croydon, and was now a widow. If you happened to have preconceptions about missionaries, she quietly undermined them. She spoke Hindi, Punjabi, Gujarati and Urdu, and when she met women in saris or shalwar and kameez waiting at bus stops she stopped to talk to them. They were delighted to be able to talk in their own language to this friendly old lady. They invited her home, plied her with spiced tea and pakora, and told her that their children learned English at school and their husbands at work, but they were stuck at home, not even able to to talk to their neighbours. Couldn't she find some English women to help them learn?

Ruth got herself a small notebook for names and addresses, went around talking to church groups, called in her friends. Their names and addresses too went into the notebook, potential learners from the front, potential tutors from the back. She paired them off, and when she had made a good match, committed the surprised tutors to visiting every week. She knew about loving her neighbour and was not afraid to tell other people how to do it.

Then she started knocking on official doors. The Community Relations Council. The Adult Education Department. I can picture it, busy men confronted by this bent-over woman, gently spoken but unshakeably persistent as she explained to them what they ought to be doing... Until it became easier to do something than to keep turning her away. The Education Department put up a salary for an adult education organiser —

I am given a small office, an empty filing cabinet, no budget, and the promise of a half-time assistant. The Director of Adult Education briefs me on my role. It is unilluminating. He really hasn't an idea. You'll need to find out from Mrs Warren, he says.

I visit her. She receives me in a small front room of a semi-detached house with lace curtains that doesn't in any way fit with her. I'm sure she was more at home in the dust of the Punjab, dressed like the women around her. This is the house of her step granddaughter, who joins us with a tea tray. Ruth is retiring to California, she says. She's just here until she goes.

She has the notebook on the coffee table between us. We go through it together, and she tells me something about each of the people in it. My head is buzzing with detail but it doesn't seem the right moment to be taking notes. I'll get the general idea and learn more from them each when I meet them. Most of the volunteers have come from her talks to church groups, of many different denominations. I ask, in passing, which is hers. She says vaguely that she doesn't have one any more, by which I understand that the business of doctrines and ritual and membership has become irrelevant.

'When do you leave?' I ask, hoping it is not soon.

'As soon as I've had my hip replaced,' she says. Then, with a smile as if to excuse herself, 'I've been needing to go for a good while, my dear.'

'Tell her,' the step granddaughter prompts; and then she does it for her. 'She's been on the waiting list for a year, and every time they say she can have it, she says she's not ready. She has been waiting to hand over to you.'

'And you took your time coming,' Ruth says drily. '

It seems this was the second time they had advertised. There were people in the first round that the Director of Adult Education thought could have done it, but Ruth wouldn't have any of them. 'They were all too professional,' she says, 'I couldn't see any of them visiting the women in their homes.'

So I got the job not *because* I was professionally qualified, but despite it. It is the greatest compliment.

She hands me the notebook.

~

I felt her mantle on my shoulders many times in the years that followed ... As I visited Asian women in their homes and got drawn in to their lives. As I briefed each new volunteer. As I cycled around town, getting to know each area, thinking of Ruth moving from one region of India and Pakistan to another, long enough in each to become fluent in four languages, then starting again somewhere else. And through it all, losing the sense that it mattered which church she was nominally connected to.

There were moments when unexpected challenges arrived, when I thought, 'I wonder what Ruth would have done?' —

A middle-aged man arrived at one of the English class centres.

With him was his young sister, Rashida Abedi, who had recently come from Pakistan. He explained that she had had meningitis and become profoundly deaf. He was long settled in Britain, and had brought her here in the hope that doctors could reverse the damage to her hearing, but nothing could be done. Now, he had applied for permission for her to stay; and she needed to learn to speak English.

How would that be possible? She had almost never heard it spoken. But one of our teachers, Mary Simpson, made it possible, skilfully adjusting her teaching style while an Urdu-speaking volunteer sat next to Rashida, transcribing in Urdu script the English words being taught so that Rashida could attempt to pronounce them. She made extraordinary progress. Soon she went on to take a range of other practical courses, and inspired us all with what is possible.

Then the Immigration Department refused her permission to stay in the UK. Her brother was a British citizen, devoted to Rashida, and desperately wanted to keep her here and support her. If she were sent back to Pakistan, she would have none of the opportunities she had here. He sought legal advice. If she had been his wife, he would have had the right to keep her with him. He told them he had no intention of marrying. Could he not keep her here instead? But as his sister she had no right to stay. The legal adviser said the only thing that might help would be to ask for a concession on compassionate grounds, and that would only have a chance if he could get a lot of people to press for it. So he came to see me. Could I organise a campaign?

It was one of those moments when life throws at you a challenge you *really* don't want to have to think about. With a full-time job and young children I had enough to do just keeping the family-work-life show on the road. I was also nervous. My own family's immigration status was not yet sorted, and I didn't want to draw the officials' attention to myself. But how to say no? Rashida was an example to all of us, in determination, in making the best of what life had handed her. How could we do nothing?

So we decided we would try. At first 'we' was me, Mary, her teachers and friends, but gradually it extended to a whole lot of other people who heard her story. We made leaflets, with 'Let Rashida Stay' as the strap-line. We started a petition, and people took it to adult education classes, churches, work places, wherever they could talk to people and get signatures. I contacted the Royal Association for Deaf People and they circulated the story to their members, country wide. The numbers signing the petition grew, and went on growing. We organised a public meeting which Rashida herself addressed in English, choking us all up. She had almost never heard the language spoken and here, a year and a half after joining our classes, she was talking to an audience of 150 people. I remember still how she began, asking our patience that her way of speaking might sound strange to us, because 'deaf people cannot hear their own voice'. Our local MP, Bernard Weatherill, was there. He was Speaker of the House of Commons and his position meant he couldn't take up the case in Parliament but he got a fellow MP to do it. A group of us went to listen on the night it was being discussed, and heard the answer. No exception could be made.

Through all those months we swung wildly and repeatedly from hope to despondency. Then just when we thought it was all hopeless, the Immigration Department gave her permission to stay.

After the campaign was over, we suggested to Rashida that she write her own story. She didn't say, 'But how can I do that in English?', just as she had not said, 'How can I address a meeting in English?' She just did it, learning what she needed to in the process. Mary edited it and we published it in English and in Urdu. It was called *From Sound to Silence*. Mary organised opportunities for Rashida to talk about it, and made journeys with her to English classes elsewhere, where she and her story inspired people with how she had overcome obstacles we could hardly imagine having to deal with.

What did I learn through all that? First, that taking action on her behalf was painless. I had come from a country where people who demonstrated often ended up in prison, and in much of the world doing the simple things we had done would have required great courage. But we were lucky to be in a situation where dissent is possible without, in most cases, having to confront police violence. Primarily what had been required of us was time, collective effort, working out who might be on our side, and asking them for their support. Easy things to give, once you've taken that first step.

We learnt also something else — that winning is occasionally possible. We never knew what the final push was that got them to agree. Had someone senior in the Home Office been touched by her case? Or had we just got to be a nuisance, and it was easier to say 'Yes' than to keep having to say 'No.'

Like Ruth, knocking on official doors eight years earlier?

You can't be sure that your own small actions will make any difference; but if you do nothing, worse might happen, and if you do something, other people might too, and there's just a chance it might have an effect.

~ 44 ~

My Turn to Speak

October 2016, Salisbury

A secondary school building has been taken over for this Saturday, and 200 women are arriving, some after journeys from miles away. The organisers have done this with flair. The place is festooned with decorations in suffragette colours. The air buzzes with stimulus and conversation. Most of the members of groups are late middle-aged or older, and the organisers want to make sure they get the perspective also of younger women, so they have invited a group of A-level students from a local school to attend. They will report back at the end of the day on what they think about the discussions.

The auditorium is packed. There are two other speakers. The first has a senior policy role in an international development agency and is talking about the UN's new Sustainable Development Goals. She is strong on topic. The Goals are an attempt to get governments to agree on actions that could redress things going wrong in the world. It's the kind of framework I used to work with daily, but sitting in this audience of women for whom the technical vocabulary is new, the challenge of communicating what the goals all add up to seems vast. I'm looking around at faces with a glazed-over look. They're trying to connect, but it's difficult. After months of negotiation, those co-ordinating this process across multiple UN agencies finally agreed on 17 goals and 169 targets, so it's hard even for people who work professionally on these issues to keep them all in their heads.

Then comes the high-profile speaker, A C Grayling, author of about 30 books on philosophy, biography, history of ideas, human rights, ethics; founder of New College of Humanities, presenter on the BBC World Service on science and society. He is an engaging speaker. He talks about the life of a 17th century woman intellectual, part of the Enlightenment movement of ideas which is the subject of his latest book. It doesn't seem particularly relevant to the conference theme, other than that Grayling feels that the thinkers of the Enlightenment contributed to making the world a better place. Perhaps it was a talk he had prepared for some other audience and has adapted for this occasion. But the women in the audience are indeed interested in everything, and his talk is well received.

My turn. When we planned this we agreed that rather than my giving a talk one of them should interview me, with lots of time for questions from the audience. Caroline Worsely is doing it. She starts asking about my own history. How did I first get involved in the issues that thread through my books? It all feels so long ago; well, it *was*. When I first became aware of grossly unequal life chances, I was a young child. When I started teaching in night-school for adults who had never had the chance of schooling, and going on anti-apartheid demonstrations in Cape Town, I was a student of 19. When we got caught up in a political crisis in Zambia I was 32. It was 30 years ago that I started working with refugees.

I think back to that young woman I was then, and in the other phases of life since, and it's as if I'm looking at someone outside myself. I have been formed by everything that has happened since. The issues are so different now, and my own consciousness so different. Do I learn anything useful by thinking about those earlier people I have been? And do the women in the audience, listening? It is all so far away from the lives they are dealing with. Perhaps it sounds as if my decisions were more highly-principled than ones they have had to make? But for each of us it's a matter of responding to what life thrusts at you, within the understanding we have at the time.

Caroline moves on to asking about my Save the Children years, the background to *Uncertain Light*. That is easier. First because I'm more used to doing it, but mainly because it's not just me, it's a cause that people can easily identify with. The difficulty is giving a sense of the actual nature of the work, how frustrating it can be working in any large organisation, and how difficult it is to feel that you personally are contributing to the fundamental aim. But I am given a lead by a young woman in the audience who has herself worked in Save the Children's head office, so she understands that. She asks me, 'When you look back on your time there, what do you feel is the most important thing you achieved?'

I have never asked myself the question, and at first I can't think of anything. It was all such a collective endeavour. Then I remember a long, tedious process that I led through layer after layer of the organisation's decision-making structures, which ultimately resulted in a change of policy. Save the Children has always been an emergency response organisation, going in speedily to crises — earthquakes, wars, tsunamis; and in the years I worked there it was gradually building up a strong profile of work in education. But in my early years the emergency responses never included education work. Those who worked on emergencies were doing things that saved lives, food, water, shelter, emergency health provision. They saw education as a longer term process, that would have to wait till the crisis was over. People working close to the problems, those in the countries where it was all happening, saw it differently. They saw that children who miss out on schooling for the years lost to the crisis seldom get back in. They saw that children suffer horrendous long-term damage from having to flee, witnessing violence, losing close family, losing your home to an earthquake — and that the adults around them are so busy trying to survive that they can hardly give them the kind of support that would help them deal with all that. They saw that just as children in refugee camps need food and shelter, they also need safe spaces to play, and adults to give them time, and schools, even if makeshift ones, where they can continue to feel that life has some structure and purpose.

Eventually the argument was won. Now, if you see an appeal from Save the Children in any of these crises, it's likely to talk about safe play spaces, keeping schools going, psychological support for children, as well as the vital food, water and health issues.

~

Time is up. Everyone streams out into the foyers, and heads for the lunch queue. The conference bookstall has 50 copies of *Uncertain Light,* and a chair for me to sit at through the lunch break, signing copies and being there for the women who are buying them to talk to. Each of them has something to say, about their own lives, and the connecting points with what I've been talking about. I wish there were longer for these conversations. This is the heart of it. The bookstall sells out, and there is still a long queue, so we go on talking.

The A-level students have already read the book before the conference, and they invite me to come and talk to their school. So perhaps something worked. Not sure that I know what. Not sure I could do it again.

~ 45 ~

Leaving It in My Hands

A quick gear change, to London for the UK launch of Ralph's book on Ghalib. It's a relief to have the focus turned off me, to be thinking about him and his unique contribution to so many others. It's just over eight years since he died. I have a photo taken almost exactly two years before that. He's sitting in a garden in Sussex where a group of us are spending a September weekend, walking and relaxing. Book in hand, of course, an 88 year old who still walks everywhere, whose mind is as it ever was, who has friends of all ages and is constantly delighted to make new ones. He looks up when I tell him I'm about to take a photo. He can't imagine why anyone needs one, but he obliges.

While I'm preparing what I will say at the launch I feel his presence, happy that I'm continuing his work. I knew you would, he says, and goes back to reading. Leaving it in my hands.

We have an appropriate venue for the launch. The Royal Asiatic Society describes itself as 'a forum for those who are interested in the languages, cultures and history of Asia to meet and exchange ideas.' They host lectures by scholars on an extraordinary range of subjects, and Ralph almost certainly attended meetings here. There are associated Asiatic Societies in India, Korea, China, Malaysia and Japan. It was set up in 1823 by an eminent Sanskrit scholar, Henry Thomas Colebrooke, and the room in which we are meeting has a bust of him which looks rather critically over my shoulder as I give my presentation. People who have been members of the Society range from Richard Burton, traveller and scholar extraordinaire, known in popular English-reading culture through his translations of *One Thousand and One Nights,* and the Bengali poet-philosopher, Rabindranath Tagore. Its library includes collections of manuscripts in Persian, Arabic, Pali, Sanskrit, Malay and Javanese.

But the real reason Ralph's book is being launched here is that an admirer of his work is the current President. Professor Francis Robinson is a historian whose focus is Muslim South Asia. He is a generation younger than Ralph and has written movingly of what he learnt from him. He reviewed each of his books as they came out, spoke at his funeral, arranged for the Royal Asiatic Society to host this event. They have mailed an invitation to their members, their technician will record the event, and they're also charmingly providing wine for people as they arrive. Ghalib would have approved – he was lyrical about the virtues of wine (and he didn't mean it metaphorically.) I said, 'What about snacks?' and to my pleasure they ordered in samosas. Just such a pity Ralph isn't here to enjoy them.

Professor Robinson introduces the event, which takes care of the scholarly context of Ralph's work. It's up to me now to pitch it at the other level. What Ralph wanted to do was to make Ghalib's poetry accessible to anyone. The mixture of people in this audience would have delighted him. The majority are older South Asians, and as I don't know most of them, they will have come in response to publicity sent out by the Royal Asiatic Society. Perhaps they come to a lot of events here? Or perhaps some of them knew Ralph? There are also younger Indians and Pakistanis, and from greeting them as they came in, it seems most came to Britain as postgraduate students. There's a scientist, an economist, a political scientist, an IT consultant. And then there are English speakers who had never heard Ghalib's name until they read *Uncertain Light*. Nor would they ever have heard of this event if I hadn't told them, so I feel they are my support team, open to hearing whatever I'm going to tell them. Mainly for the English speakers, I have come prepared with cards, bookmark shaped, on each of which is a translated ghazal couplet, and put them on the seats around the room. Before we begin there's already a buzz of conversation as people pick them up and start talking about them.

I talk about Ralph's life-long work, how I came to be helping him. Then I highlight points he thought important about Ghalib's life and work, illustrated by the couplets on the bookmarks. An Urdu speaker reads each couplet in Urdu, and I read the English translation…

Pondering the nature of existence:
> When nothing was, then God was there; had nothing been, God would have been
> My being has defeated me: had I not been, what would have been?

His self-deprecating humour — this couplet addressed to someone he is wooing, who is not responding:
> I grant that you are right, Ghalib is nothing
> But if you get him free, then what's the harm?

His rejection of fundamentalist religion:
> The mosque is ruined, so I bring its stones into the city
> And build myself a house there in the unbelievers' lane.

Urdu speakers living in London don't get many opportunities to spend an evening listening to Ghalib. For them it probably doesn't matter what I say, they are just loving the examples. Many of them can complete well known couplets, and do so, so it becomes a participatory event. For the English speakers, it's an eye-opener to experience the obvious enthusiasm of the Urdu speakers around them as each couplet is recited.

It seems to please everyone, and the whole experience gives me as much pleasure as it does anyone else. It's completely different from talking about my own books. I have no doubt about what I can offer, or whether people will be interested. Having Ralph introduce me to Ghalib opened up new experiences for me. I am delighted to have the chance to spread that further.

As I travel home afterwards I have one of those moments when it seems completely natural to chat to someone no longer alive. Ralph is thoroughly contented at the whole event; and he's also ticking me off. 'It's ridiculous to have doubts when you're talking about your own books,' he says. 'It's no different from talking about mine. You offer it, and it's up to them if they are interested. If they're not, what does it matter?'

~ 46 ~

Three Principles

November 2016, Shrewsbury

Shrewsbury is putting on its first literature festival, and I am here at the invitation of one of the organisers, whom I got to know at the poetry festival in Much Wenlock. I have come early, so I can spend time exploring the old town centre. Shrewsbury's best known resident was Darwin, and the town is full of places connected with him. My session will be held in the Unitarian Chapel, where Darwin as a boy attended services with his mother. I look in on it. It always helps to get a sense of the venue beforehand.

This one surprises me. It's my first close encounter with Unitarianism and I discover they don't have a theology. Instead they have three principles, inscribed on the inside walls of this simple building — *Freedom, Reason, Tolerance*. I am sufficiently impressed that I do a bit of googling and discover that three significant

19th century novelists were strongly influenced by Unitarianism. Elizabeth Gaskell grew up with it. Charles Dickens, who had a strong aversion to any form of conventional religion, gravitated towards it as an alternative. And for George Eliot, who in childhood had a dominating father with very dogmatic beliefs, it was learning about Unitarianism that encouraged her to read widely in science, philosophy and literature. She took Darwin's ideas seriously at a time when established religions were in uproar about them. She talked about a new 'Religion of Humanity' and said she hoped that her books would help her readers 'to imagine and to feel the pains and joy of those who differ from themselves in everything but the broad fact of being struggling, erring human creatures.'

I'll be happy to have my session here, with all those vibes in the air around me.

~

For the past week I have been struggling through a miasma of that misery called the Common Cold. I have had almost no voice. I cancelled everything else, have been speaking as little as possible, and trusted in Paracetamol, Vitamin C, herbal remedies and sleep. I am still working my way through packets of tissues and don't move anywhere without throat lozenges, but hopefully by Sunday I will be able to rejoin the company of those who can speak.

Meanwhile I am listening to the other writers. My most interesting new discovery is Paul McVeigh, here to talk about his first novel. *The Good Son* is told in the voice of a ten year old boy growing up during The Troubles of 1980s Belfast. I read it in the week before coming here, while getting through all those tissues. Its sharp dialogue and vivid characters make it warm and funny while at the same time it's a sensitive, sometimes heart-stopping account of the effect on a child of living with constant, inescapable violence. The boy is both delightfully cocky and terrified, with good reason. The family relationships are intensely felt, and McVeigh captures so well the power that adults and older children have over younger ones. He talks about coming from a background where nothing could be talked about, 'From the "huge unexploded bomb" type secret, to "Mum buying a new blouse and having to pretend to my Dad it was old" type'. When as a teenager he read Anaïs Nin's journals, 'these exposing personal enquiries into emotion and excavations of the truth, it transformed my concept of the territory of the written word. To this day I cannot write anything unless I'm certain of its absolute emotional truth.'

~

Sunday, and luckily my voice is back. A book group that has been reading *Uncertain Light* have invited me to get together with them for lunch before my session. Then we all go over to the chapel, where copies of all my books have been set out and people are beginning to arrive. One is a long-lost friend who now lives in a small town in Shropshire and has journeyed here specially. I am delighted to see her. We will go somewhere for tea afterwards and catch up on each other's lives. A woman in her late eighties arrives — another friend! We knew each other slightly in Zambia. She's had a long career in adult education in Africa, and has been loyally reading my books over all the years I've been writing them. She moves slowly, with lungs that are obviously compromised, but intellectually she is as sparky as ever.

I am to be interviewed by Tim Cook, formerly a BBC Radio Shropshire journalist. We met briefly at the Wenlock Festival where he too was taking part in the Big Read of Shakespeare's sonnets. Earlier this morning we had our first proper conversation. I'm impressed by the depth of his preparation. He has read all my novels and says he would like to ask questions about how each of them grew out of events in my own life. By now I am used to questions of that kind, but Tim's sensitive prompts lead to something deeper. He gets me telling the story of the political crisis that thrust us suddenly out of Zambia and landed us in Britain, shell-shocked and with two confused young children. I don't often talk about it.

It was an insecure time but very long ago, so it's not emotionally difficult to talk about. It's just that I can't find a way to tell the story briefly —

~

For eight years we worked in the newly independent country of Zambia. I taught at a school till our children were born, and Robert at the university which in those initial years had to rely almost totally on foreign teachers. We both loved being there, and as we knew we couldn't go back to South Africa, hoped to stay.

Then it all fell apart. Students organised a demonstration criticising government policy. The university was closed, 30 students were taken off to prison, and the rest put on buses and taken back to the rural areas where their families lived. Robert had had nothing to do with the demonstrations but when students were arrested (no charges brought, just locked away) he and another lecturer started a petition among university teachers, politely asking for the release of the students. Police arrived at our home in the small hours of the morning, ransacked Robert's study, and took him away.

It took ten days for a lawyer to discover where he was. A small number of other lecturers had also been taken, and the officials denied all knowledge of the arrests. When we found them, we got to visit once a week for 20 minutes — enough for me to see that he was in a poor way. He could say nothing about what was happening. Later we learnt that after intensive questioning for several days it must have become clear to their interrogators that there was nothing to investigate, so they were simply dumped back into solitary confinement. While friends took care of our children, I was knocking on official doors, and phoning friends in the UK, asking them to contact Amnesty International, to get press coverage, to do anything to prevent Robert and the others from just rotting there.

I also had to make a plan. It was almost certain that if he and the other lecturers were released they would be immediately sent back to their own countries. In our case that would have been disastrous. Robert had been openly working alongside people in the ANC, the African National Congress, the leading movement opposing the apartheid regime. In South African law that was treason, enough to put him in prison for years. The only other country where we had family ties was Britain, for we both had British-born mothers. When I finally got to see the British High Commissioner he said, as if it were obvious, that there must be a reason Robert was in prison, and why would Britain want to allow a potential trouble-maker in? Our mothers being British gave us no right to enter. That would only apply if it was our fathers.

Everything that happened after that is a blur, the details washed out by the trauma. But eventually, after Robert's aunt in Britain had sent a statement that she would support us if necessary, I acquired the desperately needed piece of paper that would allow him to enter Britain. Temporarily.

Suddenly after two months he and the others were released and had to leave the country in 48 hours. He flew to Britain; I followed a couple of weeks later with our two very small children. We had no idea what would happen next.

~

Those first months after we arrived … A time of retreat, like injured creatures. Safe, and grateful to be so, but at a loss. Landed from the sky in a place where we had never expected to live. Speaking and behaving as someone normal, but underneath the thinest layer of skin, feeling cut off from everything that had always constituted normality. No script to fall back on, making it all up each day. Not able to conceive yet of a different future, just coping with each day, no energy beyond that to take initiative …

I saw all that later in the eyes of the recently arrived refugees I worked with. It's there in the first chapters of *A Shield of Coolest Air,* when Rachel arrives so suddenly from a political crisis in

South Africa. And after she has begun to take root, she recognises it again in the eyes of the recently arrived Somali woman she meets in the playground of their children's school.

Everything that made a new kind of life possible came from the kindness of those around us. Friends, but also strangers. Friends who had been in Zambia took us in for the first month. They scarcely had room but they cooked meals, got us out walking with the children and noticing the first signs of spring, kept daily life moving. Then Robert's aunt gave us a temporary home. His grandmother had died a year earlier and her small retirement flat was still there, so we used it. But now? We could not have been more grateful to them all, but we had to move on ...

It's there in *If You Can Walk, You Can Dance*, each time the 'normal' in Jennie's life collapses under her and she has to find a way to start again, to make sense of life anew in a different place.

Robert's difficult transitions ... He was great with the children but had lost his own role in the world. Two months in solitary confinement in prison had had a deeply damaging effect. Another ex-Zambia friend got his university department to take him on as a research associate. He had no duties. There was a small stipend for two months; after that, if for official purposes he needed a place of work, he could stay unpaid. A space where he could hide until he felt stronger.

I found a job teaching English to foreign students in a nearby town. I rented a place for us to live in a village in the downs, making a safe nest in the middle of nature. Robert stayed home with the children. We got a nursery place for the youngest so Robert could put in an appearance at the university, but having taken her to the nursery he went straight to the library and spoke to no one. Each small step towards a new normal helped. Don't think too far ahead. Live each day for what it can be ...

It's all there in *Uncertain Light*, that state of mind, when Tessa and Ben have to suddenly leave one life and start another. I gave them our village, our first year. They were different people with a different history, but I knew exactly how they would feel.

My books are novels not autobiography, but we know certain things from the roads we have travelled. Things that happen at times of crisis, the moments when you have to journey without a map, get imprinted in bold on your inner eye.

~

Deep winter as my train back from Shrewsbury heads east, away from the setting sun. It's still afternoon but the light is disappearing from the world. I'm tired and I don't feel like reading. I stare out of the window at the silhouette world that passes by.

How strange that I found myself talking about all that old history. Actors sometimes talk about the qualities of different audiences. Today I felt that, felt people listening, intent, with me all the way.

I check my phone. Already there are two messages from people who were in that audience. One says, 'Thanks for coming to Shrewsbury, for stating your truth quietly, for recording events which need to be heard even more loudly through your wonderful books.'

What is 'my truth'? I live a quiet life. In a world of gross inequality I am profoundly privileged. I love what most people love — those closest to me; friends; shared interests; having time to do my own things. The only thing that might have made me seem different, to the woman who texted me or to others in that audience, is that I have lived through politically charged times. But that was an accident of history, not my choosing, as it was not my choosing to be born to privilege in a deeply divided society.

The question is how we react to such things, and that too is partly luck. I was lucky to have grown up among adults who saw the humanity in everyone they encountered, who felt the injustices around us and did what they could to mitigate them. I was lucky that they encouraged their children to think and question, and that they answered our questions honestly. That as far as it was possible in their place and time, they tried to live by those three principles

— Freedom, Reason, Tolerance. I was lucky that my antennae for all those things were alerted early, and have never switched off.

My truth; passed on to me by others.

STORIES NOT YET TOLD

~ 47 ~

When Artists Go to Work

December 2016

I'm trying to assimilate the US presidential election results, and the dread prospect of who is now sitting in the White House.

Looking for a tonic against political depression, I found this from Toni Morrison. She wrote it in 2004, after a previous disastrous presidential election, the one when George Bush got re-elected a year and half after invading Iraq:

> "I am staring out of the window in an extremely dark mood, feeling helpless. Then a friend, a fellow artist, calls. He asks, 'How are you?' And instead of 'Oh, fine, and you?' I blurt out the truth: 'Not well. Not only am I depressed, I can't seem to work, to write; it's as though I am paralyzed, unable to write anything more in the novel I've begun. I've never felt this way before, but

the election…' He interrupts, shouting: 'No! No, no, no! This is precisely the time when artists go to work, not when everything is fine, but in times of dread. That's our job!' "

So. Writing is not a form of retreat. It's a way of being sharply engaged.

As one humanitarian and political disaster has followed another, I have shed my modesty and got behind the message that is bigger than me. Can't stop now. There are stories waiting to be told, other lives I have been formed by, that have never got into what I have written. People whose beings I want to keep alive by writing them.

Here's one.

~

I have a particular connection with what's going on in the United States because I spent a year as an exchange student in Seattle, living as part of a warm, wonderful family. Fran Miller, the mother in that family, is 95 now. We have stayed in touch through all the decades since, and I phone her every couple of months.

In these last months she has been in a state of constant, undimmed political outrage. Her daughter tells me that they have been trying to persuade her not to watch the news because it makes her so angry.

'I will *never*,' she says, 'say *President* and That Man's Name in the same sentence.'

Fran remembers U.S. Presidents who to me are just history. She and her husband Jim learnt their Democratic allegiance as young people during the Roosevelt era. While Jim was away in the army she was at home with a child, and a mother-of-two when Truman authorised the dropping of atomic bombs on Japan. Through the Eisenhower years she was the all-competent runner-of-the-household who had not had a paid job since the birth of her first child, but that did not in the least define her. Her four children grew up to an accompaniment of her unflagging political indignation.

The year I was there we all listened together to Kennedy speaking to the nation about the Cuban missile crisis. In the Johnson years she followed intently the alternating triumphs and despair of the Civil Rights momentum, and the escalating disaster of the US war in Vietnam. Through the decades beyond, her letters to me were punctuated by comments about 'that idiot in the White House'. Before Obama became a presidential candidate she and Jim were talking about him as the hope for the future. Her grown children and grandchildren campaigned for him, and at a distance I rejoiced with them all over his election.

Now this, the Man with the unmentionable name.

~

Fran and Jim helped me become myself in more ways than I could find words for. It was part of the ethos of the student exchange that I referred to them as 'my American mother and father' but the relationship never felt anything like that. I needed no substitutes and nor did they. It was simply an act of generosity that led them to open their home, along with a belief in internationalism. The organisation that arranged the exchanges, the American Field Service (AFS) had started as an ambulance service in the war, staffed by pacifists exempted from combat roles. After the war they invested in young people, convinced that friendships formed young across national boundaries would contribute to international understanding. I've heard cynical criticisms of this kind of programme as yet another aspect of US imperialism, but that doesn't fit what I experienced. There was no ideology to which we were exposed, just a trust that something good would come of placing young people in willing families. The openness and warmth created a feeling of almost belonging, but far from dimming my powers of thinking for myself, it gave them a huge impetus.

I came into their household as a young almost grown-up person, and that's how they behaved with me. Jim was large, affectionate, humorous, tolerant, steady. He had wanted to be a writer, but straight out from the army had a young family to support, and found work in advertising. Fran was petite, lively, magnetically drawn to learning new things, an avid self-educator, reading to challenge herself. She always had an evening course on the go. When I arrived it was Italian literature. I'm sure she got me to talk about what I was reading, but what I remember is the constant stimulus she provided simply by being herself, by responding to life as a series of mind-opening adventures. A lifetime later I haven't begun to catch up with all the things she was reading that I put on my 'one-day' reading list.

It was formative simply realising that things I had taken for granted were not the only way to do things, that families can function in different ways, education can take different forms, social inequalities have distinct histories in different societies. Of course I had known this as an idea, but making the many small adaptations to living it is another matter, and has a dramatically maturing effect. It gave me also a filter for reacting to things that would happen later. However distressed I am by what happens politically in the US, however distant I feel from aspects of its contemporary culture, I am never tempted to generalise about 'Americans'. I know that there is nothing I feel about Trump that isn't felt even more strongly by millions of people like Jim and Fran and their children.

The family had a small-holding in a beautiful valley called Issaquah. It was then out in the country, and I was gutted when I went back 30 years later to discover it was now a built-up suburb of greater Seattle. There was a stream at the bottom of the garden, tree-covered hills rising on the other side, and a paddock for the couple of horses they kept. She and Jim had grown up in Eastern Washington, and riding was as natural to them as skiing to Norwegians. At weekends she got us all helping with the outdoor tasks, over-riding adolescent complaints. I remember Jim and Jim junior, then about ten, cutting back undergrowth and handling a bonfire, and Fran laughing that the males of the species could always be tempted into a job that involved destruction. I followed her around as we clipped the edges of the lawn and she talked about Dostoevsky, or the amount of federal revenue going on the space race when there still weren't enough schools and houses for the disadvantaged. The occasional short-term boyfriends who came my way I remember mainly because of Fran's talking, half-joking, half-serious, about how she felt responsible for not letting anything untoward happen. I was a late developer and nowhere near considering sexual activity, but she wasn't taking chances. 'What am I going to say to your parents if you get caught up with some unsuitable guy?' she said. This was 1962. The first contraceptive pills had only just become available and few parents would have talked with their daughters about the possibility of using it, but Fran had her own way of prompting caution. Her guideline was hilarious. 'Would you share your toothbrush with him? If not, think again.'

She ran the farm, managed two households, brought up a family of four (with me, five), all with such calm competence that I only registered in later years that it had been the true art that conceals art. Meals arrived, housework was done, plans were made, outings arranged, children listened to, political arguments fielded with her mother, homework supervised — it all just happened, and she still had apparently limitless energy left to sit discussing issues after meals. One by one the others would get tired of it and peel off to do their own thing, and I was left still listening. Years later her daughter told me she had felt excluded by those constant conversations. I was taking over her mother, and with the self-focus of youth, I was insensitively unaware that it might have any impact on the others. I am sure Fran was aware of it, and probably talked with her own girls about being tolerant with me.

She had been determined that her three daughters would have the kind of stimulating education no one had thought appropriate for girls in her youth, so the school they went to, and I with them, was a small independent girls school with high academic standards and a broad humanist curriculum. The girls felt, or maybe just said they felt, grieved that they were missing the normal American school experience, and along with it the contact with boys. For me it was a positive experience — small classes, young and imaginative teachers, stimulating new subjects that made learning an adventure, all totally different from my own earlier school experience. But Fran knew it was important also for me to get an idea of a more typical American school, and arranged for me to spend a couple of weeks in the local high school. I have a vague memory of crowded corridors and locker rooms where the volume control was set at max and I hardly understood the rapid street-wise repartee. There were a lot of black kids at the school and several of the teachers were active in a chapter of CORE, the Congress on Racial Equality, that was growing rapidly in the north to support civil disobedience actions in the southern states. A few weeks after my year came to an end volunteers from that group were on the march on Washington where Martin Luther King made his 'I have a dream' speech.

Ever since that year Fran has kept me connected. Postcards, photos, letters, following me around the world. She writes always in capital letters, curly ones, hard to decipher. I have only to see that familiar handwriting on an envelope to be taken back to those vivid conversations about what she was currently reading. For a few years she and Jim lived in Germany when he had arranged a transfer with his company, and we got to see each other several times. She was then, in typical Fran style, studying German, German history, Renaissance art, and more. I date each of our brief times together by the world affairs that she wanted to discuss. Reagan, the Iran-Contra affair, Gorbachev, the Berlin Wall. After Jim retired her constant curiosity morphed into joint explorations. Flipping through her cards now I find one that says, 'Jim and I have become *serious* birders'. The card has a painting of a gallinule, a waterbird I have no memory of ever having seen, with a reminder from her that she and I saw one together once on a walk 30 years earlier. Another card says, 'We've discovered the amazing geology of this region — a wonder, right under our feet, that we stupidly ignored all these years.' One year they brought their two oldest granddaughters on a European holiday, and we all had a few days together in Yorkshire. I remember her calling urgently to Jim to stop the car so she could jump out and photograph a field of rape, full, startling yellow. Star, at 16, the age of their granddaughters, was with us, and so was Ralph. He and Jim discovered that as young men during the war they had been stationed within a few miles of each other, near the Burma border. I can still hear Fran laughing at them as they exchanged stories. 'You two old soldiers!'

When I joined Save the Children, 30 years after my year in Seattle, I took a month off between jobs to spend with them. They had hired a house on the Washington coast for the summer, looking out across the Pacific, where their grown children and grandchildren took turns to come and spend time with them. I had just published *A Shield of Coolest Air*. Somalia was one of the few countries Fran had never read anything about, so she sat me down more or less as soon as I had arrived and said, 'Tell me about it.'

~

Jim and Ralph died in the same year. Since then I have tried to remember to phone Fran every few months, though often time has passed faster between calls than I have noticed. Each time she wants first to hear about my family and our doings, and then to know what I think about whatever has been in the news. She is now studying palaeontology. Her grandson was a lead palaeontologist in a hugely significant fossil discovery, the Snowmastodon Project in Colorado. It became a family affair — Jim Jnr was one of the structural engineers lifting the discoveries, and others in the family were among the hundreds of volunteers at the site. A thousand miles to the north Fran was following every stage of the process, determined to keep up and understand.

She, Jim and their family are not in any of my books, but what they helped me experience is there in them all. She will always be for me an example of how to live vividly, carrying in herself the determined engagement that makes every day worth something, whatever people with power are doing to undermine the values we live by.

I have lived since then in three countries, been engaged in the cultures of others, had the chance to work with people in remote places that few visit even as tourists. But the process of noticing what is going on around me, of seeing differences and feeling beneath them the more fundamental similarities, that started in my year in Seattle, from the safest and most loving base.

~ 48 ~

Walking Across Mountains

I take the bus down Tooting High Street in London, heading to an event organised by a group called Wandsworth Welcomes Refugees. Not, this time, to talk about my own books but to interview my friend Shabibi Shah, a refugee from Afghanistan, about hers.

To anyone who knows South London, Tooting represents Asian food markets and sari shops, the best samosas, and a High Street where you can pass people speaking most of London's 120 languages. There's a literary link even here, and a history of political challenge to the authorities. Next to the large indoor Tooting Market is a chapel where Dissenters met in secret to escape persecution. Among them was Daniel Defoe. Apart from writing *Robinson Crusoe* (said to be, after the Bible, the book translated into the largest number of languages), he produced more than 300 works, of which a good number were political pamphlets.

We are meeting further down the street, in a music-venue-cum-bar. When everyone is assembled, I get Shabibi to talk about her autobiography, *Where do I belong?* It's an extraordinary story of her escape from danger, walking across mountains with very young children to a refugee camp in Pakistan, and from there, by an unlikely set of events, finally to London. Now, a widow with grown children, she acts as a foster mother to young unaccompanied asylum seekers from Afghanistan.

Before she had to flee, Shabibi was a journalist and a poet in her own language, Farsi. In addition to all other losses, changing countries meant losing her writing voice. She had almost no English when she came, and a myriad family issues to be handled before she could think of herself. But she eventually became competent enough in English to write her story. She's not IT-confident, but she has friends who are, so now the book is out, self-published, and the story is so striking that The Guardian ran an interview with her about it. She has since written a novel on a similar theme, also in English. She reads widely in both Farsi and English, she is in a book group where all the others are native English speakers, but she regrets that she will never be able to write in English with the facility and subtlety that she once could in Farsi. I said, 'Why don't you write in Farsi and we could get it translated?' That doesn't any longer feel an option, because it's over 20 years since she used her own language regularly outside the family. But she still writes Farsi poetry, some of which she posts on FaceBook. I wish I could read it.

She is nervous about this public appearance, though she has no need to be. What bothers her is not only natural modesty, it is that she has to do it in English. She need not have worried. The story tells itself, and holds everyone's attention. At the back of the packed room I see two teenage girls listening, rapt, inspired by this amazing woman who walked across mountains.

At the table where people queue to buy her book, our friend Mary Simpson and I are displaying the *Our Lives Press* booklets that came out of the English classes we used to work with in Croydon. Each is about 50 small pages, large print, simply told autobiographies by people who have come as adults to live in Britain. Some knew English well enough to write their own story, others told it to a volunteer-scribe who wrote it down as it was told, corrected the English, and checked it back with the author. A small group of us run the project. We encourage people to write their stories, we publish them, and go around English classes to tell others about them. They're great reading material for people new to English because the language is naturally simple and the stories rivetingly real. Rashida Abedi's *From Sound to Silence* tells of the impact of deafness. Helene Ramazani, author of *Achieving against the odds,* escaped from the Congo when her life was in danger, to arrive in England, completely alone in a strange country, unable to speak the language. A young Albanian woman tells how she was sold to traffickers and forced into sex-work. Somehow she managed to escape and make a new life with her daughter. Her story, *Never Give Up,* had to come out under an assumed name, Kristy Krasniqi, to avoid her being traced by her traffickers. Babush Tesfay's *Finding the Unexpected* tells how he escaped the war between Ethiopia and Eritrea, in both of which he had relatives.

Faizia Zaman's story, *Standing on my own two feet,* tells how the idea of writing her story came about. A group of us had gone to listen to Sharan Jeet Shan speak, one of the first British South Asian women to write her autobiography, *In My Own Name.* Faizia was inspired by her story and in the train coming back I said, 'You should write your own.' She had been educated to college level before she came to Britain, but like many people she couldn't believe anyone else would be interested in her story. Yet with the dedicated help of an English speaking friend she did it — how, as a Bangladeshi woman new to life in Britain she was suddenly widowed and had to learn to cope on her own. She had five young children, no obvious way to support herself, and knew little about how systems worked in this new country. Faizia is no longer alive but her children, all university educated, are proud of all that she made possible for them, and that she wrote the story.

The first in the series is in one way the most remarkable, because Asha Mohammed, a Somali refugee, had never learnt to read in her own language. When I said, 'Asha, you should write your story!' she clearly thought I was slightly crazed. But with the help of a volunteer scribe she did it, describing in a down-to-earth, humorous way her first days and months in England. When it was done, she was not particularly satisfied. She had told only a fraction of the experiences she had been through, she said. So she gave it a title which is one of my favourites — *So many things I could have written.*

~ 49 ~

An Invitation to Tea

A flip back to the years of writing *Uncertain Light* ... I am describing a young woman walking from an underground station to meet an elderly woman she doesn't know ...

I realise that this isn't just any road I am picturing, it is a particular road. It's decades since I walked it, but suddenly everything about it is vivid in my memory — the turning, the trees that line it, the entrance to the building, and once inside, everything that speaks of the woman who lived there.

Ever since I was asked to talk about how to make the world a better place, I've been thinking about her, for she was someone who, quietly, but life long, did just that.

We met soon after Robert and I had arrived from Zambia. He was still prison-shocked, confidence shattered. We were anxious about money. What I earned scarcely covered the rent. For other costs we were using up our small stock of savings. And after that was gone? A friend who understood our situation knew of an organisation that gave small grants to refugee academics. It had been set up in the 1930s to help scholars who were at threat from the Nazis, finding them places in British and American universities; and it still continued. The friend got Robert to send in his details. He was embarrassed. The organisation had the impressive name of the Society for the Protection of Science and Learning, and the idea that helping him would be protecting learning made him want to creep into a shell.

A letter arrived telling him he had been awarded a grant. It was modest, but it would see us through a year. A lifeline. The letter was signed by Esther Simpson. She followed it up with a phone call, inviting us to tea.

We made the journey to London, all four of us, walking that road from the underground station. We arrived at her flat to find a little, ordinary-looking elderly woman, who began talking as if she had known us for years. In our still insecure state she succeeded in making everything feel comfortably ordinary. She made us tea in her tiny kitchen, with cakes bought in from a local Viennese restaurant. Her desk was covered in papers and letters, representing her continuing engagement with all the scholars she had helped. There were photographs around the room of their children of all ages, some in graduation gowns.

Despite the photographs, it was not a room that was used to children — too much to bump into, with possibly valuable things on small tables. But something about the atmosphere made our girls perfectly behaved. They sat on their chairs politely and accepted second helpings of cake and chatted perkily when spoken to. She asked their dates of birth — she said she liked to send birthday cards to the children of her scholars. I asked, amazed, how many cards that was in a year. 'Well,' she said, 'by the end of the War there were over 600 scholars, but there have been many more since.

And of course many of their children now have children, so I have rather last count. But they're all in my birthday list, so I go by that.'

By the time we left it had become clear that Esther *was* the Society for the Protection of Science and Learning. There was a Board of Trustees, but apart from that she did it all, with all the paperwork in boxes in her spare room. She had been running it for 43 years, and for the last 25 years, voluntarily.

~

It was only gradually that I learnt her story. She was born in 1903, which happens to be the year my father was born. As I think about the paths her life took, I have a parallel story in my mind, of a boy growing up 6,000 miles away but formed by some of the same major events of the time, the legacy of the horrors of World War, which turned them both into pacifists.

Esther was a child of Jewish immigrants who had fled from pogroms in Russia to Leeds. The family name was Sinovich. Her father worked in a garment factory. No one who knew her in later years could remember her talking about her childhood years, except for the education that formed her. She got a scholarship to university, studied languages, and was a gifted violinist. In her twenties she was secretary to the International Fellowship of Reconciliation, one of many organisations formed in the wake of the first World War that hoped to make sure there would never be such a war again, by fostering links between individuals across countries.

From 1928 until 1933 she worked in their office in Vienna. In the immediate post-war years there had been immense poverty in Vienna but by the time she got there things had improved greatly and she loved her time there. She was earning very little but the things she enjoyed doing were cheap or free — music, friendships with like-minded people, and getting out into the country. Her delight was always playing chamber music, and in the lively musical culture of Vienna in those years she played regularly in string quartets with professional musicians.

In 1933 she met a young Hungarian physicist, Leo Szilard. He had been working in Berlin with Einstein and had left immediately Hitler came to power, and was concerned about what would happen to Jewish and anti-Nazi academics. William Beveridge, director of the London School of Economics, got together vice chancellors of several British universities and together they set up an Academic Assistance Council, to help find academic posts elsewhere for university teachers and researchers who were being dismissed from their own universities on racial, political or religious grounds, or were in danger. Esther asked Szilard to see if there might be a job for her with the Council. She received a cable inviting her to come as soon as possible. With very little confirmed funding, all they could offer her was a temporary job at two pounds ten shillings a week, about a third of what she was currently earning. That didn't bother her. She was not yet 30 and knew she could always find another job if necessary. So she took it. She said later, 'This was something that I could do. Well, you could say it was a call.'

Early on the organisation's name changed to the Society for the Protection of Science and Learning, to emphasise that while they were helping individual refugees, they were securing for everyone the intellectual contribution those scholars would collectively make to society. Perhaps to facilitate her work, Esther too quietly changed her name and became Esther Simpson; and it was perhaps around this time that she became a Quaker.

When she started work at the Council, there was already a backlog of letters from people seeking help. Through the next years they kept coming, and the pressure never let up. From two small rooms loaned to them by the Royal Society, Esther was processing applications, contacting institutions where people could be placed, and dealing with awesome amounts of bureaucratic red tape to get permission for them to come into Britain. For scholars already eminent in their fields it was easy to find places. Universities in Britain knew they were privileged to get them. But many were less well known or at an early stage in their careers, and it was a major problem to find places, particularly if they didn't know English well enough to be able to take on a teaching post. The strategy then was to find a university willing to have them as research scholars without pay until they were able to take up teaching posts, and meanwhile they were supported by grants from the Society. Finding placements at universities was only the start. Esther was on the case offering support and advice in all their settlement issues, and trying to arrange for their families to join them.

By the time war was declared the Society had managed to place over 600 academics in British, American and Canadian universities. From then on it became almost impossible for people to get out of Nazi-controlled areas. Now there was a new challenge. Britain began interning 'enemy aliens', regardless of whether they were refugees from Nazi occupied territories. Now the director and trustees of the Society were lobbying the British government for the release of the scholars they had helped save, and Esther was preparing dossiers, taking notes at meetings, and often doing the lobbying herself, in countless letters politely but utterly persistently nagging a sluggish bureaucracy to respond. Her work was in one sense undramatic — endless form filling, detailed paper work, minutes of meetings, tens of thousands of letters — but she did it with unconditional commitment. Max Perutz, one of her 'family', as she described them to a friend, said she had an 'iron toughness in the face of officialdom.'

She worked continuously. She had no concept of working hours, weekends or holidays. While there were people needing help, she was busy dealing with their cases. The only personal thing she made time for was making music with others, several evenings a week. At the outbreak of war the Society's office had moved to Cambridge. She had learnt to ride a bicycle, and through the dark evenings of the blackouts she cycled to rehearsals with her violin case strapped to her back. Soon a quartet she was part of was being asked to perform at airfields and soldiers' camps. In talking about it years later there was no sense that she felt she had given up anything, just gratitude for the richness of friendships she gained through doing it. She never married, but she adopted the families of the scholars she worked for as if they had been her own.

The work didn't stop when the war ended. She was then helping to reunite families of the scholars, and responding to requests to try to track those who had not escaped. But by 1951 funding for the SPSL was winding down, and she needed to find some other form of income. She became secretary of an organisation called the Society for Visiting Scientists, who agreed that she could carry on the work of the SPSL, unpaid, from their office. Every few years there would be a new political crisis and work ballooned. In 1948 she was helping to place refugee scholars from Czechoslovakia; in 1956 from Hungary; in 1968 again from Czechoslovakia and Poland; through the 1960s and 1970s from politically oppressive regimes in South Africa, Argentina, Chile, Greece.

In 1966 the Society for Visiting Scientists had run out of funding and her paid job ended. She was then 63; for most of her working life she had been on minimal pay and she had few financial resources. Six of the scholars whom she had helped organised an appeal among the others, by then scattered world-wide, and raised enough to enable her to buy a flat. The appeal letter had said, 'What we all probably remember best is that she was always there, that her life centred round one problem only, how to help all of us.'

~

Retirement was not a concept she understood. She simply carried on running the SPSL voluntarily from her flat, and so lucky for us, and hundreds of others, that she did. She had some kind of honorary status at the Royal Society, in whose building she had worked in the first years of the Academic Assistance Council. She invited us to a meal there once, as I'm sure she did with many others, underneath the gaze of previous Fellows in their dark heavy-framed portraits. Because her talk was always about the scholars whose lives she had been bound up with, and whose subsequent stellar careers she followed with the greatest interest, she could sound as if she were name-dropping to impress, but it simply was the fact that so many of those she had became closest to were extremely eminent. Among them there were 16 Nobel Prize winners, and over 100 Fellows of the Royal Society (scientists) and of the British Academy (humanities and social scientists). But she was equally loyal in her friendships with others, like us, who didn't become well known. Someone said she had the happy talent of not taking in statistics or abstract concepts about humanity, but of focusing only on individual people.

In the late 1980s a researcher called Ray Cooper had the idea of studying the influx of Second World War refugee academics to Britain, and someone told him he should speak to Esther. It didn't take long for him to realise what an extraordinary story hers was, and he asked her permission to record their conversations. The results, along with all her papers, are now lodged in the library of the University of Leeds. It's clear that she had to be continually prompted to talk about herself . Mostly she wanted to talk about all the scholars she had worked for, and what they went on to do, and the countless people she had made music with or otherwise befriended through her work. The recordings are full of delightful vignettes. There's one about Wittgenstein, who was not a refugee but who had gone out of his way to help a colleague who was. During the war he gave up his position at Cambridge because he said that with a war on it was ridiculous to be teaching philosophy. He wanted to do something useful, so he took a job at Guy's Hospital as a porter. They insisted he eat with the doctors rather than the porters, which he said was a pity, for the porters were a much more interesting group of people.

By the time Cooper put together extracts from those interviews as a book, Esther was 89, and as mentally spritely as ever. An event was organised for its launch. She stressed that the event was for 'Ray's book', as if it had little to do with her; but she was obviously hugely enjoying the fact that it had brought together so many people who were important to her. We were in the company of elderly scholars, two of whom spoke with a light and loving touch about what she had done for them and for hundreds of others. One was Ernst Gombrich, author of *The Story of Art* – perhaps the best known art historian in the world, with a string of honours and awards. The other was Max Perutz, molecular biologist, a Nobel Prize winner.

Walter Adams, who had headed the Society through its crucial early years, once described how he had been amazed at her tireless energy and unfailing good nature. 'Yours was a truly personal success, the giving of yourself and your friendship unstintingly in a way that literally changed the cultural history of the world.'

~

I see her now as she was the last time we visited her in her home. She was in her eighties. Our younger daughter Star was still at school, and came with us. Esther was delighted to learn that Star was playing the cello, and immediately presented her with her own copy of the score of the Beethoven quartets. She talked about how much joy she had always had playing them. She could no longer because her hearing wasn't up to it, but she hoped Star would get as much pleasure from them as she had. None of us told her that Star wasn't quite at that level yet.

I see her room, with the papers everywhere, the photographs of 'her' children. I gifted that room to Greta in *Uncertain Light,* and along with it something of Esther's spirit.

CREATIVE PROCESSES

~ 50 ~

Why Do We Do It?

We read because we've been read to, or found our own way to books. There are societies without books, and children surrounded by books who never acquire the habit, but for those who do, the delight of disappearing into a story feels completely natural. No need to ask why.

But why do we write them?

Novelists seem to get asked this far more often than other writers, historians, for instance, biographers, journalists, writers of cookbooks. Maybe that's because making up fictional people seems such a bizarre thing to do. Unless you are one of those who does it.

I thought at first that 'Why?' was almost a non-question. 'Stories have been percolating in my mind since my childhood,' says Kerri Sakamoto, Japanese Canadian. But in the week after my hip replacement, when my concentration level was minimal, I distracted myself by rooting around to see what answers other novelists give. Here's a sample, randomly chosen, just ones I found revealing:

Joseph Conrad: My task is, by the power of the written word to make you hear, to make you feel. It is, before all, to make you see. That, and no more — and it is everything.

Katherine Mansfield: Would you not like to try all sorts of lives? One is so small. That is the satisfaction of writing. One can impersonate so many people.

George Orwell: When I sit down to write a book, I do not say to myself, 'I am going to produce a work of art.' I write it because there is some lie that I want to expose, some fact to which I want to draw attention, and my initial concern is to get a hearing.

Graham Greene: Writing is a form of therapy. Sometimes I wonder how all those who do not write, compose or paint can manage to escape the madness, the melancholia, the panic fear which is inherent in the human situation.

Simone de Beauvoir: When I used to read books that moved me deeply, such as George Eliot's The Mill on the Floss, I wanted terribly much to be, like her, someone whose books would be read, whose books would move readers.

James Baldwin: You write in order to change the world, knowing perfectly well that you probably can't, but also knowing that literature is indispensable to the world... The world changes according to the way people see it, and if you alter, even by a millimeter the way people look at reality, then you can change it.

Maya Angelou: We write for the same reason that we walk, talk, climb mountains or swim the oceans — because we can ... We have some impulse within us that makes us want to explain ourselves to other human beings.

Gao Xingjian: Writing eases my suffering. It's my way of reaffirming my own existence.

Isabelle Allende: I just need to tell a story. It's an obsession.

Each story is a seed inside of me that starts to grow and grow, like a tumour, and I have to deal with it sooner or later.

Vikram Seth: What started me was ignorance, and what kept me going was obsession. I needed to know how it would finish.

Amy Tan: I may be writing something fictional, but something will click, some element that is part of a memory. It's like my brain suddenly coming into sync with the brain I had in the past.'

Hilary Mantel: You don't become a novelist to become a spinner of entertaining lies: you become a novelist so you can tell the truth.

Hamid Ismailov: Thinking about the dire state of my country, I felt that perhaps people needed some light, some positive heroes who stood strong in the face of all the upheavals and adversities in their lives.

Colm Toibin: I write with a sort of grim determination to deal with things that are hidden and difficult.

Malorie Blackman: I started writing in part to redress the imbalance regarding ethnic diversity in children's literature that I felt acutely as a child, but the ethnic identity of my characters is never the whole story. What inspired me to write was a love of stories and reading.

Chimamanda Ngozi Adichie: I write because I have to. I also write because I want and hope to be read.

Clearly, a variegated species. From six continents and eleven countries. Just over half are women, several gay or bi-sexual. Ethnically diverse. Their writing-lives span a century and a half — if you're wondering about the order, it's by date of birth. But there's one thing they all have in common. They don't just vaguely enjoy writing fiction, they feel impelled to do it.

~ 51 ~

Too Good to be True

I've been reflecting on some of the more personal reactions to my books.

In one book group, a warm, relaxed group who have known each other for years, there is a moment of spiky disagreement. A woman says she thinks Rahul, the pivotal character in *Uncertain Light*, 'too good to be true'. Someone else disagrees. I wait to see what others will say.

'Too good to be true' is associated with Victorian romanticism, the pure young women in Dickens' novels, for instance, where all his other characters are warts-and-all. Or Louisa May Alcott and

Eleanor Porter's girls — high spirited, often tom-boys, but whose social training always triumphed, so the 'truth' of their experience was always being adjusted to fit. The word 'do-gooder' implies a suspicion that people are not actually as good as they like to make out.

In the group there's an air of reticence. Does that mean they aren't sure what they think? I ask the woman who made the 'too good to be true' comment to say more, and she begins listing Rahul's flaws. He is self-driven to the point of selfishness, inconsiderate of the needs of those close to him – qualities which you might think would disqualify him from being thought 'too good'.

There's something else going on here, some irritant like a pebble in your shoe. That Rahul, or someone like him, could exist I know, for I have met them. But maybe she hasn't? Or maybe she has known someone who had some of his qualities but was even more flawed? If she can't imagine herself making the choices he made, maybe she can't believe anyone would? Whatever it is, it's clear that he made her cross, and what irritated her even more was that he didn't have that effect on the people in the story.

Someone else in the group quietly says that to her Rahul seems a Christ-like figure. It's an unexpected comparison. There is nothing either religious or messianic about his story. I think her brave for saying it — and why should that be?

~

Later I'm talking to a friend who has just finished reading the book. She too has the 'too good to be true' reaction. When I probe a little as to what she means, she quickly takes it upon herself. 'Maybe I'm just jealous.'

Of?

'Of someone having all those talents,' she says.

But again, why? We hear about people with unusual talents all the time, and mostly we can simply admire.

'All those languages,' she says.

She speaks three fluently herself, and can get by in a couple more. All European languages. Does it seem more impressive to speak Urdu and Persian?

As it happens, she and I have each recently been to a funeral. We move on to talking about how, listening to people sharing their memories of the person who had died, we learnt things about them that we hadn't known. If we *had* known them in their life-time, it would have given us a different insight into them.

It's connected. Rahul's story emerges in *Uncertain Light* through the memories of those closest to him, who are all reacting to his sudden and confusing disappearance. The emotional truth for people in that situation is that they hold on to the things about him that they most value. When they remember things that irritated or upset them, they seem so much less important when faced with actual, final loss.

~

Tangentially, or perhaps not, I am remembering a review of my book, *Somewhere More Simple*. The reviewer said that there were moments when he wanted to throw the book against the opposite wall. No indication why. He didn't suggest that he thought it a useless novel. Elsewhere in the review he said some very positive things about it, including that at moments it has 'a Peter Grimes tragic potential.' But something had provoked him. What?

For me the vehemence is a clue. I doubt if he would have felt that strongly unless the story had at some level worked for him, enough for him to care about the characters — until something triggered a reaction of, '*NO! Why did she* [the author, me] *let the guy do that?*' Because *he* [as a person, not a writer] wouldn't have done so, in that situation? Or had encountered something like it, and had been upset by it ? Or irritated ?

I have now met the reviewer. We were at the same festival. He was there as a star, I as a minor participant, so I didn't expect to get to speak to him, but I listened with interest and I liked everything I heard. He was warm, lively, and encouraging of other writers. That made me even more curious about the throwing-it-at-the-wall reaction, so when I found myself near him in a crowd I introduced myself and said, 'You once reviewed a book of mine.'

'Yes, I remember,' he said. That review was eight years ago, and he reviews lots of books. Perhaps he had seen my name in the programme and that had jogged his memory? But it was enough to encourage me to risk the next step. I reminded him of the throwing-against-a-wall comment and said I'd always wanted to know what that was about.

It was immediately obvious that he hadn't needed reminding. He laughed, passed it off with a light remark, and was clearly not going to be drawn. Well, why should he? It might have taken too long to explain. Or been too personal.

So I'm still wondering.

Irritation is an odd thing. It can be sparked off by something apparently trivial, but it cuts sharply. And if you lay your soul bare in writing, you can't avoid irritating some of the people some of the time.

~

The potential for goodness exists in us all. It is every bit as much a part of real life as any of its opposites. That it is difficult to convey in fiction is partly because of a reaction against an earlier tendency in writers (reflecting their times) to refuse to face up to complex reality.

There are fashions in literature, as in everything else. Terry Eagleton, literary scholar and critic, talks of a tendency in 20th century fiction to take it for granted

> "that families will be dysfunctional, individual lives unfulfilled and relationships cockpits of gladiatorial combat ... For writers like Fielding and Dickens, cheerfulness is quite as real as gloom, which isn't the case with Sebald or Graham Greene. Suffering for

them is fundamental in a way that bliss can't be, and certainly easier to knock a story out of. For the modern age, there is, many would say, something phoney about the very idea of happiness. Even the word has a naff ring to it ... 'Contentment', with its inescapable overtones of munching grass, isn't much of an improvement, while 'ecstasy' comes in the shape of tablets."

It's easiest to see this when crossing cultures. I first became aware of it when I was introduced to Urdu poetry. Urdu poets express despair and longing with an intensity that to British readers seems almost embarrassingly over-the-top. It's not that anyone doubts that despair can be extreme, but cultures differ widely in how they feel it is appropriate, or effective, to express it.

Even within any one culture, what seems an effective way of conveying emotional truth can change with dramatic suddenness. The characters in Terence Rattigan's plays expressed depth in constrained, understated ways which audiences in the 1940s and 1950s found extremely moving. By the late 1950s he had been shoved out of fashion by dramatists of the angry young men generation, for whom relationships were only being 'truly' depicted if they were in the style Eagleton called 'gladiatorial combat'.

The change in fashion is not just a sign of changing values in society. It is also partly media-driven — stress, tension and disaster sell news, and also books. In the films that we see, the media stories we are exposed to, anger, violence and tortured emotions are everywhere. Fashion models need to look blank, turned off, unemotional. For the young, anxious to fit in, it's safest to be 'cool', a cultivated, uninvolved, detachment, though interestingly the word itself is ambiguous, because it is also used to express real approval. 'Wicked', as used by the young, describes something unequivocally positive, a use that people of my parents' generation would have found incomprehensible.

At another level goodness never goes out of fashion. When people become tearful at something in a story, a film, a play, it's often at a tender, generous moment rather than a sad one. It could be something as simple as a loving gesture at a moment of need, or perhaps something heroically admirable; either way, it surprises us by getting to us in a deep place.

Each writer of fiction makes unconscious choices as well as conscious ones on which aspects of the human condition to portray, and how to express the 'truth' of that condition. But we are less free than we like to think in making those choices.

~

Ernest Hemingway: 'All good books are alike in that they are truer than if they had really happened, and after you are finished reading one you will feel that all that happened to you.'

But you can only be sure what feels true to you. There are reasons in the lives of each of us that will make a story believable to one when it is not so to another.

~ 52 ~

Practise Any Art

My granddaughter Isla is creating dragons. Out of Fimo, but actually out of the extraordinary fertility of her imagination. She works peacefully and with complete absorption, rolling the soft substance between her fingers to make wings and legs and ears to add to the sausage-shaped body, and a small family of dragons takes shape as I watch. They're not your normal species of dragon, but their features are certainly not random, for there's a family likeness about the long heads and short bodies. Beyond species, they have personality, each looking at me differently from those miniature beady eyes.

All that from rolling very small bits of Fimo.

'Practise any art,' wrote the American novelist Kurt Vonnegut, 'music, singing, dancing, acting, drawing, painting, sculpting, poetry, fiction, essays, reportage — no matter how well or badly

— not to get money and fame, but to experience becoming, to find out what's inside you, to make your soul grow.'

That quotation has scooted around the internet, variously misquoted, so I entertained myself by tracking to find out who he said it for. In 2006 a teacher at a New York high school got her students to write to their favourite author and invite them to visit the school. Vonnegut was the only one to reply. He said that at 84 he no longer made public appearances but he sent them those words instead. I bet they were glad they asked in time, for he died the next year.

Isla doesn't need anyone to tell her to practise any art. It's what she does all the time, mostly making things with her hands; and occasionally she checks on what I'm up to. She has been asking for years if I've written a book for children yet. What a waste to have a granny who writes books, but only for adults.

I've told her that writing for children is a lot more difficult — that it's a long time since I was a child — that I don't know what it would be about.

Clearly, these are lame excuses.

'Pirates,' she suggested. 'Treasure. Magic.'

'That's not really my thing,' I said, 'I write more about things that could really happen to people.'

'Like Jacqueline Wilson?'

But immediately she decided, No, there's only one Jacqueline Wilson.

I retreated. 'I just can't get started. I think we'll have to do it together.'

She was onto it, instantly. We were on our way home from a bookshop choosing a present for her cousin, who is three, and before we got off the bus she was half way through inventing one. She didn't have to think what it would be about, she knew immediately — a story about children going to an animal centre to find a pet, and choosing one unsuitable animal after another. 'And funny,' she said. When we were home she dictated, I typed. It came out in occasional rhyme, and it *was* funny.

An hour later the story was there. I had made occasional suggestions. She decided without hesitation if they were a good idea, but mostly they were dismissed. The story was hers, I was just the scribe. Press 'Print' and out it came, fully formed. Amazing.

Her élan gives me courage.

~

My own creative process? You'd think after all these years I'd be more in command of it than I am. Each time I am in a pause between books I make notes for myself about what I might write next. I look back at those notebooks and I have to laugh. They all say the same things, and I have never carried out my excellent advice to myself. The next one is going to be a *short* book, I tell myself each time, so it doesn't take me seven years. And I'm going to start with a *plot*, a simple one preferably, with stages clearly worked out.

Ah, the plot — there's the rub. I have a fellow sufferer, I discovered, in Edith Nesbit, author of *The Railway Children*. She struggled with plots. Luckily I've never had anything like the pressure to produce them that she was under. Her supposedly charming husband was useless at supporting them financially, but casually generous at filling the house with people he had taken an interest in, so in addition to the pressure of being the main earner she was left to run the house for a large, constantly changing group of people. One of them told how she came in to breakfast one day and asked, 'Can someone please give me a plot?'

What actually happens in my case is almost the exact opposite of what I repeatedly tell myself I'm going to do. Some thought, feeling, perception, works away inside me, and sends me to start typing. Only gradually do I begin to understand where it might go. At that point I have to go back to the beginning and see which of all the tentative drafts might be worth taking on that journey. When I'm feeling positive I think of this process as organic; otherwise, as frustratingly amorphous. But it's mine, and I'm stuck with it.

Even for work and academic writing I've never found it

easy to put down headings and subheadings of a topic and then write around those. I have a reputation for writing clearly, but that's only arrived at after many stages. I jump in to the middle of a topic, thoughts suggest other thoughts, spiralling outwards. Everything seems to connect. It all becomes too diffuse and I have to try and rein it in. In writing fiction I rejoice in being free of the expectations of logical order that non-fiction requires, but at some point I realise that I have to begin imposing some kind of shape on all that organically generated material. The free-wheeling part of my brain works best in the early morning, the logical editing part later in the day. I have to keep the balance on the side of morning writing otherwise the shape that my editing brain puts on what I've written risks becoming a straitjacket. Often I'll edit a section in the afternoon, be pleased with the result, and discover next morning that it's dull and lifeless.

~

I run through in my mind Kurt Vonnegut's rolling list of art forms that one might practise. I'm a dabbler, enjoying having a go at whatever. I have done a couple of paintings, no more, but being with children has given me excuses for making other things. I have played around with recorders, and sing in a choir, but don't kid myself that my voice contributes anything more than enthusiasm. For years I worked hard at the violin, and in my dreams would be playing quartets, but I know it's never going to happen. Languages are endlessly fascinating to me, but I'm only fully competent in one. And yet, delightfully, life has given me the chance to watch from the margins the work of a great translator of Urdu poetry, and to find a role helping to make his translations available.

It's through Ralph's work that I have discovered an organisation called the Poetry Translation Centre that gives people the chance to dabble in the creative art of moving between languages. They run an unusual type of workshop to give people an experience of what goes into translating a poem. You can take part whether you know the language of the poet or not. A language specialist provides a literal translation of a poem and, with an English poet, leads the group as they discuss each line, and work towards an English version. The director of the Centre heard me talk at the London launch of Ralph's Ghalib book, and invited me to do a session on Urdu poetry — and it was only after I accepted that I discovered that I couldn't do it on Ghalib. They only do living poets. *Definitely* beyond my competence. But by now I was hooked on the idea, and didn't want to turn up the chance.

Consider now the luck of having Rakhshanda Jalil as a resource in my life. She's the translator/literary historian who chaired the launch of Ralph's book on Ghalib in Delhi, and we've since become friends. So I ask Rakhshanda if she will help me prepare for the Poetry Translation session.

We choose Zehra Nigah, an Urdu poet I met years ago through Ralph, and then again last year in Lahore. She's 80 now and has been writing quietly incisive poems about women since she was a teenager. We chose her extraordinary poem *Mai bach gayi, ma*, 'I was saved, Mother'. It's the voice of a girl killed at birth, who quietly lists all the indignities she has been spared by not being allowed to live. It's very powerful. We go through it phrase by phrase with the workshop group, only some of whom know Urdu. It is of course Rakhshanda who is the actual translator, but we all have a sense of having co-created.

~ 53 ~

The Business of Agents

February 2017, London Book Fair

I'm a tad overwhelmed to be here. The London Book Fair fills the vast Kensington Olympia exhibition centre. It's a mass of constantly moving people, circulating slowly past publishers' stands around several floors, under a huge atrium. I go upstairs. Looking down on them all, they're like ants milling around a disturbed nest.

I look in on an upper floor area called the IRC, where people sit at desks in rows that seem to stretch half a mile, each talking one-to-one. The buzz of rapid words is like bees. For people who work in international development IRC means the International Rescue Committee. Here, I see from the notice, it means the International Rights Centre. Still in humanitarian mode I am momentarily impressed that there is so much publishing on the subject of human rights ... Ah, now I see, it's the other kind of 'Rights' — book publishing Rights, translation Rights. Wake up, Marion. These are all literary agents I see before me, negotiating deals and advances. That's the Premier League, and I'm a spectator.

I have actually, foolishly, booked a meeting with one of them. For all the sensible talking I do to myself, there's a hidden part of me that thinks how much fun it would be to be discovered by a literary agent, who would love my books and find a mainstream publisher to take them on, and get them far more readers than I ever can. It's not entirely impossible. There are occasional writers to whom that has happened. Mary Wesley's first novel for adults was published when she was 71. She kept going for 20 years, ten best-sellers, three million copies, one of Britain's most successful novelists. Obviously I'm not thinking in those terms, but it is inspiring to know there was a woman who overcame all the age-ist reactions and blasted her way into being widely read.

I was given an introduction to this agent by someone in the publishing world who heard me talk at a festival. She was extremely kind, and gave me introductions to five agents; only this one has responded. I try to discreetly check out which of the sea of desks is hers. When I locate her, she is listening to a young and highly articulate writer. She seems very caught up with her. I know already that nothing will come of this. I'm the wrong age, not pushy enough, don't have a new book ready for her to take on which is obviously going to be a best seller. Why would she try and place a book already published by a small independent that closed after three books?

My turn. She starts by telling me how hard it is to be an agent in these dire times for publishing. I sympathise. In passing she mentions a child, and we have a pleasant chat about the difficulties of juggling parenting and career.

And that's that.

~

My position among writers, I have learnt in these years of travelling, is ambiguous. Among those who earn their living by their books, I am an outsider. At literary festivals we have interesting encounters, but if conversation turns to the business of being published it quickly becomes clear that I am not part of their world. On a couple of occasions I have appeared alongside well known writers who gave out a strong vibe of 'What is she doing here?' It was difficult to account for their need to put that obvious distance between us. They were women several decades younger than me, whose novels have cross-cultural settings, as mine do. I could not possibly have been seen as a threat — at my age? And clearly not going anywhere they have set their sights on. But there it is.

To the many people who write but have not yet been published, I appear to be someone who has made it. That my books exist, that I can hold up copies to show, that I have been invited places to talk about them, all this is evidence that I have climbed an apparently unassailable rock face. The very fact that I don't have a major publisher behind me gives them hope — maybe they too can make it? Some ask if I will read their as-yet-unpublished-book and give them an opinion. I wish I didn't have to disappoint most of them. Others ask if I can advise them on how to get a publisher. The answer to that is easier: I wish I knew. A few writers who have got their books out on their own have given me copies, and I have posted short reviews on-line, as others have done for mine. Many of those books have opened up to me things I would never have stumbled on otherwise. That my books have not easily found publishers alerts me to a simple truth. A book that has not found a publisher may be the very one you want to read.

If I have low days when I think about agents and publishers, there are other days when pleasant surprises arrive. While I was learning to walk again I heard that *Uncertain Light* had been shortlisted for the international Indie Book Award for fiction. It's a prize based out of the US, for independently published books, that is, small publishers or self-published. A package arrived in the post with rolls of glitzy stickers that I could put on copies of books, a gold circle with the name of the prize surrounding the word *Finalist*. The Indian publishers were bringing out a new edition, and they included a sticker image in the cover design, and put something about it on their website.

It's all a bit unreal. Great, of course, that the judges liked the book, but I hardly needed that anymore. I had been in the company of appreciative readers for over a year. They're the ones I can imagine, and feel warmed by.

~

I have arranged to have lunch with my cover designer, Andrew Corbett. I owe to him the covers of all four of my novels, and I never get tired of them. Each captures something of the quality of the experience that went into that story. We are joined by our friend, Mohammed Umar, who is a phenomenon of self-publishing and optimism. His novel *Amina*, about a woman growing up in a Muslim family in Northern Nigeria, and challenging the limitations of society, has been taken on by small independent publishers across the world and translated into 33 languages. All this unaided by any agent. These are mostly in countries where books don't sell widely so of course he makes no money from them, he's just happy to reach new readers. Now he has written a novel called *The Illegal Immigrant*, something he himself was at one time. 'Most illegal immigrants would rather forget their experience,' he says, 'but me, I felt I had to confront it. This is how people live.' It's almost as common a story as the one about a woman trying to escape patriarchy, so I have full confidence this book will go the same way. His buoyant, irrepressible energy is a good antidote to the lingering picture of all those dead-serious agents upstairs.

I have one more meeting, for which I have to thank Rakhshanda Jalil, my Urdu-translating friend. I'm early, so I get a coffee, watch the endless movement of people around me, and remember the conversation with Rakhshanda six months ago that got me here —

'What's happening with your own writing?' she asks.

I laugh. Rakhshanda is the most astonishingly productive writer I know. Essays, reviews, translations, new studies of prominent Urdu writers, every few months there seems to be something new. Perhaps she imagines a similar rate of output from me?

I explain. I've been touring. I write a blog. I'm editing a book of Ralph's, which is slow work. Grandchildren. Life. There's no room for more.

'Well, what about getting another of your books published in India?'

Well, of course I'd love that, but who? and why would they?

She promptly gives me the name of one of her publishers and suggests I contact them. Niyogi Books. 'It's a family-run business,' she says, 'a husband and wife team. They're a charming couple.'

I check them out. No home-spun outfit this, they produce an amazing range of beautiful books, including by authors I greatly admire.

Rakhshanda introduces us by email. I get a friendly reply from Tultul Niyogi. They have looked at my website and would be interested to see *If You Can Walk, You Can Dance.* Where can they get hold of a copy to have a look at?

I am sure it's the Commonwealth Writers Prize that has got her this far, for it is far better known in India than in the UK. I get a friend in Delhi who has a copy to get it couriered to her, but the flare of excitement dies quickly. They're in the business of publishing so they have to ask themselves questions about potential market. It's hardly likely that a novel mostly set in Africa will be commercially viable in India.

It doesn't take her long to get back to me. She is definitely considering it. 'We can pitch it to the vast number of women readers of the Indian sub-continent,' she writes, 'as well as for reading material for university courses in Women's Studies, African Literature, World Literature and Sociology.'

I feel breathless at her optimism.

Her husband will be at the London Book Fair soon, she writes. Could I meet him there? —

And here he is, coming towards me. Bikash De Niyogi is charming, as Rakhshanda said, but not in a smooth way. He's energetic, straight-talking, a man with a mission that he thoroughly enjoys. He talks easily about his own journey. He worked for years in printing and advertising but had always loved books, and 11 years ago he used the money he had made in printing to get his own new publisher off the ground. His practical experience means that he knows how to produce books to the highest standard. As for the choice, 'I decided, I'll only publish good books. I'll never compromise. I may not make huge money, but I can pull it off.'

When it's fiction he leaves the decision to his wife. She thinks *If You Can Walk, You Can Dance* is a good book, so that's it.

I've seen from the website that they have plenty of high profile authors, so they can carry a few unknowns, and how lucky for me that I get to be one of them.

We sign a contract.

So we're off again, my books and I, at the start of another surprising leg of this journey.

~ 54 ~

Musical & Other Inspirations

There's a traditional Zimbabwean musical instrument that I have had a long-standing yen to learn to play. It's called *mbira,* a small hollow wooden box with metal strips. In *If you can walk, you can dance*, Jennie was given an mbira by an old man in Swaziland, and carried it around with her on her journeys. I have had two of them for years, and love the sounds I've heard others make on them. Now finally I'm being let into its secrets.

At SOAS, the School of Oriental and African Studies, where Jennie in the story studied African languages and music, I join an introductory course on how to play it. My ears and thumbs struggle with the rhythms and unexpected sounds. The teacher-performer, Linos Magaya, learnt it as a child in Zimbabwe, playing in the open savannah. His co-teacher is English and learnt from him. We in the small class come from Asia, Africa, Europe and the UK, from musical traditions as varied. We learn on the simpler hollow wooden boxes, while the ones Linos and Tim play on are embedded in large calabashes from which the mesmeric sound resonates.

Next day I am struggling to remember the complex patterns my thumbs have to negotiate. It's just a five day course, and at the end of it I feel even more of a beginner than when I started, but my ears have definitely woken up. I can *hear* differently. I am at the point where Jennie began, sitting on the ground in a village in Swaziland.

Knowing that *If you can walk, you can dance* is coming back has spurred me to start tracking back to the sources of inspiration that gave it life. All those years ago two composers of contemporary classical music talked to me about their own creative processes. Both were eminent, and generous. I had approached them out of the blue and they gave me time. Lots of time.

I want to tell them now that the book is coming out again. I am not sure if they will remember me — but they do. Judith Weir, who gave the book a warm endorsement to go on the cover, is now Master of the Queen's Music, the musical equivalent of Poet Laureate, the first woman ever in that post. Michael Finnissy, I discover, lives in rural Norfolk. It so happens that I am booked to go soon to Norwich to give a talk, so I take a chance and ask if we might meet again. He agrees at once, though it will mean a train journey. It's in character with what I remember of him. He is free from any sense of self-importance.

April 2017, Norwich
So here I am at the University of East Anglia, to talk to a group of international MA students, invited by Caitlin, my friend and ex-colleague who teaches here. I'm very happy to see her, but somehow I hadn't taken in that it's not my books the students want to hear about, they want to know how to get into a career in international

development. I feel inadequate to help them. I am ten years out of touch. I do my best to recover my lost persona and think about what these young people might find useful.

At the back of the room are two middle-aged women. I notice them as I'm talking because they are so different from the others in this classroom. After it is over they come up to talk to me. I had assumed they were mature students but they are simply people who have discovered my books through a friend. They checked out my website, discovered I would be talking somewhere at the university, located (how?) a poster telling them which room in this vast and confusing campus it would be at — and here they are. I am stunned. Audiences at events, in my experience, come only as the result of a lot of organised effort. That these two women cared enough to go searching amazes me.

One of them works on health issues internationally and has been spreading the word to her friends in other countries. 'There's a book group in Addis Ababa that's been reading it,' she says. 'They'd love to do a Skype conversation with you about it.'

They inspire me to keep believing that all this journeying has an effect.

Caitlin drives me back to the station. While I settle in a café with a book to wait for Michael, I am thinking back to how we first met. It was in my first years of learning to play the violin in the Late Starters Orchestra. They organised summer courses, and commissioned composers to devise works for us that would be play-able at our level yet musically exciting. Michael was one of those. One of Britain's leading contemporary composers, and a pianist who performs at prestigious venues on several continents, he still spent considerable amounts of time encouraging others to make music, at whatever level they could.

All that was part of the inspiration for the musical themes in what became *If you can walk, you can dance*. I interviewed five of the composers that I met on those courses. There's a character in the book who is a composer and I was trying to get a sense of how he might have gone about composing. The essential thing I learnt was that the process is more or less impossible to explain, and completely individual, as it is for writers. Michael volunteered to read an early draft of the book. It was at a stage when it was far too long and unwieldy, and his comments were very helpful in thinking about how to focus it more. He was pleasingly matter-of-fact in the way he talked about how he worked. One thing I still remember: 'It's impossible for me to compose something unless I have parameters,' he said. 'But if someone says, we need a 20 minute piece for a secondary school wind band, I can do it.'

I think about what I am currently working on. Lots of images, fragments, but no idea yet of structure. Maybe I need to start defining the parameters —

Michael comes in to the café, a tall, quietly spoken man, as warm and easy as I remember. We talk for an hour before my train arrives, a more personal chat than we have had before. I feel that through reading my book he knows more about me than I do about him, but no, that's not right — I have spent many hours listening to his music. Neither medium is autobiographical; but they're both an intuitive way to connect with what is central to the other.

I remind him of how he took the trouble of putting together some cassettes of his own music for me. Listening to them took me on an extraordinary journey that, more than anything else I learnt in those days, helped me imagine what motivated the (very different) composer in my story. The first of his compositions that I listened to was a set of piano pieces, with Michael playing, called *English Country Tunes*. To call the title ironic doesn't do justice to it. From the first note it explodes with intense, complex, clashing sound, erupting from an inner life that is startling to encounter from someone with such an apparently quiet way of being, and expressing things beyond what I could find words for. I had the impression of meeting someone to whom the technicalities of music had never presented the slightest difficulty, so that to compose within accepted structures would have been a self-limiting exercise. What made it possible for me to connect with it was that he is so easy to like, and as articulate with words as he is with music. What he *said* about it made the kind of sense I wanted to learn to hear in the music itself, and gradually began to.

I tell him there's going to be a re-launch celebration for the book. Will he come?

'Sure,' he says.

~

June 2017

And now it's happening. *If You Can Walk, You Can Dance* is out in the world again. The Niyogi Books edition in India has had five reviews and counting. It has been shortlisted for a prize at the Bangalore Literary Festival. A friend travelling in Sikkim, high in the Himalayas, sends me a photo of it prominently displayed in a bookshop.

In Battersea, where I live, the relaunch is being celebrated by a gathering of 90 people from every stage on my own journey, and those who helped inspire its themes. My violin teacher-friend Wendy Staal plays unaccompanied Bach. Judith Weir and Michael Finnissy talk about the way music is portrayed in the book. The community choir that lights my Tuesday evenings sings songs from three continents, and Adam, our choir leader, gets everyone singing a traditional Zulu song that women revived in the apartheid years, affirming their own resilience. At SOAS the ethno-music department hosts a second launch, with music provided by Linos Magaya and Tim Lloyd on the mbira. At both of them Alastair Niven, for 20 years chair of the Commonwealth Writers Prize, speaks about the significance of this most cross-cultural of literary prizes. 'I am invited to many launches,' he says, 'but a *re*-launch is special, for it's a sign that a book has lasted.'

With us are people from all the stages of my life. Friends I have recovered from years back, scattered across the world, but with the internet shrinking distance. People I got to know because they wrote to me about the book and what it meant to them. New people who have come into my life as a direct result of this journey — people first met in reading groups, libraries, literary festivals. The two women who came to my event in Norwich have journeyed to London for this, others from equally far away. I marvel when I think back to how much has changed in two years. I was writing in isolation before. No longer.

There is a moment in one of the celebrations when it seems to me that the story itself is taking on new meanings. The actor Paterson Joseph, whom I first met at the event to celebrate Mandela's life, has agreed to read an extract from my book. I am more than touched. He has fitted this in between filming for a new television series and performing his own solo play about Ignatius Sancho. Sancho, born an African slave, became a noted 18th century British gentleman, actor, musician, the first black Briton to vote in a parliamentary election. Now Paterson's voice is giving life to the reactions of Jennie in my story, taking us into an imaginary village in Malawi, a way of life that he, like almost everyone listening, has never experienced.

The one person who can perhaps visualise it from life is Doreen Siame, once a schoolgirl in my class in Zambia, now a newly rediscovered friend. Afterwards she sends me a message about impressions of the event, with all those disparate people coming together. 'There was a feeling of connectedness, a sense of belonging.'

~ 55 ~

Road Ahead Blocked

The road ahead is flooded. There are warning signs up: Road blocked. Find an alternative route.

Through the years I have been travelling, the rate of climate disasters has been speeding up. Cyclones, sea level rising, arctic melting. But we keep on, apparently unable to change direction.

A few landmarks, local and personal:

2015, Boxing Day: As I am getting ready to travel to India, Storm Eva breaks over Hebden Bridge in Yorkshire where my daughter May and her family live. Floods devastate the town, the fifth in as many years. As the waters subside, the community rallies once again to help clear debris and restore damaged premises.

2016, April: While I am reading a Shakespeare sonnet at the Wenlock Poetry Festival, Southern Africa is suffering a prolonged drought. Eight countries record the lowest rainfall in 35 years.

Crops have failed, millions will face hunger. We hear stories from our close relatives and friends. Cape Town, a city of over 4 million, is likely to run out of water.

2017, June: As we relaunch *If you can walk, you can dance,* intense summer heat causes wildfires in Portugal to blaze out of control. A young couple pack their three small children into a car, to drive out of the valley and escape the thickening smoke. They're cousins of our granddaughter Omni. Their home, a lovingly restored old farmhouse, is destroyed. All their tools are gone with it. Our daughter Star and their friends start a funding appeal to buy them new tools.

Robert and I go to see Al Gore's climate change film, *An Inconvenient Sequel: Truth to Power.* It's extremely powerful. The message, Change direction, while there's still time.

There are about five people in the cinema.

~

Perhaps it's connected, but I've lost energy for the journey. My blog has drifted into internet space. I need to retreat, and discover where my own creative process is leading.

I go down a few dead ends. I have been invited to contribute to an anthology of stories written in response to the environmental crisis. Great, but I've never yet been able to write fiction to someone else's plan. I adapt one of my blog pieces, *Tales I Tell My Grandchildren,* and the tolerant editor accepts it.

I discover a piece I wrote during my first years in Save the Children, about landing in Mogadishu in the middle of a civil war. There's something about it that still seems relevant so I decide to work on it. It becomes *What Was Once A City.* Now it's written I wonder what to do with it. I find there are a couple of prizes for short memoirs, so I submit it.

Why do I bother with prizes? It's a practical matter. If I get onto a shortlist, it creates a peg on which to hang another bit of promotion. I don't enjoy doing my own promotion but I'm realistic. No one other than me is doing it, so it has become my job. I didn't write my books to let the copies gather dust.

I'm not looking for bookings in my diary but the occasional talks about my books still happen. The library service in Wiltshire gets in touch. I had contacted them a year ago, heard nothing for months, and now they are suddenly keen to have me. There's a festival in Harwich; I get an invitation through a long-ago friend who now lives there. A writer in Shropshire invites me to talk to her writing group. The National Women's Register, whose regional conference I spoke at in Salisbury, asks me to become their first patron. I am gob-smacked. I am happy to be publicly associated with them, it's an organisation that fulfils a valuable function, but what they need, I tell them, is someone famous who can get them media attention. They come back with plans of what they would and would not expect of me. In return, they say, I will get invitations to speak to local groups. So really, what to say except I'm delighted.

Winter sets in, and at my latest library talk, no one turns up. The weather is terrible, and I wonder if the librarian's done any pre-publicity? There's a poster up, but not prominent. When I agreed to the date, I didn't focus on the fact that it's the night before Halloween. Of course no one will come. The librarian and I chat for half an hour in the deserted, echoing library while outside a storm builds up, truly worthy of the timing. I ask for suggestions for books that might tempt our seven-year old grandson into reading more. She gives me a copy of a *Beast Quest* book from a huge pile that the publisher has donated. If you don't have seven-year old boys in your life, you might need to be told that this is a bestseller series (18 million copies so far), ghost written by many incarnations of the imaginary Adam Blade. Judging by the cover pictures, the books are many variations on the theme of St George and the dragon.

Our polite wait-for-a-non-existent-audience over, I go out to battle in Beast Quest style against the now vicious wind and rain to get home. It is no ordinary storm. It feels ominous, a warning from the planet.

Why do I do this? I just want to stay home and get somewhere with my own writing.

March 2018

I'm on the Sussex coast now, to speak to the Winchelsea Literary Society about 'A Sense of Place' in my fiction. Places form people. From the earth we came, to the earth we belong. Some places we love without being aware of how much until we have to leave. Each generates atmospheres of its own, reflected in our souls. Landscapes constrain or enable, make certain stories possible and others impossible. Cities as much as countryside. In *A Language in Common* newly arrived South Asian women meet in draughty halls for English classes, and form friendships within the safety of that small world. The novelist Anita Desai said of one of these stories, 'You have an ability to fully create a world and draw the reader down into it so that one can almost feel and even smell it, it is so close.' ... In *Somewhere More Simple* it is the small-scale, intimate beauty of the Scilly Isles, the margins of sea and land, that define people's lives — the wild flowers, the gaunt majesty of rocky headlands. One reviewer said that the islands were almost a character in the story, and that feels right. I have been close enough to imagine wanting to belong.

Winchelsea itself is an evocative place. I can imagine already a story emerging here. It's a small medieval town on the coast of East Sussex. As its name says it was once on the sea, but over centuries its harbour silted up so that it became stranded inland and lost its trade across the channel, a small reminder that the places we take for granted are not immutable. My early morning walk is in the fertile Weald area among remains of an old pollarded forest, looking out over green fields. The house I'm staying in, home of my friend Jonty, goes back centuries, with wonky floor boards and odd corners. Browsing the bookshelf in the bedroom I am given is a journey in itself, fragments of life going back decades, books that have accumulated, travelled, been packed and unpacked in new homes. All here.

When I am writing, I see and feel each place as if I were moving through it with the people in the story. I approach with a long shot, then the camera moves in. Until the *place* is realised, nothing in the story moves as it should.

~

Things perk up. *Uncertain Light* has been shortlisted for the International Rubery Book Awards, which someone described (a trifle hopefully) as 'the Booker of Independent Publishing'. My memoir about landing in Mogadishu has won first prize, in not one but two memoir competitions. Two different judges. That's good for morale. The Fish Publishing prize, based in Cork in Ireland, will get my story published in an anthology, and comes with a sizeable number of Euros that will get Robert and me to Ireland for the launch, and a holiday.

August 2018

We've been back from Ireland a few weeks when I see a news photo of a 15 year old school girl with plaits on the steps outside the Swedish Parliament. She is holding a homemade notice that translates as 'School Strike for Climate'. By December Greta Thunberg is addressing the UN Convention on Climate Change. She is extraordinarily knowledgable, articulate, and without fear. In January 2019 she challenges the assembled world leaders at Davos: Our house is on fire. Why do we not react?

February 2019

Another flood in Hebden Bridge, even more devastating than the last. It's national news, and two of our grandchildren are interviewed for TV as they help clear the debris. School Strikes for Climate are happening in over 60 towns and cities in the UK now, with 15,000 students taking part. All of our grandchildren are there, aged five to 17, in two different cities. 'I'd be in school if the world was cool,' says their poster.

In March a million students across the world are demonstrating.

By April everything seems to be moving. Star gets an amazing new job as an environmental consultant. May is preparing local school children to give presentations on climate change. Robert has for years been a full-time local environment campaigner. May and her family come from Yorkshire to join Extinction Rebellion protesters who are occupying prominent sites in central London. Five of them sleep on mattresses on the floor of our small flat. Plus dog Meg. Not sure how many hours Meg and the children will want to be sitting down on the street watching police try and move people, so my role is to bring them to join the adults about lunch time. I myself am not up for sitting in the streets, so I'm glad to be able to make some small contribution. We approach rather warily. As someone is being lifted into a police van (she is floppy-heavy as a sack of potatoes) May starts spontaneously singing. People around her join in the refrain line, something about Love. It's a magic moment. An eager young trainee reporter wants to interview her. She gathers the children around her and holds a wriggling Meg as they film. He asks her what the song was. Turns out she made it up, right then.

In September four million people take part in climate actions around the world.

~

As if released by the seismic shifts around me, my writing begins to take shape. First to emerge is a story that I've been commissioned to write. This has never happened to me before, and I am amazed. It's for the Isles of Scilly. What could be more fortuitous? I'm one of five writers, one for each island, who will produce a 'walking story' that traces a route across the island. The stories will come out in audio versions, downloadable so that people can follow the route and listen as they walk. A simple concept, but a challenge — how to coordinate the development of a story with the pace of a country walk? Each has its own mood and process.

Robert and I have a week there, quietly on our own. While he does his own writing I walk my route. On one day I am accompanied by Nikki Banfield, a young woman who grew up on the island, went away, and came back to work for the Isles of Scilly Wildlife Trust. We have hardly set off before we are hit by a sudden hail storm, blowing in out of an apparently clear Atlantic sky. We shelter under pine trees, get soaked, go on. The sun comes out and the colours are extraordinary. Every few yards I learn something new. Nikki has childhood memories attached to places, and her job has made her alert to the link between nature and human use of the land, and what needs to be done to protect it.

Touching Base emerges, my small fictional tribute to this unique and fragile environment.

~ 56 ~

Stories Acted Out

Back to the beginning: Bloemfontein, the early 1950s:
My mother is, for the moment, a Queen, mother to King Darius of
Persia. I stand close to her, holding her hand. I am seven, and the
King's daughter. It is I, the princess, who look out over the parapet
and see the Persian troops massing for the coming battle with
Alexander the Great. My father, King Darius, is totally confident.
He asks me lightly what he should do with Alexander when he
captures him. I say, 'Put him in a cage with Marduk,' my pet lion
cub. But Darius will be defeated and flee, and after that the stage
will be dominated by powerful strange men making decisions
about what is to happen to us. I cling to the Queen Mother, the
only person who has any influence over Alexander. Everyone else
is scared of him but he listens to her. Though he is our Enemy, he

has been won over by her dignity, and ends up calling her Mother. It is a psychological switch that has amazed historians, but I believe in it implicitly.

Terence Rattigan's *Adventure Story* is the last play the Bloemfontein Repertory Society will put on in the (once) Grand Theatre, where we look past fraying velvet curtains to a vast auditorium. Backstage there are holes in the roof and pigeons roost there, dropping little white piles onto the floorboards below. My next appearance is in a draughty school hall, transformed into a medieval village in England where superstition is rife after Halley's comet is seen shooting across the sky, *A Tail of Fire*. Now my mother is a shrewish woman who will not allow her daughter to marry for love. By a twist of the comic plot she has been put in the stocks alongside the father of the young man her daughter loves. My brother and I are in a crowd of village children, mocking them.

Skip a year, and I'm a page in *As You Like It,* watching in some amazement the goings-on of the adults in the forest.

Stories, acted out in front of us, by real people. The magic caught me young, and has never deserted me. It is probably the reason why it came naturally to me to make up stories myself.

~

The Bloemfontein Reps was set up before my brothers and I were born. Mom and Dad were founder members. Astonishing for such a small community, they put on five plays a year for over 30 years, pausing only during the War. In our home, supper was early because either Mom or Dad had to be off for a rehearsal. They took turns to be home in the evenings while the other was either acting or directing. Three evenings a week, for five weeks, then three nights of performances, and everyone taking part had day jobs.

Along with scores of play-scripts that Mom brought home from the library there were books on every aspect of stage-craft — lighting, costumes, set design, make-up. Everything had to be learnt, and then taught to the stream of newcomers who had never done anything like this before. I would watch Mom working out moves for a play she was about to do. She set it all out on a chessboard, with a diagram of the stage and where all the furniture would be. The chess pieces were the characters in the play. She started at the point of greatest emotional tension, arranged them where they needed to be for that, then worked backwards from that.

Everything about the way play scripts were set out appealed to me. The descriptions of the setting, spelled out down to the last occasional table and lampshade in those 1950s plays. Stage directions: *Enters left, Exits right.* I liked the authority of a script. At family meal times everyone was trying to tell Mom or Dad something, all at the same time. In a play there were arguments enough to be real, but the playwright decided who had to speak next, and nothing could disturb that order.

Sometimes I was allowed to sit in on rehearsals, and watch the story unfolding bit by bit. The drama behind the drama was as interesting as what the audience finally saw. In *Adventure Story* the number of set changes would have challenged a well-resourced professional company — the palace in Babylon, a temple in Delphi, royal military tents, a battle field. The sets were designed by Darius himself (in normal life an engineer) who was doubly acting, because he was pretending he didn't have any personal interest in the young director, Megan Craddock, when everyone could see he did. The set changes were driving the stage manager frantic. He was Austrian, with a strong accent and a low tolerance for chaos. Dad, who wasn't in this play but was always looked to when things got tricky, came to the next rehearsal and talked quietly with him. Things got calmer backstage.

I was allowed to stay up for the Saturday night party after the last performance, always held in our house if Mom or Dad had been in the play. Megan was presented with an award For Bravery, for tackling such a complex play. After I was sent off to bed I lay awake listening to the sound of Mom playing the piano, while increasingly uninhibited voices sang 'The Foggy Foggy Dew'. Bursts of laughter as people retold stories about things that had gone wrong, that frisson of near-disaster that is hilarious afterwards. I drifted to sleep, remembering the way Mom had held herself, regal, as she told Alexander the Great that he was being Very Foolish.

Human dramas, packaged and labelled — but not always safely. By being allowed in on the fringes of these vividly acted-out stories of adult relationships, I was being exposed to issues I would never have found in books thought suitable for children or young teenagers. I am remembering the terror of watching as Siggy Tiger threatened a young girl with rape. On stage, that is, in a play called *Johnny Belinda*. It's about a deaf-mute girl in an isolated farming community in Canada. Her father and all their neighbours dismiss her as an idiot, unteachable. A coarse neighbour (Siggy) sees his chance to take sexual advantage of this girl who can't call out for help. Did I even understand what he was planning? I was a skinny 12 year old, still far from adolescence. But though I might have had no words or even concepts for lust or sexual dominance, I certainly understood the air of menace. It was visceral. The rape was off stage, of course, but that didn't stop it getting under my skin, just watching him watch her.

Now, more than 60 years later, I google to find the playwright. Elmer Blaney Harris, prolific, all-but-forgotten. This was his most successful play, based on a real incident on Prince Edward Island. I search the internet in vain for a secondhand copy of the play. I check the drama publishers, Samuel French. Their catalogue comes up with it, but they have only a reference copy. Finally I find it in the British Library and I sit there for one afternoon, experiencing it all over again. I see now what passed me by, when aged 12 and riveted by Siggy Tiger's dominating body-language, that the play is less about the rape itself than about the power of malicious gossip. In that narrow-minded community, the blame is pinned on the Doctor, the girl's friend and protector, the only person in that enclosed world who sees in her a full human being, trapped in isolation. He has taught her to communicate by gesture, elicited her devotion, till caring turned to love. No one else has taken any interest in the girl; so when she is discovered to be pregnant, he is the obvious suspect. He is charged, almost destroyed. He only just manages to evade conviction through the testimony of the wife of the man who raped the girl.

I emerge into the light, still lost in it.

~

The British Library is my regular place of work these days. This extraordinary collection, the book part of the British Museum, has every book ever published in the UK and much more besides. Like any other registered user, I can summon up long-forgotten out-of-print books and old newspapers from across the ex-British empire, and they will be retrieved from vaults in Yorkshire and delivered here for me to read. I can't yet say what I'm working on — it feels like it might all crumble if I try and put words around it — but I've found a form of words, gratefully adopted from an Australian historian, Tom Griffiths. I'm at the 'amassing clay' stage:

'I find that one must first amass the clay, the raw material of reality, building up the rough form, gathering much more than one can eventually keep. Then begins the careful paring away, the sculpting and moulding, the tweaking out of detail. The final reality emerges, and one could believe that it was always there, trapped in the clay, awaiting discovery and release.'

Amassing clay is messy but very absorbing. Right now my hands are covered in the stuff, and I'm only just beginning to see what might emerge.

My mother.

She has been gone 27 years, but since I set out travelling with my books she has been there, not in the shadows, something much more present than that. She was there when I took her maiden name as my publishing name ... As I rose early to look at Beverley Minster ... As I reflected on why appreciating poetry comes naturally to me ... As I packed to go to India, and in my own unsettled state about the coming journey I remembered how apprehensive she felt before each long-distance flight to visit us, but how she did it nevertheless ... She was there listening as I read a Shakespeare sonnet on his anniversary, for it was from her that I first heard his words spoken aloud ... She travelled with me back to Scotland, as I remembered stories of her childhood ... As I react to what's going on politically, I am steadied by the values that came from her and my father.

Of all my books, the only one she saw was *A Language in Common,* which came out two years before she died. She was 82 at the time, living in a retirement home called Siesta, a name that made her indignant, as if one's last years were a process of going quietly to sleep, she said. I dedicated the book to her. She was absurdly touched, and admitted to being shy when she showed the book to others in the home, in case they thought she was boasting about the dedication.

A few years before she died I started writing down things she had told me about her early life, and my memories of growing up with her. I sent it to her. She pointed out the few things I'd got wrong, and I pressed her to write her own childhood memories. She did, in her neat handwriting on foolscap sheets of paper, and finished it aged 83. She died two years later.

I am journeying back towards her now, to touch base again with all she was, and all I drew from being her child. The plays she acted in and directed have become my route to rediscovering the woman she was, aside from being our mother. She was also a teacher and a librarian. What I realise now, belatedly, is that theatre was not an extra, it was her real creative vocation.

Even when she was not personally involved in a play, she was reading them and proposing them to others. Most of the plays they did were recent, written by their contemporaries, had been on Broadway or the West End and had just been released for amateurs. The city library got in sets of plays for amateur groups around the country. She must have read hundreds of them, and passed the ones she thought were worth something to those who were next in line to direct a play.

From memory, from other people's memories, from programmes in the scrap books of friends passed on to their children, I have tracked down over 90 of the plays she herself was involved in. Most are forgotten now, but the British Library has them, and I have read them all. Through them I am getting a glimpse into the inner life that she carried.

~ 57 ~

Rediscovering My Mother

In the flat Fen country of Norfolk there have been dramatic rains. The Great Dyke has broken and the land is flooded. A convent set on high ground takes in local people whose homes are under water, and also two prison officers whose vehicle has been trapped in the flooded roads, with a young woman prisoner whom they are transporting to the gallows, convicted of the murder of her brother. One of the senior nuns, Sister Mary Bonaventure, becomes convinced of her innocence, and despite the Reverend Mother's disapproval manages to protect her until the true story emerges.

Charlotte Hastings' *Bonaventure* was a West End success in 1949. Now, directly after its release for amateur productions, the Bloemfontein Reps is putting it on, with my mother in the title role, as Sister Bonaventure. There's a photo of her wearing the starched winged headdress of the nuns of that particular order. The young convicted woman is seated, lost in her own intensity. Sister Bonaventure stands behind, looking down at her, equally absorbed. Her hands on the young woman's shoulder and forehead seem to be transmitting courage, silently willing her to be calm.

It was a production I was too young to see. Nearly 70 years later, paging through back copies of Bloemfontein's local newspaper in the British Library, I find a review. It takes me right back to the feeling of being in a bare hall, with poor acoustics and none of the advantages of a theatre stage. Yet it's clear the reviewer was transported. The headline is 'A Touch of Acting Genius'. He talks of Megan Craddock's exceptional performance as the young woman, but he credits my mother, Kathleen Marquard: 'Maybe I am not wrong in thinking that Miss Craddock was superb merely because Kathleen Marquard coaxed her to be so; impelled her to be so by the sheer restraint and calm she showed.'

~

The roles she played were often set in confined social settings, where the pressures were unspoken, and individuals had to work out complex dilemmas privately. It's not difficult to see the undertow of significance. Ten years after *Bonaventure* she was again a nun, taking a difficult stand to protect someone. In Maurice McLoughlin's *A Letter from the General* she was the Reverend Mother in a teaching mission in East Asia. In the midst of a civil war, hurried arrangements are being made to evacuate the nuns but she holds out because she is secretly sheltering a priest on the run.

Reading these plays now, I experience them differently, closer perhaps to how Mom herself might have, reflecting the concerns of an adult life in complex times. Through those years, while the political situation got ever more dire, there was an unstated interplay between the reality in the world out there, about which they personally could do little, and the energy they put into creating alternative lives in the theatre. Dad was on the phone constantly, encouraging people to take part, to overcome their shyness and give acting a go, or to those more experienced, to try their hand at directing (at that time called 'producing'). Their social world was Bloemfontein's white middle-class community, and primarily those for whom English was their effective first language. The plays they produced in no way reflected, let alone confronted, the social and political issues that surrounded them and that they were constantly compromised by. There were as yet almost no plays being written in South Africa that reflected the central issue of race that dominated the political landscape around us. Athol Fugard, pioneer of an anti-apartheid theatre, was still only 23 years old. It was some years before he would produce his first plays that were shown (illegally) to racially mixed audiences. His later co-workers John Kani and Winston Ntshona were children still, growing up as I was during the 1950s while the net of oppressive apartheid laws drew tighter, constraining their lives in ways I would not begin to understand until I was an adult.

At one level the Bloemfontein Reps was a theatre of escapism. But it was also much more than that, a reaching out to connect culturally beyond, reflecting human challenges and moral dilemmas in other worlds than their own. That can be said of all theatre, anywhere. These same plays were being put on by amateur dramatic societies all over Britain, and there was usually just as big a gulf between the daily lives of the actors and the social world represented on stage. But the best plays have a capacity to tap in to a humanity anywhere, and a universal resonance. If that were not so no one would still be producing Shakespeare, and Arthur Miller's *Death of a Salesman* would not have been performed in countries across the globe.

~

She had been to schools headed by early advocates for women's education, and all her life was an independent minded woman.

Dad appreciated that in her, though it may have taken some shaking down in their early married years to reach the pattern of settled equality between them that I knew when I was a child. She told me once that when they were newly married she heard that one of Dad's elderly aunts had commented it was a pity that he and she argued so much. She was highly indignant. They weren't arguing, she said, she was just standing up for herself. She was laughing as she told me, but still indignant.

I see that quality in some of the earliest plays the Reps put on. In J M Barrie's delightful one-act *The Twelve Pound Look*, a successful man with the usual Edwardian patriarchal attitudes accidentally meets his ex-wife. She had disappeared in what to him had always been mysterious circumstances. It turns out there is no secret except that she wasn't going to put up with being patronised any longer, and found herself a much preferable life as a typist. It's there more stridently in Clemence Dane's 1934 play, *Moonlight is Silver*, where she and Dad played joint leads as a newly married couple. The reviewer was clearly riveted by her performance. When the husband gives way to unfounded jealousy and refuses to believe his wife's explanation, she says, 'I'm not going to be bullied, and over-ruled and explained away, and have my whole mind beaten up.'

The comedy parts she chose to play had the kind of humour that grows out of sensitive characterisation. In Emlyn Williams' gentle but pointed comedy, *The Late Christopher Bean*, she was the Welsh housekeeper, Gwennie, who subverts traditional class roles by outwitting the self-satisfied doctor's family. That would have appealed to her innate sense of justice. In her father's family in Scotland, her aunts and cousins had 'gone into service' in middle-class houses. I was too young to see that play but it was a role people talked about years later.

Feminist she undoubtedly was; rebel she was not. She once described herself as a social coward. In a way it was true, for she minded unduly what other people in their small-town community would think. She suffered agonies of apprehension when her grown children did things which might not be approved by those around her, and I suspect the suffering was mostly regret at her own lack of courage. When one of her sons came home with shoulder length hair, her main concern was to ensure that her more conservative friends didn't see him looking like that. She herself didn't like the hair length but adjusted to it as she adjusted to much else that her children presented her with. She was braver in facing far bigger challenges, as when first a son and later a son-in-law were arrested by the political police and kept in solitary confinement for months. Her inner moral compass was never in doubt. She knew which things mattered and which didn't.

A role that I remember particularly vividly connects with that tension in her. In Terence Rattigan's *Separate Tables,* set in a dreary residential hotel in an English seaside town, she played Mrs Railton-Bell, a domineering, judgemental widow who revelled in self-righteous outrage when one of the residents was caught in a minor sexual scandal. It was unnerving to see my mother fully inhabiting a character so utterly different from her own – she who made no judgements about the choices of others and would have been incapable of carping criticism or malicious gossip. But perhaps it was through watching her become someone different that I was becoming more aware of her, as *herself.* Kathleen Marquard, whose name appeared in the programmes, and who had an extraordinarily versatile inner life.

~

Dad once said, 'Mom's a good actress, but she's an outstanding producer.' He was right — and not just right, but generous. He produced as many plays as she did, and well. He was the warmest of men and for those taking part he made the process fun as well as illuminating. The one I remember with greatest affection is John Patrick's *The Curious Savage,* about an elderly woman whose children get her admitted to a genteel mental hospital, the sign of instability being that she has made a will leaving her considerable fortune to whimsical causes rather than to her grasping and already-well-off offspring. As all the other unusual residents rally around her, a gentle farce plays out, cheerfully undermining assumptions about who is sane. That had resonances for the society we lived in, where the crazy injustices of discrimination on the grounds of race were accepted by those around us as 'normal'.

Mom as a director did her share of crowd-pleasers, but when she had a choice she looked for challenge. She took emotionally dense plays, and evoked in her untrained actors an identification with their roles that made the plays powerfully real. She tackled unusual topics ... J B Priestley's *They Came to a City* is about people's ability, or inability, to handle the possibility of social change ... Mary Hayley Bell's *Duet for Two Hands* is on the ethics of medical experiments. One of the few plays of which she kept a photo, so I assume it was one of the most significant for her, was Pamela Hansford Johnson's *Corinth House*. Set in a claustrophobic boarding house, the central dynamic revolves around a retired teacher being confronted by an emotionally disturbed ex-pupil who forces her to question her earlier actions.

Several of the plays she directed explored the complex half-buried emotions of women in apparently conventional situations. In Leslie Storm's *Black Chiffon* it is the perfect wife and mother who goes to pieces after her son's marriage. In Wynyard Browne's *The Holly and the Ivy*, the young daughter of a country vicar cannot decide between the conflicting demands of continuing to make life comfortable for her loved but out-of-touch widowed father, and moving on to make a life of her own. A play in which the gender roles feel closest to the times and the society she was living in was R F Delderfield's *The Orchard Walls* — mid-1950s, when both in Britain where Delderfield wrote it and in white Bloemfontein where the Reps were playing it, married women in middle-class families had been pushed back into housewife-and-mother roles. I was the only one among my friends whose mother had a job outside the home. In the play a popular principal of a girls' school is faced with the choice of continuing with the work in which she excels, or joining the man she almost married earlier and following him to where *his* work takes him. Two of the Reps' most talented younger women created the production, one acting the central role, one directing. Both women looked up to my mother as a wise friend, and confidant in difficult times. I cannot prove it, but I feel sure that it was she who found this play, and that she probably also mentored the director.

~

She directed her last play when she was 61. It seems so young to have stopped, at the height of her experience. The decision was probably prompted by Dad's health. He had had a heart attack a couple of years earlier, and was never free of anxiety about a recurrence. I had left home by then, and I have no memory of hearing about the play in her letters. Was I so preoccupied with my own life that I hardly focused? I heard about it only once I had started trying to track Mom's life in theatre. My cousin Anne had done the props for the production, and had vivid memories of watching my mother work with the actors. She could remember neither the name of the play nor the playwright, only that it was set in an arctic research station many feet under the snow where the pressures of isolation were extreme, and tensions almost unmanageable. An all-male cast. The main entrance onto the stage was via a ladder that went up into the rafters.

I googled till I had wrung dry the resources of the internet. I tried 'antarctic' as well as 'arctic'. I trawled lists of plays that came out in the couple of years before it was produced. I emailed people working in arctic research stations to see if by any chance they knew of such a play. Eventually I found it in the place I should have looked first. Among the handful of Reps photos Mom had left was a small photo of an all-male cast of a play. On the back, in her handwriting, 'My last play, before I retired firmly' — and, wonder of wonders, a programme.

It was called *Breaking Point,* and the playwright was William

Fairchild. Wikipedia told me he was mainly known in his day as a screen writer. The play was first performed on the professional London stage in 1962, and since then only a few times by amateur groups. It's a far better play than its early demise suggests, a thriller that starts quietly, building up small irritations among those living this lockdown life. One of them disappears in the icy world above, and is found dead; clearly murdered. His father, who has been funding the research project, arrives to close it down and to find out what happened to his son. Each of these men has his own reason for having disliked the murdered young man. Anne had marvelled at how my mother had drawn from her cast, some of whom had never acted before, the gradual release of extreme emotion that men at that time were so unused to being allowed to express. At a critical point one of them had to break down and weep. When that happened in performance, she said, there was a gasp of shock through the audience.

What reserves did my mother draw on, to tap so powerfully into things she herself hadn't experienced but knew to be real? A kind of imaginative remembering, that enabled her to inhabit the range of characters she herself played, and to evoke in untrained actors qualities that they didn't know they had?

We each only have one life; but there is no limit to the number we can imagine.

~ 58 ~

How Long Can You Stay?

It's 70 years since I watched my mother tell Alexander the Great he was being very foolish, over 30 since my first stories were published, five since I set off travelling with *Uncertain Light*. That's my writing story in brief, I guess. So far.

'How long can you stay?' Ralph used to ask when I visited him in his last year. But the more pertinent question was, how long could he stay? People I love have gone already. Every few months, it seems, we lose another. I feel them with me still, in the influences that have made me who I am, in the conversations we still have in my mind. But they are not here to laugh in response, to hug, to look after. Turn to look the other way, and so short a span of my own life lies ahead. How did I get here without noticing?

That our lives will end is, of all facts, the most inescapable, yet we seem psychologically structured so as to be unable to absorb it. We think, we feel, we love, therefore we are. How to conceive of a time when there will be no 'I' to love those close to me, to watch the sunrise, to feel the grain of the tree trunk beneath our encircling arms?

The writing journey doesn't end. But why would you want it to?

'If my doctor told me I had only six minutes to live,' Isaac Asimov said, 'I wouldn't brood. I'd type a little faster.'

And looking for readers? That too will continue as long as anything I write gets published. Writers and readers are in a symbiotic relationship. We need each other. Books don't fully exist until they are read. With each new reader I learn about, I feel that we are travelling together a short distance. Brief encounters, but no less meaningful for that. When I am gone my books will almost certainly join the millions that were enjoyed in their day and have now disappeared. But another future is also possible, and why not fantasise? It could be a spiral that will slowly gain momentum. I will not be here to notice if it does, but that's not what it's about.

Going forward without a map is complicated, but there isn't much choice. Maps need constant updating, and it's we ourselves who will have to do it. We follow our best instincts, try to be grounded in our understanding of what matters, but life keeps throwing up new challenges. When I set out I could not have imagined that I would be writing these last pages as the world is in lockdown, trying to limit the spread of a pandemic. But nor could we have foreseen that people in the well-fed parts of the world would be finding it possible to do without things they once regarded as essential. How to build on that, to avert the more fundamental threat of climate change? How to stay responsive, yet not be blown off course?

We reach out in two directions, back to understand where we have come from, and forward to where our grandchildren might be going. We marvel at the natural world, while our ways of life daily threaten it. We hug the five-hundred-year old tree, to celebrate it, to imaginatively protect it.

Perhaps writing is also a form of tree-hugging. Each moment moves by so fast. You think you'll never forget it, but you do. We write to capture what it is to be alive.

Points Along the Way

Numbers refer to chapters.

Inspirations

Fiction writers

Chimamanda Ngozi Adichie 50
Louisa May Alcott (1832–1888) 51
Isabelle Allende 50
Maya Angelou (1928–2014) 50
Isaac Asimov (1920–1992) 58
Margaret Atwood 9
Jane Austen (1775–1817) 7
James Baldwin (1924–1987) 50
Susan Barker 16
J M Barrie (1860–1937) 33 57
Simone de Beauvoir (1908–1986) 50
Malorie Blackman 50
Adam Blade 55
Enid Blyton (1897–1968) 19
Chaucer (1343–1400) 29
J M Coetzee 16
Joseph Conrad (1857–1924) 50
Daniel Defoe (1660–1731) 48
Anita Desai 55
Charles Dickens (1812–1870) 46 51
Fyodor Dostoevsky (1821–1881) 47
George Eliot (1819–1880) 46 50
Henry Fielding (1707–1754) 51
Anna Funder 16
Jane Gardam 18
Elizabeth Gaskell (1810–1865) 46
Graham Greene (1904–1991) 50 51
Mohammed Hanif 31
Ernest Hemingway (1899–1961) 51
Khaled Hosseini 15
Hamid Ismailov 50
Lisa Jewell 18
Manju Kapur 27
Laszlo Krasznahorkai 16
Marina Lewycka 18
Sara MacDonald 17
Paul McVeigh 46
Katherine Mansfield (1888–1923) 50
Hilary Mantel 50
Hisham Matar 15
Herman Melville (1819–1891) 9
Edna St Vincent Millay (1892–1950) 15

Rohinton Mistry 9
Toni Morrison (1931–2019) 47
Alice Munro 9
Edith Nesbit (1858–1924) 52
Ben Okri 9
Michael Ondaatje 9
George Orwell (1903–1950) 9 50
Sigitas Parulskis 16 22
James Patterson 9
Jerry Pinto 30
Eleanor Porter (1868–1920) 51
Philip Pullman 10
Premchand (1880–1936) 26
J K Rowling 9 33
Nyantara Sahgal 26
Kerri Sakamoto 50
W G Sebald (1944–2001) 51
Vikram Seth 9 50
Lionel Shriver 15
John Steinbeck (1902–1968) 8
Amy Tan 50
Colm Toibin 50
Leo Tolstoy (1828–1910) 12 21
Mohammed Kabir Umar 53
Kurt Vonnegut (1922–2007) 52
Sarah Waters 18
Mary Wesley (1912–2002) 53
Jacqueline Wilson 52
Virginia Woolf (1882–1941) 13
Gao Xingjian 50

Poets

Sadruddin Ayni (1878–1954) 4
Carol Caffrey 34
Jonty Driver 16 19 55
Faiz (1911–1984) 7 10 31-32
Rasul Gamzatov (1923–2003) 7 10
Ghalib (1797–1869) 11 20 26-27 30-
    31 34 45 52
Hadraawi 21
Hafiz (1315–1390) 4
Sayyid Mohammed Abdille Hasan
    (1856–1920) 21

List of Illustrations

Direction of Travel: Signpost on the coastal path, North Devon
1   Travelling to remote places [Photo: Mamdou Traore]
2   The writer at sixteen, Bloemfontein
3   Khoja-Iskhok village, Tajikistan [Photo: Mikhail Romanyuk]
4   'Generous Mamlakat': portrait of a Tajik woman [Photo: Mikhail Romanyuk]

Heading off alone: Crossing over the Rockies to Eastern Washington, USA
5   An NGO worker leads a training session, Tajikistan [Photo: Eric Gourlan, OSCE]
6   Indian village [Photo: Compassion International]
7   Tajik soldiers patrol the Afghan border in the civil war, Tajikistan*
8   Farm road, Hebden Bridge
9   Beach on St Mary's, Isles of Scilly
10   Country path, Wiltshire
11   Coming to terms with social media
12   Ready for the book launch

In Search of Readers: Book signing, Wenlock Books, Shropshire
13   Faqirchand Booksellers, Khan Market, New Delhi [Photo: Aaliya Waziri]
14   Listener Women's Book Festival programmes, New Zealand, 1999
15   Appearing in the public eye. [Book cover: Andrew Corbett]
16   Norwich cathedral cloisters [Photo: David Iliff; Creative Commons: CC BY-SA 3.0]
17   Dawn over the harbour, Penzance
18   West Towers, Beverley Minster [Photo: Beverleyminster.org]

Inspirations along the way: Walking in the Surrey Hills
19   Migrating birds, Extremadura, Spain [Photo: Martin Kelsey]
20   Young herder, Zambia, painting by Clement Mufuzi
21   Nomadic family on the move, Somalia*
22   Singing to raise awareness of violence against women, Ghana [Photo: new.wn.com, Jan 2016]

Travelling with a book: Exploring Masjid Wazir Khan, Lahore
23   Making heavy weather of travelling
24   The Outer Ring Road, New Delhi
25   Hindutva demonsrator [Photo: AFP Outlook India, 21 Jan 2013]
26   Between seminar sessions, Hyderabad University
27   Mosque in Panch Sheel Park, New Delhi

I am grateful for permission to use the photos which are credited. Those marked * have appeared in many places on the internet, but I have not been able to identify the copyright holder. I will be grateful for information which will enable me to credit them. All other photos are mine.

Acknowledgements

My thanks to all those whose experiences have informed my writing, made the journey delightful by their warmth, read drafts, published and promoted my books, hosted events, stimulated me by their writing, inspired me by their lives. None of my own journey would have happened the way it did without them. Alongside those named here are many more unnamed. They will know which part of the story owes something to them.

On the production of this book I am particularly grateful to Becky Joynt for technical support, Andrew Corbett for creating a cover that captures its spirit, Jen Marshall Haugen for helping launch it, and Rosemary Wailes, a geographer who said she would never set out anywhere without a map, which spurred me to provide more signposts. My greatest debt is to Greg Lanning who generously commented on successive drafts, used his film-maker's eye to help me finalise the selection of visuals, and kept me encouraged.

Robert Molteno has been the best possible lockdown companion, and our daughters have sustained us with their love. The book is dedicated to our grandchildren, who hugely enrich our lives — in the hope that we will all be able to make the changes needed to protect their future.

www.marionmolteno.co.uk